NEW FAVORITE BRAND NAME
COOKIE COLLECTION

PUBLICATIONS INTERNATIONAL, LTD.

ISBN: 0-7853-0311-1

Library of Congress Catalog Card Number: 93-84430

Pictured on the front cover: *Top row, left:* Dreamy Chocolate Chip Cookies *(page 83); Center:* Linzer Hearts *(page 184); Right:* Chocolate Peanut Butter Squares *(page 205). Bottom row, left:* Almond Toffee Triangles *(page 46); Center:* Peanut Butter and Chocolate Cookie Sandwich Cookies *(page 128); Right:* Almond Cream Cookies *(page 210).*

Pictured on the back cover: *Top row, left:* Double Chocolate Dream Cookies *(page 88),* Mini Chocolate Clouds *(page 211),* Butterscotch Fruit Drops *(page 211); Center:* Versatile Cut-Out Cookies *(page 186); Bottom:* Outrageous Brownies *(page 18). Bottom row, left:* Pineapple Almond Shortbread Bars *(page 72); Center:* "Radical" Peanut Butter Pizza Cookies *(page 150); Right:* Almond Toffee Squares *(page 45).*

1   2   3   4   5   6   7   8

Manufactured in U.S.A.

Microwave ovens vary in wattage. The microwave cooking times in this publication are approximate. Use the cooking times as guidelines and check for doneness before adding more time. Consult manufacturer's instructions for suitable microwave-safe cooking dishes.

Contents

Before You Begin 4
Fundamentals for foolproof cookie baking

Blockbuster Brownies 10
Dreamy chocolate bars for die-hard chocoholics

Bountiful Bars 40
Wonderful spread-and-bake treats ready in a snap

Champion Chippers 78
Dozens of delightful ways to make the king of cookies

Surprisingly Simple 108
Homemade goodies for hurry-up days

Kids' Creations 128
Snack-time confections for cookie jars and lunch boxes

Especially Elegant 158
Fanciful creations for those special occasions

Homemade Holiday 180
Merry masterpieces for festive munching

Acknowledgments 214

Index 215

BEFORE YOU BEGIN

Cookies — who can resist a chocolate chip when it's still warm from the oven and oozes chocolate all over your hands? Can you pass up a chewy oatmeal with its plump juicy raisins, crunchy walnuts and just a hint of fragrant cinnamon in every bite? Of course you can't. You're hooked. So is the rest of the country, because cookies have become America's most popular snack food.

Compact, portable and delicious, cookies are the perfect go-anywhere, anytime treat. Whether at home in a brown-bag lunch or on a silver tea tray, their versatility and diversity makes them the definitive all-occasion goodie.

From the simplest drop cookie to the fanciest chocolate-dipped, if you read the following cookie baking basics before you begin you'll be assured of sensational results every time.

Measuring Ingredients

Dry Ingredients: Always use standardized measuring spoons and cups. Fill the appropriate measuring spoon or cup to overflowing and level it off with a metal spatula or knife.

When measuring flour, lightly spoon it into the measuring cup and then level it off. Do not tap or bang the measuring cup since this will pack the flour. If a recipe calls for "sifted flour," sift the flour before it is measured. If a recipe calls for "flour, sifted," measure the flour first and then sift.

Liquid Ingredients: Use a standardized glass or plastic measuring cup with a pouring spout. Place the cup on a flat surface, fill to the desired mark and check the measurement at eye level. When measuring sticky liquids, such as honey and molasses, grease the measuring cup or spray it with non-stick

cooking spray before filling; this assures tha the sticky substance won't cling.

Melting Chocolate

Make sure the utensils used for melting chocolate are completely dry. Moisture caus es chocolate to "seize," which means it be comes stiff and grainy. If this happens, add $1/2$ teaspoon shortening (not butter) for each ounce of chocolate and stir until smooth Chocolate scorches easily, and once scorched cannot be used. Follow one of these three methods for successful melting:

Double Boiler: This is the safest method because it prevents scorching. Place the chocolate in the top of a double boiler or in a bowl over hot, not boiling, water; stir until smooth. (Make sure that the water remains just below a simmer and is one inch below the bottom of the top pan.) Be careful that no steam or water gets into the chocolate.

Direct Heat: Place the chocolate in a heavy saucepan and melt over very low heat, stir ring constantly. Remove the chocolate from heat as soon as it is melted. Be sure to watch the chocolate carefully because it is easily scorched when using this method.

Microwave Oven: Place an unwrapped 1-ounce square or 1 cup of chips in a smal microwavable bowl. Microwave on HIGH (100% power) 1 to $1^1/2$ minutes, stirring after 1 minute. Stir the chocolate at 30-second intervals until smooth. Be sure to stir micro waved chocolate since it may retain its origi nal shape even when melted.

Toasting Nuts

Toasting nuts brings out their flavor and fra grance, and makes them crisp. Spread the nuts in a single layer on a rimmed baking sheet. Bake in a 325°F oven for 8 to 10 min utes or until golden. Shake the pan or stir the nuts occasionally during baking to ensure even toasting. The nuts will darken and become crisper as they cool. To toast a small amount of nuts, place them in a dry skillet over low heat. Stir constantly for 2 to 4 minutes or until the nuts darken slightly and are fragrant.

Toasting Coconut

Spread the flaked coconut in a thin layer on a rimmed baking sheet. Bake in a 325°F oven for 7 to 10 minutes. Shake the pan occasionally during baking to promote even browning and prevent burning.

Tinting Coconut

Dilute a few drops of food coloring with $1/2$ teaspoon milk or water in a small bowl. Add 1 to $1^1/3$ cups flaked coconut and toss with a fork until evenly tinted.

GENERAL GUIDELINES

Take the guesswork out of cookie baking by practicing the following techniques.

- Read the entire recipe before beginning to be sure you have all the necessary ingredients and utensils.
- Remove butter, margarine and cream cheese from the refrigerator to soften, if necessary.
- Toast, chop and grind nuts, peel and slice fruit, and melt chocolate before preparing the cookie dough.
- Measure all the ingredients accurately and assemble them in the order they are listed in the recipe.
- When making bar cookies or brownies, use the pan size specified in the recipe. Prepare the pans according to the recipe directions.
- Adjust oven racks and preheat the oven. Check oven temperature for accuracy with an oven thermometer.
- Follow recipe directions and baking times exactly. Check for doneness using the test given in the recipe.

PREPARATION TIPS

The seemingly endless variety of cookies can actually be divided into five basic types: bar, drop, refrigerator, rolled and shaped. These types are determined by the consistency of the dough and how it is formed into cookies.

Bar Cookies: Bar cookies and brownies are two of the easiest cookies to make—simply mix the batter, spread it in the pan and bake. These cookies are also quick to prepare since they bake all at once rather than in several batches placed on a cookie sheet.

Always use the pan size specified in the recipe. Substituting a pan of a different size will affect the cookies' cooking time and texture. A smaller pan will cause the bars to become cake-like and a larger pan will produce a flatter bar with a drier texture.

Most bar cookies should cool in the pan set on a wire rack until barely warm before cutting into bars or squares. Try cutting bar cookies into triangles or diamonds for a festive new shape. To make serving easy, remove a corner piece first; then remove the rest.

Sprinkle bar cookies with powdered sugar for a simple garnish. Dress up frosted bar cookies by topping with nuts, chocolate chips or curls, or dried or candied fruit.

Drop Cookies: These cookies are named for the way they are formed. Spoonfuls of soft dough are dropped onto a cookie sheet and flatten during baking. Space the mounds of dough about 2 inches apart on cookie sheets to allow for spreading unless the recipe directs otherwise.

Spoonfuls of dough that are uniform in size and shape will finish baking at the same time. To easily shape drop cookies in uniform size, use an ice cream scoop with a release bar. The bar usually has a number on it to indicate the number of scoops that can be made from one quart of ice cream. The handiest sizes for cookies are a #80 or #90 scoop. This will yield about one rounded teaspoonful of dough for each cookie.

Refrigerator Cookies: Refrigerator doughs are perfect for advance preparation. Tightly wrapped rolls of dough can be stored in the refrigerator for up to one week or frozen for up to six weeks. These rich doughs are ready to be sliced and baked at a moment's notice.

Always shape the dough into rolls before chilling. Shaping is easier if you first place the dough on a piece of waxed paper or plastic wrap. If desired, you can gently press chopped nuts, flaked coconut or colored sugar into the roll. Before chilling, wrap the rolls securely in plastic wrap or air may penetrate the dough and cause it to dry out.

Use gentle pressure and a back-and-forth sawing motion when slicing the rolls so the cookies will keep their round shape. Rotating the roll while slicing also prevents one side from flattening.

Rolled Cookies: Rolled or cutout cookies are made from stiff doughs that are rolled out and cut into fancy shapes with floured cookie cutters, a knife or a pastry wheel.

Chill the cookie dough before rolling for easier handling. Remove only enough dough from the refrigerator to work with at one time. Save any trimmings and reroll them all at once to prevent the dough from becoming tough.

To make your own custom-designed cookie cutters, cut a simple shape out of clean, heavy cardboard or poster board. Place the cardboard pattern on the rolled out dough and cut around it using a sharp knife.

Shaped Cookies: These cookies can be simply hand-shaped into balls or crescents, forced through a cookie press or pastry bag into more complex shapes, or baked in cookie molds.

By using different plates in a cookie press or different tips on a pastry bag, spritz cookies can be formed into many shapes. If your first efforts are not successful, just transfer the dough back to the cookie press or pastry bag and try again. The dough itself can be flavored or tinted with food coloring and the pressed shapes can be decorated before baking with colored sugar or candied fruit.

BAKING

The best cookie sheets to use are those with little or no sides. They allow the heat to circulate easily during baking and promote even browning. Another way to promote even baking and browning is to place only one cookie sheet at a time in the center of the oven. If the cookies brown unevenly, rotate the cookie sheet from front to back halfway through the baking time. If you do use more than one sheet at a time, rotate the cookie sheets from the top to the bottom rack halfway through the baking time.

When a recipe calls for greased cookie sheets, use shortening or non-stick cooking spray for best results. Lining the cookie sheets with parchment paper is an alternative to greasing. It eliminates clean up, bakes cookies more evenly and allows them to cool right on the paper instead of on wire racks. Allow cookie sheets to cool between batches; the dough will spread if placed on a hot cookie sheet.

Most cookies bake quickly and should be watched carefully to avoid overbaking. Check them at the minimum baking time, then watch carefully to make sure they don't burn. It is generally better to slightly underbake, rather than to overbake, cookies. Here are some guidelines that describe when different types of cookies are finished baking:

Cookie Type	Doneness Test
Fudge-like Bar Cookies	Surface appears dull and slight imprint remains after touching surface with fingertip
Cake-like Bar Cookies	Wooden toothpick inserted into center comes out clean and dry
Drop Cookies	Lightly browned and slight imprint remains after touching surface with fingertip
Refrigerator Cookies	Edges are firm and bottoms are lightly browned
Rolled Cookies	Edges are firm and bottoms are lightly browned
Shaped Cookies	Edges are lightly browned

Most cookies should be removed from cookie sheets immediately after baking and placed in a single layer on wire racks to cool. Fragile cookies may need to cool slightly on the cookie sheet before being moved. Always cool cookies completely before stacking and storing. Bar cookies and brownies may be cooled and covered with aluminum foil or plastic wrap to store in the baking pan.

STORING

Unbaked cookie dough can be refrigerated for up to one week or frozen for up to six weeks. Rolls of dough should be sealed tightly in plastic wrap; other doughs should be stored in airtight containers. Label dough or container with baking information for convenience.

Store soft and crisp cookies separately at room temperature to prevent changes in texture and flavor. Keep soft cookies in airtight containers. If they begin to dry out, add a piece of apple or bread to the container to help them retain moisture. Store crisp cookies in containers with loose-fitting lids to pre-vent moisture buildup. If they become soggy, heat undecorated cookies in a 300°F oven for 3 to 5 minutes to restore crispness.

Store cookies with sticky glazes, fragile decorations and icings in single layers between sheets of waxed paper.

As a rule, crisp cookies freeze better than soft, moist cookies. Rich, buttery bar cookies and brownies are an exception to this rule since they freeze extremely well. Freeze baked cookies in airtight containers or freezer bags for up to six months. Thaw cookies and brownies unwrapped at room temperature. Meringue-based cookies do *not* freeze well and chocolate-dipped cookies will discolor if frozen.

TIPS FOR SENDING COOKIES

Bake soft, moist cookies that can handle jostling rather than fragile, brittle cookies that might crumble. Brownies and bar cookies are generally sturdy, but avoid shipping those with moist fillings and frostings since they become sticky at room temperature. For the same reason, shipping anything with chocolate during the summer or to warm climates is also risky.

Wrap each type of cookie separately to retain flavors and textures. Cookies can also be wrapped back-to-back in pairs with either plastic wrap or foil. Bar cookies should be packed in layers the size of the container, or they can be sent in a covered foil pan as long as the pan is well-cushioned inside the shipping box. Place wrapped cookies as tightly as possible in snug rows inside a sturdy shipping box or container.

Fill the bottom of the shipping container with an even layer of packing material. Do *not* use popped popcorn or puffed cereal as it may attract insects. Place crumpled waxed paper, newspaper or paper towels between layers of wrapped cookies. Fill any crevices with packing material, and add a final layer at the top of the box. Ship the container to arrive as soon as possible.

WEIGHTS AND MEASURES

Dash = less than ⅛ teaspoon

½ tablespoon = 1½ teaspoons

1 tablespoon = 3 teaspoons

2 tablespoons = ⅛ cup

¼ cup = 4 tablespoons

⅓ cup = 5 tablespoons plus 1 teaspoon

½ cup = 8 tablespoons

¾ cup = 12 tablespoons

1 cup = 16 tablespoons

½ pint = 1 cup or 8 fluid ounces

1 pint = 2 cups or 16 fluid ounces

1 quart = 4 cups or 2 pints or 32 fluid ounces

1 gallon = 16 cups or 4 quarts

1 pound = 16 ounces

SUBSTITUTION LIST

If you don't have:	Use:
1 teaspoon baking powder	¼ teaspoon baking soda + ½ teaspoon cream of tartar
½ cup firmly packed brown sugar	½ cup granulated sugar mixed with 2 tablespoons molasses
1 cup buttermilk	1 tablespoon lemon juice or vinegar plus milk to equal 1 cup (Stir; let mixture stand 5 minutes.)
1 ounce (1 square) unsweetened baking chocolate	3 tablespoons unsweetened cocoa + 1 tablespoon shortening
3 ounces (3 squares) semi-sweet baking chocolate	3 ounces (½ cup) semi-sweet chocolate morsels
½ cup corn syrup	½ cup granulated sugar + 2 tablespoons liquid
1 whole egg	2 egg yolks + 1 tablespoon water
1 cup honey	1¼ cups granulated sugar + ¼ cup water
1 teaspoon freshly grated orange or lemon peel	½ teaspoon dried peel
1 teaspoon pumpkin pie spice	Combine: ½ teaspoon cinnamon, ¼ teaspoon nutmeg and ⅛ teaspoon *each* allspice and cardamom

EQUIVALENTS

Almonds, blanched, slivered	4 oz. = 1 cup
Apples	1 medium = 1 cup sliced
Bananas	1 medium, mashed = $\frac{1}{3}$ cup
Butter or margarine	2 cups = 1 lb. or 4 sticks 1 cup = $\frac{1}{2}$ lb. or 2 sticks $\frac{1}{2}$ cup = 1 stick or 8 tablespoons $\frac{1}{4}$ cup = $\frac{1}{2}$ stick or 4 tablespoons
Chocolate	1 (6-ounce) package chocolate chips = 1 cup chips or 6 (1-ounce) squares semisweet chocolate
Cocoa, unsweetened	1 (8-ounce) can = 2 cups
Coconut, flaked	$3\frac{1}{2}$ oz. = $1\frac{1}{3}$ cups
Cream cheese	3-oz. package = 6 tablespoons 8-oz. package = 1 cup

Flour
  White or all-purpose
  Whole-wheat
	
	1 lb. = $3\frac{1}{2}$ to 4 cups
	1 lb. = $3\frac{3}{4}$ to 4 cups

Honey, liquid	16 oz. = $1\frac{1}{3}$ cups
Lemons	1 medium = 1 to 3 tablespoons juice and 2 to 3 teaspoons grated peel
Marshmallows	1 cup cut-up = 16 large or 160 miniature

Milk
  Evaporated
 	
  Sweetened, condensed
	
	5-oz. can = $\frac{5}{8}$ cup
	12-oz. can = $1\frac{1}{2}$ cups
	14-oz. can = $1\frac{1}{4}$ cups

Oranges	1 medium = 6 to 8 tablespoons juice and 2 to 3 teaspoons grated peel
Pecans, shelled	1 lb. = 4 cups halved, $3\frac{1}{2}$ to 4 cups chopped
Raisins, seedless, whole	1 lb. = $2\frac{3}{4}$ to 3 cups
Shortening	1 lb. = $2\frac{1}{2}$ cups

Sugar
  Granulated
  Brown, packed
  Confectioners' or
    powdered
	
	1 lb. = $2\frac{1}{2}$ cups
	1 lb. = $2\frac{1}{4}$ cups
	1 lb. = $3\frac{3}{4}$ to 4 cups, unsifted

Walnuts, chopped	$4\frac{1}{2}$ oz. = 1 cup

BLOCKBUSTER BROWNIES

Minted Chocolate Chip Brownies

³/₄ cup granulated sugar
¹/₂ cup butter or margarine
2 tablespoons water
1 cup semisweet chocolate chips or mini semisweet chocolate chips
1¹/₂ teaspoons vanilla
2 large eggs
1¹/₄ cups all-purpose flour
¹/₂ teaspoon baking soda
¹/₂ teaspoon salt
1 cup mint chocolate chips
Powdered sugar for garnish

Preheat oven to 350°F. Combine sugar, butter and water in medium microwaveable mixing bowl. Microwave on HIGH (100% power) 2¹/₂ to 3 minutes or until butter is melted. Stir in semisweet chips; stir gently until chips are melted and mixture is well blended. Stir in vanilla; let stand 5 minutes to cool. Beat eggs in chocolate mixture, 1 at a time. Add combined flour, baking soda and salt; mix in mint chocolate chips. Spread into greased 9-inch square baking pan.

Bake 25 minutes for fudgy brownies or 30 minutes for cakelike brownies.

Remove pan to wire rack; cool completely. Cut into 2¹/₄-inch squares. Sprinkle with powdered sugar, if desired.   *Makes about 16 brownies*

Peanutty Picnic Brownies

1 package DUNCAN HINES® Fudge Brownie Mix, Family Size
1 cup quick-cooking oats (*not* instant or old-fashioned)
1 egg
¹/₃ cup water
¹/₃ cup CRISCO® Oil or CRISCO® PURITAN® Oil
³/₄ cup peanut butter chips
¹/₃ cup chopped peanuts

1. Preheat oven to 350°F. Grease bottom of 13×9-inch pan.

2. Combine brownie mix, oats, egg, water and oil in large bowl. Stir with spoon until well blended, about 50 strokes. Stir in peanut butter chips. Spread in prepared pan. Sprinkle with peanuts. Bake at 350°F for 25 to 28 minutes or until set. Do not overbake. Cool completely. Cut into bars.
Makes about 24 brownies

Minted Chocolate Chip Brownies

Rich 'n' Creamy Brownie Bars

Rich 'n' Creamy Brownie Bars

Brownies

    1 package DUNCAN HINES®
        Chocolate Lovers' Double Fudge
        Brownie Mix
    2 eggs
    1/3 cup water
    1/4 cup CRISCO® Oil or CRISCO®
        PURITAN® Oil
    1/2 cup chopped pecans

Topping

    1 package (8 ounces) cream cheese,
        softened
    2 eggs
    1 pound (3 1/2 cups) confectioners
        sugar
    1 teaspoon vanilla extract

1. Preheat oven to 350°F. Grease bottom of 13×9-inch pan.

2. For brownies, combine brownie mix, fudge packet from Mix, 2 eggs, water and oil in large bowl. Stir with spoon until well blended, about 50 strokes. Stir in pecans. Spread evenly in prepared pan.

3. For topping, beat cream cheese in large bowl at medium speed with electric mixer until smooth. Beat in 2 eggs, confectioners sugar and vanilla

extract until smooth. Spread evenly over brownie mixture. Bake at 350°F for 45 to 50 minutes or until edges and top are golden brown and shiny. Cool completely. Refrigerate until well chilled. Cut into bars.

Makes about 48 bars

Peanut Butter Paisley Brownies

    1/2 cup butter or margarine, softened
    1/4 cup peanut butter
    1 cup granulated sugar
    1 cup packed light brown sugar
    3 eggs
    1 teaspoon vanilla extract
    2 cups all-purpose flour
    2 teaspoons baking powder
    1/4 teaspoon salt
    1/2 cup (5.5-ounce can) HERSHEY'S Syrup

Preheat oven to 350°F. Blend butter and peanut butter in large mixer bowl. Add granulated sugar and brown sugar; beat well. Add eggs, 1 at a time, beating well after each addition. Blend in vanilla. Combine flour, baking powder and salt; add to peanut butter mixture.

Spread half of batter in greased 13×9-inch pan. Spoon syrup over top. Carefully spread with remaining batter. Swirl with spatula or knife to marbleize. Bake for 35 to 40 minutes or until lightly browned. Cool; cut into squares.

Makes about 36 brownies

Peanut Butter Paisley Brownies

Fudgy Bittersweet Brownie Pie

Fudgy Bittersweet Brownie Pie

1 (12-ounce) bittersweet chocolate
   candy bar, broken into pieces
1/2 cup butter or margarine
2 large eggs
1/2 cup sugar
1 cup all-purpose flour
1/2 teaspoon salt
   Vanilla ice cream
   Prepared hot fudge sauce
   Maraschino cherries (optional)

Preheat oven to 350°F. Melt chocolate and butter in small, heavy saucepan over low heat, stirring constantly; set aside. Beat eggs in medium bowl with electric mixer at medium speed, 30 seconds. Gradually beat in sugar; beat 1 minute. Beat in chocolate mixture, scraping down side of bowl once. Beat in flour and salt at low speed until just combined, scraping down side of bowl once. Spread batter evenly in 10-inch tart pan with removable bottom.

Bake 25 minutes or until center is just set. Remove pan to wire rack; cool completely.

To serve, cut brownie into 12 wedges. Top each piece with a scoop of vanilla ice cream. Heat fudge sauce in small microwaveable bowl or glass measuring cup in microwave oven on HIGH (100% power) until hot, stirring once. Spoon over ice cream; top with a cherry, if desired. *Makes 12 brownies*

Kahlúa® Mudslide Brownies

2 cups all-purpose flour
1/2 teaspoon baking powder
1/2 teaspoon salt
2/3 cup butter
4 squares (1 ounce *each*)
  unsweetened chocolate, chopped
3 eggs
1 1/2 cups granulated sugar
4 tablespoons KAHLÚA®
2 tablespoons Irish cream liqueur
1 tablespoon vodka
3/4 cup coarsely chopped walnuts
  (optional)
  Kahlúa® Glaze (recipe follows)
  Whole coffee beans (optional)

Preheat oven to 350°F. Combine flour, baking powder and salt in small bowl. Melt butter and chocolate in small saucepan over low heat; set aside. Beat eggs and granulated sugar in large bowl until light. Beat in flour mixture, chocolate mixture, 4 tablespoons Kahlúa®, Irish cream and vodka. Fold in walnuts. Pour into greased 13×9-inch baking pan.

Bake just until toothpick inserted into center comes out clean, about 25 minutes. *Do not overbake.* Cool in pan on wire rack. Spread with Kahlúa® Glaze. Decorate with whole coffee beans, if desired. Cut into squares.

Makes about 24 brownies

Kahlúa® Mudslide Brownie

Kahlúa® Glaze

1 1/4 cups powdered sugar
3 tablespoons KAHLÚA®

Beat together powdered sugar and 3 tablespoons Kahlúa® in small bowl until smooth.

Chocolate Chunk Blonde Brownies

1/2 cup (1 stick) margarine or butter, softened
1 cup firmly packed brown sugar
1 cup granulated sugar
4 eggs
2 teaspoons vanilla
2 cups all-purpose flour
1 teaspoon CALUMET® Baking Powder
1/4 teaspoon salt
1 package (8 ounces) BAKER'S® Semi-Sweet Chocolate, coarsely chopped
1 cup chopped nuts

Preheat oven to 350°F.

Beat margarine, sugars, eggs and vanilla until light and fluffy. Mix in flour, baking powder and salt until well blended. Stir in chocolate and nuts. Spread in greased 13×9-inch pan.

Bake for 30 minutes or until toothpick inserted into center comes out with moist crumbs. **Do not overbake.** Cool in pan; cut into squares.

Makes about 24 brownies

Prep Time: 20 minutes
Bake Time: 30 minutes

German Sweet Chocolate Cream Cheese Brownies

Brownie Layer

   1 package (4 ounces) BAKER'S®
      GERMAN'S® Sweet Chocolate
   1/4 cup (1/2 stick) margarine or butter
   3/4 cup sugar
   2 eggs
   1 teaspoon vanilla
   1/2 cup all-purpose flour
   1/2 cup chopped nuts

Cream Cheese Layer

   1 (4-ounce package)
      PHILADELPHIA BRAND®
      Cream Cheese, softened
   1/4 cup sugar
   1 egg
   1 tablespoon all-purpose flour

Preheat oven to 350°F.

Microwave chocolate and margarine in large microwavable bowl on HIGH (100% power) 2 minutes or until margarine is melted. **Stir until chocolate is completely melted.**

Stir 3/4 cup sugar into chocolate mixture. Mix in 2 eggs and vanilla until well blended. Stir in 1/2 cup flour and nuts. Spread in greased 8-inch square pan.

Mix cream cheese, 1/4 cup sugar, 1 egg and 1 tablespoon flour in same bowl until smooth. Spoon over brownie batter. Swirl with knife to marbleize.

Bake for 35 minutes or until toothpick inserted into center comes out with fudgy crumbs. **Do not overbake.** Cool in pan; cut into squares.

Makes about 16 brownies

Prep Time: 20 minutes
Bake Time: 35 minutes

Brownie Candy Cups

Brownie Candy Cups

   1 package DUNCAN HINES®
      Chocolate Lovers' Double Fudge
      Brownie Mix
   2 eggs
   1/3 cup water
   1/4 cup CRISCO® Oil or CRISCO®
      PURITAN® Oil
   30 miniature peanut butter cup
      candies, wrappers removed

1. Preheat oven to 350°F. Place 30 (2-inch) foil liners in muffin pans or on cookie sheets.

2. Combine brownie mix, fudge packet from Mix, eggs, water and oil in large bowl. Stir with spoon until well blended, about 50 strokes. Place 2 level measuring tablespoons batter in each foil liner. Bake at 350°F for 10 minutes. Remove from oven. Push 1 peanut butter cup candy in center of each cupcake until even with surface of brownie. Bake 5 to 7 minutes longer. Remove to cooling racks. Cool completely.

Makes 30 brownie cups

Coconut Crowned Cappuccino Brownies

6 squares (1 ounce each) semisweet
   chocolate, coarsely chopped
1 tablespoon freeze dried coffee
1 tablespoon boiling water
$1/2$ cup sugar
$1/4$ cup butter or margarine, softened
3 large eggs, divided
$3/4$ cup all-purpose flour
$1/2$ teaspoon baking powder
$3/4$ teaspoon ground cinnamon
$1/4$ teaspoon salt
$1/4$ cup whipping cream
1 teaspoon vanilla
$3/4$ cup flaked coconut, divided
$1/2$ cup semisweet chocolate chips

Preheat oven to 350°F. Melt chocolate squares in small, heavy saucepan over low heat, stirring constantly; set aside. Dissolve coffee in boiling water in small cup; set aside. Beat sugar and butter in large bowl until light and fluffy. Beat in 2 eggs, 1 at a time, scraping down side of bowl after each addition. Beat in chocolate and coffee mixture until well combined. Add combined flour, baking powder, cinnamon and salt. Beat until well blended. Spread evenly into greased 8-inch square baking pan.

For topping, combine cream, remaining 1 egg and vanilla in small bowl; mix well. Stir in $1/2$ cup coconut and chips. Spread evenly over brownie base; sprinkle with remaining $1/4$ cup coconut. Bake 30 to 35 minutes or until coconut is browned and center is set. Remove pan to wire rack; cool completely. Cut into 2-inch squares.

Makes about 16 brownies

Best Brownies

$1/2$ cup butter or margarine, melted
1 cup sugar
1 teaspoon vanilla extract
2 eggs
$1/2$ cup all-purpose flour
$1/3$ cup HERSHEY'S Cocoa
$1/4$ teaspoon baking powder
$1/4$ teaspoon salt
$1/2$ cup chopped nuts (optional)
   Creamy Brownie Frosting (recipe
   follows)

Preheat oven to 350°F. Blend butter, sugar and vanilla in large bowl. Add eggs; beat well. Combine flour, cocoa, baking powder and salt; gradually blend into egg mixture. Stir in nuts.

Spread in greased 9-inch square pan. Bake for 20 to 25 minutes or until brownie begins to pull away from edges of pan. Cool; frost with Creamy Brownie Frosting. Cut into squares.

Makes about 16 brownies

Creamy Brownie Frosting

3 tablespoons butter or margarine,
   softened
3 tablespoons HERSHEY'S Cocoa
1 tablespoon light corn syrup or
   honey
$1/2$ teaspoon vanilla extract
1 cup confectioners' sugar
1 to 2 tablespoons milk

Cream butter, cocoa, corn syrup and vanilla in small mixer bowl. Add confectioners' sugar and milk; beat to spreading consistency. Makes about 1 cup frosting.

Coconut Crowned Cappuccino Brownies

Outrageous Brownies

1/2 cup MIRACLE WHIP® Salad
    Dressing
2 eggs, beaten
1/4 cup cold water
1 (21.5-ounce) package fudge
    brownie mix
3 (7-ounce) milk chocolate bars,
    divided
    Walnut halves (optional)

Preheat oven to 350°F.

Mix together salad dressing, eggs and
water until well blended. Stir in
brownie mix, mixing just until
moistened.

Coarsely chop two chocolate bars; stir
into brownie mixture. Pour into greased
13×9-inch baking pan.

Bake 30 to 35 minutes or until edges
begin to pull away from sides of pan.
Immediately top with 1 chopped

Outrageous Brownies

chocolate bar. Let stand about 5 minutes
or until melted; spread evenly over
brownies. Garnish with walnut halves,
if desired. Cool. Cut into squares.
Makes about 24 brownies

Prep Time: 10 minutes
Bake Time: 35 minutes

Sweets-for-the-Sweet Brownies

6 tablespoons margarine
1/2 cup unsweetened cocoa
1/4 cup *plus* 2 tablespoons plain
    nonfat yogurt
1 cup sugar
2 egg whites *or* 1 egg
1/2 cup all-purpose flour
1 teaspoon vanilla extract
1 cup miniature marshmallows
1 cup "M&M's"® Plain or
    "M&M's"® HOLIDAYS® Plain
    Chocolate Candies (Valentine's)
1/4 cup unsalted dry roasted mixed
    nuts

Preheat oven to 350°F. Grease 8-inch
square baking pan; set aside. In
medium heavy-gauge saucepan over
medium-low heat, melt margarine. Stir
in cocoa until smooth. Remove from
heat; stir in yogurt, sugar, egg whites,
flour and vanilla extract until smooth.

Spread batter evenly into prepared pan.
Bake 20 to 25 minutes or until center
feels dry. Remove from oven. Sprinkle
top with marshmallows. Return to oven
3 to 4 minutes or until marshmallows
are puffed, but not brown. Remove
from oven and immediately sprinkle
"M&M's"® and nuts over top. Press into
marshmallows; cool completely before
cutting. Cut into squares.
Makes about 12 brownies

Double "Topped" Brownies

Brownies

1 package DUNCAN HINES®
   Chocolate Lovers' Double Fudge
   Brownie Mix
2 eggs
1/3 cup water
1/4 cup CRISCO® Oil or CRISCO®
   PURITAN® Oil
1/2 cup flaked coconut
1/2 cup chopped nuts

Frosting

3 cups confectioners sugar
1/3 cup butter or margarine, softened
1 1/2 teaspoons vanilla extract
2 to 3 tablespoons milk

Topping

3 squares (3 ounces) unsweetened
   chocolate
1 tablespoon butter or margarine

1. Preheat oven to 350°F. Grease bottom of 13×9-inch pan.

2. For brownies, combine brownie mix, fudge packet from Mix, eggs, water and oil in large bowl. Stir with spoon until well blended, about 50 strokes. Stir in coconut and nuts. Spread in prepared pan. Bake at 350°F for 27 to 30 minutes or until set. Cool completely.

3. For frosting, combine confectioners sugar, 1/3 cup butter and vanilla extract. Stir in milk, 1 tablespoon at a time, until frosting is spreading consistency. Spread over brownies. Refrigerate until frosting is firm, about 30 minutes.

4. For topping, melt chocolate and 1 tablespoon butter in small bowl over hot water; stir until smooth. Drizzle over frosting. Refrigerate until chocolate is firm, about 15 minutes. Cut into bars.

Makes about 48 brownies

Double "Topped" Brownies

Buckeye Cookie Bars

1 (18 1/4- or 18 1/2-ounce) package
   chocolate cake mix
1/4 cup vegetable oil
1 egg
1 cup chopped peanuts
1 (14-ounce) can EAGLE® Brand
   Sweetened Condensed Milk
   (NOT evaporated milk)
1/2 cup peanut butter

Preheat oven to 350°F (325°F for glass dish). In large mixer bowl, combine cake mix, oil and egg; beat on medium speed until crumbly. Stir in peanuts. Reserving 1 1/2 cups crumb mixture, press remainder firmly on bottom of greased 13×9-inch baking pan. In medium bowl, beat sweetened condensed milk with peanut butter until smooth; spread over prepared crust. Sprinkle with reserved crumb mixture. Bake 25 to 30 minutes or until set. Cool. Cut into bars. Store loosely covered at room temperature.

Makes 24 to 36 bars

Praline Brownies

Brownies

> 1 package DUNCAN HINES®
>   Chocolate Lovers' Milk
>   Chocolate Chunk Brownie Mix
> 2 eggs
> 1/3 cup water
> 1/3 cup CRISCO® Oil or CRISCO®
>   PURITAN® Oil
> 3/4 cup chopped pecans

Topping

> 3/4 cup firmly packed brown sugar
> 3/4 cup chopped pecans
> 1/4 cup butter or margarine, melted
> 2 tablespoons milk
> 1/2 teaspoon vanilla extract

1. Preheat oven to 350°F. Grease 9-inch square pan.

2. For brownies, combine brownie mix, eggs, water, oil and 3/4 cup pecans in large bowl. Stir with spoon until well blended, about 50 strokes. Spread in prepared pan. Bake at 350°F for 35 to 40 minutes. Remove from oven.

3. For topping, combine brown sugar, 3/4 cup pecans, melted butter, milk and vanilla extract in medium bowl. Stir with spoon until well blended. Spread over hot brownies. Return to oven. Bake for 15 minutes longer or until topping is set. Cool completely. Cut into bars.

Makes about 16 brownies

Praline Brownies

Frosted Maraschino Brownies

Frosted Maraschino Brownies

> 24 red maraschino cherries
> 1 package (23.6 ounces) brownie
>   mix, *plus* ingredients to prepare
>   mix
> 2 cups powdered sugar
> 1/2 cup *plus* 1 tablespoon butter or
>   margarine, softened, divided
> 3 tablespoons milk
> 2 tablespoons instant vanilla
>   pudding mix
> 1 ounce sweet baking chocolate

Preheat oven to temperature directed on brownie mix. Drain cherries, reserving juice for another use. Blot cherries with paper towel; set aside. Prepare and bake brownie mix according to package directions in 13×9-inch pan; cool completely in pan on wire rack.

For frosting, in medium bowl, beat sugar, 1/2 cup butter, milk and pudding mix until smooth. Cover; refrigerate until slightly thickened. Spread frosting over cooled, uncut brownie in pan. Arrange cherries in rows over frosting. In small saucepan over low heat, melt chocolate and remaining 1 tablespoon butter; stir to blend. Cool slightly. Drizzle chocolate mixture over brownie. When chocolate is set, cut into bars.

Makes about 24 brownies

*Favorite recipe from **National Cherry Foundation***

Fudgy Mocha Brownies with a Crust

1¼ cups unsifted flour, divided
¼ cup sugar
½ cup *cold* margarine or butter
1 (14-ounce) can EAGLE® Brand
    Sweetened Condensed Milk
    (NOT evaporated milk)
½ cup HERSHEY'S Cocoa
1 egg
2 tablespoons coffee-flavored
    liqueur *or* 1 teaspoon instant
    coffee dissolved in 1 tablespoon
    hot water
1 teaspoon vanilla extract
½ teaspoon baking powder
¾ cup chopped nuts
    Fudgy Mocha Frosting

Preheat oven to 350°F. In medium bowl, combine *1 cup* flour and sugar. Cut in *cold* margarine until mixture resembles coarse corn meal. Press firmly on bottom of 13×9-inch baking pan. Bake 15 minutes. Meanwhile, in large mixer bowl, beat sweetened condensed milk, cocoa, egg, remaining ¼ *cup* flour, liqueur, vanilla and baking powder until well blended. Stir in nuts. Spread evenly over baked crust. Bake 20 minutes or until center is set. Cool. Spread with Fudgy Mocha Frosting. Store tightly covered at room temperature.   *Makes 24 to 36 brownies*

Fudgy Mocha Frosting: In small saucepan over low heat, melt 3 tablespoons margarine or butter; add 3 tablespoons HERSHEY'S Cocoa and 1 tablespoon water, stirring constantly until mixture thickens (do not boil). Remove from heat; add 1 tablespoon coffee-flavored liqueur. Gradually beat in 1½ cups confectioners' sugar until smooth. Add additional water, 1 teaspoon at a time, until desired consistency. Makes about 1 cup.

Fudgy Mocha Brownies with a Crust

Oatmeal Brownies

⅔ cup granulated sugar
⅓ cup water
3 tablespoons CRISCO® Oil
½ teaspoon vanilla
2 egg whites, lightly beaten
½ cup all-purpose flour
⅓ cup quick oats (*not* instant or old
    fashioned)
¼ cup unsweetened cocoa powder
¾ teaspoon baking powder
⅛ teaspoon salt
1 teaspoon confectioners sugar

1. Preheat oven to 350°F. Oil 8-inch square pan lightly.

2. Combine granulated sugar, water, oil, and vanilla in medium bowl. Stir well. Add egg whites. Stir well.

3. Combine flour, oats, cocoa, baking powder and salt. Add to sugar mixture, stirring well. Pour into prepared pan.

4. Bake at 350°F for 23 minutes or until toothpick inserted in center comes out clean. Cool. Sprinkle with confectioners sugar. Cut into bars.

Makes about 12 brownies

Decadent Blonde Brownies

1/2 cup butter or margarine, softened
3/4 cup granulated sugar
3/4 cup packed light brown sugar
2 large eggs
2 teaspoons vanilla
1 1/2 cups all-purpose flour
1 teaspoon baking powder
1/2 teaspoon salt
1 package (10 ounces) semisweet
    chocolate chunks
1 jar (3 1/2 ounces) macadamia nuts,
    coarsely chopped

Preheat oven to 350°F. Beat butter, granulated sugar and brown sugar in large bowl with electric mixer at medium speed until light and fluffy. Beat in eggs and vanilla. Add combined flour, baking powder and salt. Stir until well blended. Stir in chocolate chunks and macadamia nuts. Spread evenly into greased 13×9-inch baking pan.

Bake 25 to 30 minutes or until golden brown. Remove pan to wire rack; cool completely. Cut into 3 1/4×1 1/2-inch bars.

Makes about 2 dozen brownies

Mississippi Mud Brownies

1 package DUNCAN HINES® Fudge
    Brownie Mix, Family Size
2 eggs
1/3 cup water
1/3 cup CRISCO® Oil or CRISCO®
    PURITAN® Oil
1 jar (7 ounces) marshmallow creme
1 container (16 ounces) DUNCAN
    HINES® Creamy Homestyle
    Milk Chocolate Frosting, melted

1. Preheat oven to 350°F. Grease bottom of 13×9-inch pan.

2. Combine brownie mix, eggs, water and oil in large bowl. Stir with spoon until well blended, about 50 strokes. Spread in pan. Bake at 350°F for 25 to 28 minutes or until set.

3. Spread marshmallow creme gently over hot brownies. Pour 1 1/4 cups melted milk chocolate frosting over marshmallow creme. Swirl with knife to marbleize. Cool completely. Cut into bars. *Makes 20 to 24 brownies*

Note: Store leftover melted frosting in original container. Refrigerate.

Extra Moist & Chunky Brownies

1 (8-ounce) package cream cheese,
    softened
1 cup sugar
1 egg
1 teaspoon vanilla extract
3/4 cup all-purpose flour
1 (3 3/8-ounce) package ROYAL®
    Chocolate or Dark 'N' Sweet
    Chocolate Pudding & Pie Filling
4 (1-ounce) semisweet chocolate
    squares, chopped

In large bowl with electric mixer at high speed, beat cream cheese, sugar, egg and vanilla until smooth; blend in flour and pudding mix. Spread batter in greased 8×8-inch microwavable dish; sprinkle with chocolate. Microwave at HIGH (100% power) for 8 to 10 minutes or until toothpick inserted in center comes out clean, rotating dish 1/2 turn every 2 minutes. Cool completely in pan. Cut into squares.

Makes about 16 brownies

Decadent Blonde Brownies

Irish Brownies

Irish Brownies

4 squares (1 ounce each) semisweet baking chocolate, coarsely chopped
1/2 cup butter or margarine
1/2 cup sugar
2 large eggs
1/4 cup Irish cream liqueur
1 cup all-purpose flour
1/2 teaspoon baking powder
1/4 teaspoon salt
Irish Cream Frosting (recipe follows)

Preheat oven to 350°F. Melt chocolate and butter in medium, heavy saucepan over low heat, stirring constantly. Stir in sugar. Beat in eggs, 1 at a time, with wire whisk. Whisk in Irish cream. Whisk combined flour, baking powder and salt until just blended. Spread batter evenly into greased 8-inch square baking pan. Bake 22 to 25 minutes or until center is set. Remove pan to wire rack; cool completely before frosting. Spread Irish Cream Frosting over cooled brownies. Chill at least 1 hour or until frosting is set. Cut into 2-inch squares.

Makes about 16 brownies

Irish Cream Frosting

2 ounces cream cheese (1/4 cup), softened
2 tablespoons butter or margarine, softened
2 tablespoons Irish cream liqueur
1 1/2 cups powdered sugar

Beat cream cheese and butter in small bowl with electric mixer at medium speed until smooth. Beat in Irish cream. Gradually beat in powdered sugar until smooth. Makes about 2/3 cup.

White Chocolate Chunk Brownies

4 squares (1 ounce each)
    unsweetened chocolate, coarsely
    chopped
$^1/_2$ cup butter or margarine
2 large eggs
$1^1/_4$ cups granulated sugar
1 teaspoon vanilla
$^1/_2$ cup all-purpose flour
$^1/_2$ teaspoon salt
1 (6-ounce) white baking bar, cut
    into $^1/_4$-inch pieces
$^1/_2$ cup coarsely chopped walnuts
    (optional)
    Powdered sugar for garnish

Preheat oven to 350°F. Melt unsweetened chocolate and butter in small, heavy saucepan over low heat, stirring constantly; set aside. Beat eggs in large bowl; gradually add granulated sugar, beating at medium speed about 4 minutes until very thick and lemon colored. Beat in chocolate mixture and vanilla. Beat in flour and salt just until blended. Stir in baking bar pieces and walnuts. Spread evenly into greased 8-inch square baking pan. Bake 30 minutes or until edges just begin to pull away from sides of pan and center is set. Remove pan to wire rack; cool completely. Cut into 2-inch squares. Sprinkle with powdered sugar, if desired.

Makes about 16 brownies

White Chocolate Chunk Brownies

Scrumptious Minted Brownies

Scrumptious Minted Brownies

1 package DUNCAN HINES® Fudge
    Brownie Mix, Family Size
1 egg
$^1/_3$ cup water
$^1/_3$ cup CRISCO® Oil or CRISCO®
    PURITAN® Oil
48 chocolate crème de menthe candy
    wafers, divided

1. Preheat oven to 350°F. Grease bottom of 13×9-inch pan.

2. Combine brownie mix, egg, water and oil in large bowl. Stir with spoon until well blended, about 50 strokes. Spread in prepared pan. Bake at 350°F for 25 minutes or until set. Place 30 candy wafers evenly over hot brownies. Let stand for 1 minute to melt. Spread candy wafers to frost brownies. Score frosting into 36 bars by running tip of knife through melted candy. (Do not cut through brownies.) Cut remaining 18 candy wafers in half lengthwise; place halves on each scored bar. Cool completely. Cut into bars.

Makes 36 brownies

Brownie Cheesecake Bars

 2/3 cup *plus* 2 tablespoons margarine
    or butter
1 1/2 cups sugar
1 1/2 cups unsifted flour
 2/3 cup HERSHEY'S Cocoa
 1/2 cup milk
   3 eggs
   3 teaspoons vanilla extract
 1/2 teaspoon baking powder
   1 cup chopped nuts, optional
   1 (8-ounce) package cream cheese,
    softened
   1 tablespoon cornstarch
   1 (14-ounce) can EAGLE® Brand
    Sweetened Condensed Milk
    (NOT evaporated milk)

Preheat oven to 350°F. Melt *2/3 cup*
margarine. In large mixer bowl, beat
melted margarine, sugar, flour, cocoa,
milk, *2 eggs, 2 teaspoons* vanilla and
baking powder until well blended. Stir
in nuts if desired. Spread in greased
13×9-inch baking pan. In small mixer
bowl, beat cheese, remaining
2 tablespoons margarine and cornstarch
until fluffy. Gradually beat in sweetened
condensed milk, then remaining *1 egg*

Brownie Cheesecake Bars

and *1 teaspoon* vanilla. Pour evenly over
brownie batter. Bake 40 minutes or until
top is lightly browned. Cool. Chill. Cut
into bars. Garnish as desired. Store
covered in refrigerator.

Makes 24 to 36 bars

Coconut-Pecan Brownies

Brownie
   1 package (4 ounces) BAKER'S®
    GERMAN'S® Sweet Chocolate
 1/4 cup (1/2 stick) margarine or butter
 3/4 cup sugar
   2 eggs
   1 teaspoon vanilla
 1/2 cup all-purpose flour
 1/2 cup chopped nuts

Topping
1 1/3 cup BAKER'S® ANGEL FLAKE®
    Coconut
 1/2 cup chopped pecans
 1/4 cup firmly packed brown sugar
 1/4 cup milk

Preheat oven to 350°F.

Microwave chocolate and margarine in
large microwavable bowl on HIGH
(100% power) 2 minutes or until
margarine is melted. **Stir until chocolate
is completely melted.**

Stir sugar into melted chocolate
mixture. Mix in eggs and vanilla until
well blended. Stir in flour and nuts.
Spread in greased 8-inch square pan.

Mix Baker's® Angel Flake® Coconut,
pecans and brown sugar in same bowl.
Add milk; toss to coat well. Spoon over
brownie batter.

Bake for 40 minutes or until toothpick
inserted into center comes out with
fudgy crumbs. **Do not overbake.** Cool
in pan, cut into squares.

Makes about 16 brownies

Prep Time: 10 minutes
Bake Time: 25 minutes

Fancy Walnut Brownies

Brownies
- **1 package DUNCAN HINES®**
  Chocolate Lovers' Walnut
  Brownie Mix
- **1 egg**
- **1/3 cup water**
- **1/3 cup CRISCO® Oil or CRISCO®**
  PURITAN® Oil

Glaze
- **4 1/2 cups confectioners sugar**
- **1/2 cup milk or water**
- **24 walnut halves, for garnish**

Chocolate Drizzle
- **1/3 cup semi-sweet chocolate chips**
- **1 tablespoon CRISCO® Shortening**

1. Preheat oven to 350°F. Place 24 (2-inch) foil liners on cookie sheets.

2. For brownies, combine brownie mix, egg, water and oil in large bowl. Stir with spoon until well blended, about 50 strokes. Stir in walnut packet from Mix. Fill each foil liner with 2 generous tablespoons batter. Bake at 350°F for 20 to 25 minutes or until set. Cool completely. Remove liners. Turn brownies upside down on cooling rack.

3. For glaze, combine confectioners sugar and milk in medium bowl. Blend until smooth. Spoon glaze over first brownie to completely cover. Top immediately with walnut half. Repeat with remaining brownies. Allow glaze to set.

4. For chocolate drizzle, place chocolate chips and shortening in small resealable plastic bag; seal. Place bag in bowl of hot water for several minutes. Dry with paper towel. Knead until blended and chocolate is smooth. Snip pinpoint hole in corner of bag. Drizzle chocolate over brownies. Store in single layer in airtight container.   *Makes 24 brownies*

Fancy Walnut Brownies

Black Russian Brownies

- **4 squares (1 ounce *each*)**
  unsweetened chocolate
- **1 cup butter**
- **3/4 teaspoon black pepper**
- **4 eggs**
- **1 1/2 cups sugar**
- **1 1/2 teaspoons vanilla**
- **1/3 cup KAHLÚA®**
- **2 tablespoons vodka**
- **1 1/3 cups sifted flour**
- **1/2 teaspoon salt**
- **1/4 teaspoon baking powder**
- **1 cup chopped walnuts or sliced**
  toasted almonds

Preheat oven to 350°F. Line bottom of 13×9-inch baking pan with parchment paper. Melt chocolate and butter with pepper over low heat. Remove from heat; set aside. Beat eggs, sugar and vanilla until blended. Stir in cooled chocolate mixture, Kahlúa® and vodka. Resift flour, salt and baking powder into mixture and stir until blended. Stir in nuts. Spread into prepared pan. Bake just until toothpick inserted in center comes out clean, about 25 minutes. *Do not overbake.* Cool completely. Cut into squares or bars.

Makes about 30 brownies

Chocolatey Rocky Road Brownies

Brownies

　1 cup butter or margarine
　4 squares (1 ounce *each*)
　　unsweetened chocolate
　1½ cups granulated sugar
　1 cup all-purpose flour
　3 eggs
　1½ teaspoons vanilla
　½ cup salted peanuts, chopped

Frosting

　¼ cup butter or margarine
　1 (3-ounce) package cream cheese
　1 square (1 ounce) unsweetened
　　chocolate
　¼ cup milk
　2¾ cups powdered sugar
　1 teaspoon vanilla
　2 cups miniature marshmallows
　1 cup salted peanuts

Preheat oven to 350°F. For brownies, in 3-quart saucepan combine 1 cup butter and 4 squares chocolate. Cook over medium heat, stirring constantly, until melted, 5 to 7 minutes. Add granulated sugar, flour, eggs and 1½ teaspoons vanilla; mix well. Stir in ½ cup chopped peanuts. Spread into greased 13×9-inch baking pan. Bake 20 to 25 minutes or until brownie starts to pull away from sides of pan. Cool completely.

For frosting, in 2-quart saucepan combine ¼ cup butter, cream cheese, 1 square chocolate and milk. Cook over medium heat, stirring occasionally, until melted, 6 to 8 minutes. Remove from heat; add powdered sugar and 1 teaspoon vanilla; beat with hand mixer until smooth. Stir in marshmallows and 1 cup peanuts.

Immediately spread over cooled brownies. Cool completely; cut into bars. Store refrigerated.

Makes about 4 dozen brownies

Brownie Sundaes For Kids

　½ gallon vanilla ice cream
　　Assorted decors
　　Chopped nuts
　1 package DUNCAN HINES®
　　Chocolate Lovers' Double Fudge
　　Brownie Mix
　2 eggs
　⅓ cup water
　¼ cup CRISCO® Oil or CRISCO®
　　PURITAN® Oil
　　Chocolate fudge ice cream
　　topping, heated

1. Preheat oven to 350°F. Line cookie sheet with waxed paper. Grease bottom of 13×9-inch pan.

2. Scoop ice cream into balls; place on lined cookie sheet. Sprinkle each ice cream ball heavily with assorted decors or chopped nuts. Place in freezer until ready to serve.

3. Combine brownie mix, fudge packet from Mix, eggs, water and oil in large bowl. Stir with spoon until well blended, about 50 strokes. Pour into pan. Bake at 350°F for 27 to 30 minutes or until set. Cool completely.

4. To assemble, cut brownies into 12 squares. Place on serving plates. Spoon hot fudge topping on top of each brownie square. Arrange garnished ice cream ball on each square. Serve immediately.

Makes 12 brownie sundaes

Chocolatey Rocky Road Brownies

Chocolate Macaroon Squares (top),
Cappuccino Brownies (bottom)

Stir in 1 cup coconut, pecans and Nestlé® Toll House® Semi-Sweet Chocolate Morsels. Set aside.

Base: Preheat oven to 350°F. In large bowl, combine cake mix, butter and egg; mix until crumbly. Press into greased 13×9-inch baking pan.

Spread Topping over Base. Sprinkle remaining ¹/₃ cup coconut on top. Bake at 350°F for 30 to 40 minutes. (Center may appear loose but will set upon cooling.) Cool completely on wire rack. Cut into 2-inch squares.

Makes about 24 brownies

Chocolate Macaroon Squares

Topping

> 1 (14-ounce) can sweetened condensed milk
> 1 teaspoon vanilla extract
> 1 egg
> 1¹/₃ cups (3¹/₂-ounce can) flaked coconut, divided
> 1 cup chopped pecans
> 1 cup (6-ounce package) NESTLÉ® Toll House® Semi-Sweet Chocolate Morsels

Base

> 1 (18¹/₂-ounce) package chocolate cake mix
> ¹/₃ cup butter, softened
> 1 egg

Topping: In large bowl, combine sweetened condensed milk, vanilla extract and egg; beat until well blended.

Cappuccino Brownies

> 1 tablespoon TASTER'S CHOICE® Maragor Bold® freeze dried coffee
> 2 teaspoons boiling water
> 1 cup (6-ounce package) NESTLÉ® Toll House® Semi-Sweet Chocolate Morsels
> ¹/₂ cup sugar
> ¹/₄ cup butter, softened
> 2 eggs
> ¹/₄ teaspoon cinnamon
> ¹/₂ cup all-purpose flour

Preheat oven to 350°F. In cup, combine Taster's Choice® Maragor Bold® freeze dried coffee and water; set aside. Melt over hot (not boiling) water, Nestlé® Toll House® Semi-Sweet Chocolate Morsels; stir until smooth. Set aside. In large bowl, combine sugar and butter; beat until creamy. Add eggs, coffee and cinnamon; beat well. Stir in melted morsels and flour. Spread into foil-lined 8-inch square baking pan. Bake at 350°F for 25 to 30 minutes. Cool completely on wire rack. Cut into 2-inch squares.

Makes about 16 brownies

Sour Cream
Walnut Brownies

Brownies

> **1 package DUNCAN HINES®**
> **Chocolate Lovers' Walnut**
> **Brownie Mix**
> **¾ cup dairy sour cream**
> **1 egg**
> **1 teaspoon water**

Chocolate Drizzle

> **½ cup semi-sweet chocolate chips**
> **2 teaspoons CRISCO® Shortening**

1. Preheat oven to 350°F. Grease 13×9-inch pan.

2. For brownies, combine brownie mix, sour cream, egg and water in large bowl. Stir with spoon until well blended, about 50 strokes. Spread in prepared pan. Sprinkle with walnut packet from Mix. Bake at 350°F for 25 to 28 minutes or until set.

3. For chocolate drizzle, place chocolate chips and shortening in small resealable plastic bag; seal. Place bag in bowl of hot water for several minutes. Dry with paper towel. Knead until blended and chocolate is smooth. Snip pinpoint hole in corner of bag. Drizzle chocolate over brownies. Cool completely. Cut into bars. *Makes about 24 brownies*

Sour Cream Walnut Brownies

Brownie Kiss Cups

Brownie Kiss Cups

> **1 package DUNCAN HINES® Fudge**
> **Brownie Mix, Family Size**
> **1 egg**
> **⅓ cup water**
> **⅓ cup CRISCO® Oil or CRISCO®**
> **PURITAN® Oil**
> **25 milk chocolate candy kisses,**
> **unwrapped**

1. Preheat oven to 350°F. Place 25 (2-inch) foil liners in muffin pans or on cookie sheets.

2. Combine brownie mix, egg, water and oil in large bowl. Stir with spoon until well blended, about 50 strokes. Fill each liner with 2 measuring tablespoonfuls batter. Bake at 350°F for 17 to 20 minutes. Remove from oven. Place 1 milk chocolate candy kiss on each cupcake. Bake 1 minute longer. Cool 5 to 10 minutes in pans. Remove to cooling racks. Cool completely.
Makes 25 brownie cups

White Chocolate Brownies

White Chocolate Brownies

1 package DUNCAN HINES®
    Chocolate Lovers' Milk
    Chocolate Chunk Brownie Mix
2 eggs
$^1/_3$ cup water
$^1/_3$ cup CRISCO® Oil or CRISCO®
    PURITAN® Oil
$^3/_4$ cup coarsely chopped white
    chocolate
$^1/_4$ cup sliced natural almonds

1. Preheat oven to 350°F. Grease bottom of 13×9-inch pan.

2. Combine brownie mix, eggs, water and oil in large bowl. Stir with spoon until well blended, about 50 strokes. Stir in white chocolate. Spread in prepared pan. Sprinkle top with almonds. Bake at 350°F for 25 to 28 minutes or until set. Cool completely. Cut into bars.

Makes about 48 small or 24 large brownies

Tip: For decadent brownies, combine 2 ounces coarsely chopped white chocolate and 2 teaspoons CRISCO® Shortening in small heavy saucepan. Melt over low heat, stirring constantly. Drizzle over brownies.

All American Heath®
Brownies

$^1/_3$ cup butter or margarine
1 square (1 ounce) unsweetened
    chocolate
1 cup sugar
2 eggs
1 teaspoon vanilla
1 cup flour
$^1/_2$ teaspoon baking powder
$^1/_4$ teaspoon salt
1 package (6 ounces) HEATH® Bits

Preheat oven to 350°F. Grease bottom of 8-inch square baking pan.

In 1$^1/_2$-quart saucepan over low heat, melt butter and chocolate, stirring occasionally. Blend in sugar. Add eggs, 1 at a time, beating after each addition. Blend in vanilla. In small bowl, mix together flour, baking powder and salt; add to chocolate mixture and blend. Spread batter in prepared pan.

Bake 20 minutes. Remove from oven; sprinkle with Heath® Bits. Cover tightly with foil and cool completely on wire rack. Remove foil; cut into bars.

Makes about 12 brownies

All American Heath® Brownies

Ultimate Designer Brownies

3/4 cup HERSHEY'S Cocoa
1/2 teaspoon baking soda
2/3 cup butter or margarine, melted and divided
1/2 cup boiling water
2 cups sugar
2 eggs
1 1/3 cups all-purpose flour
1 teaspoon vanilla extract
1/4 teaspoon salt
3/4 cup (3 1/2-ounce jar) macadamia nuts, coarsely chopped
2 cups (12-ounce package) HERSHEY'S Semi-Sweet Chocolate Chips, divided
Vanilla Glaze

Preheat oven to 350°F. Grease 13×9-inch baking pan or two 8-inch square baking pans. In medium bowl, stir together cocoa and baking soda; blend in 1/3 cup melted butter. Add boiling water; stir until mixture thickens. Stir in sugar, eggs and remaining 1/3 cup melted butter; stir until smooth. Add flour, vanilla and salt; blend well. Stir in nuts and 1 1/2 cups chocolate chips. Pour into prepared pan(s). Bake 30 to 35 minutes for square pans or 35 to 40 minutes for rectangular pan or until brownie begins to pull away from sides of pan. Cool completely.

Prepare Vanilla Glaze; spread on top of brownie. Cut brownie into triangles. Place remaining 1/2 cup chips in top of double boiler over hot, not boiling, water; stir until melted. Put into pastry bag fitted with small writing tip. Pipe signature design on each brownie.

Makes about 24 brownies

Ultimate Designer Brownie

Vanilla Glaze

2 tablespoons butter or margarine
1 tablespoon milk
1/4 teaspoon brandy extract
1/4 teaspoon rum extract
1 cup powdered sugar

In small saucepan over low heat, melt butter in milk. Remove from heat; add brandy and rum extracts. Gradually add powdered sugar, beating with wire whisk until smooth. If glaze is too thick, add additional milk, 1/2 teaspoon at a time. Makes about 1/2 cup glaze.

Butterscotch Brownies

1 cup butterscotch-flavored chips
$^1/_4$ cup butter or margarine, softened
$^1/_2$ cup packed light brown sugar
2 large eggs
$^1/_2$ teaspoon vanilla
1 cup all-purpose flour
$^1/_2$ teaspoon baking powder
$^1/_4$ teaspoon salt
1 cup semisweet chocolate chips

Preheat oven to 350°F. Melt chips in small, heavy saucepan over low heat stirring constantly; set aside. Beat butter and sugar in large bowl until light and fluffy. Beat in eggs, 1 at a time, scraping down side of bowl after each addition. Beat in vanilla. Beat in melted butterscotch chips. Add combined flour, baking powder and salt. Beat until well blended. Spread batter evenly into greased 9-inch square baking pan.

Bake 20 to 25 minutes or until golden brown and center is set. Remove pan from oven and immediately sprinkle with chips. Let stand about 4 minutes until chocolate is melted. Spread chocolate evenly over top. Place pan on wire rack; cool completely. Cut into 2$^1/_4$-inch squares.

Makes about 16 brownies

Rich Chocolate Caramel Brownies

1 (18.25- to 18.5-ounce) package devil's food or chocolate cake mix
1 cup chopped nuts
$^1/_2$ cup butter or margarine, melted
1 cup *undiluted* CARNATION® Evaporated Milk, divided
35 light caramels (about 10 ounces), unwrapped
1 cup (6-ounce package) NESTLÉ® Toll House® Semi-Sweet Chocolate Morsels

Preheat oven to 350°F. In large bowl, combine cake mix and nuts; stir in butter. Stir in $^2/_3$ *cup* evaporated milk (batter will be thick). Spread half of batter into greased 13×9-inch baking pan. Bake 15 minutes.

In small saucepan, combine caramels and *remaining* $^1/_3$ *cup* evaporated milk. Stir over low heat until caramels are melted. Sprinkle Nestlé® Toll House® Semi-Sweet Chocolate Morsels over baked layer; drizzle caramel mixture over top. Drop remaining batter by heaping teaspoons over caramel mixture. Return to oven for 20 to 25 minutes (top layer will be soft). Cool completely before cutting into bars.

Makes about 48 brownies

Variation: For Rich Chocolate Butterscotch Brownies, pour 12.25-ounce jar of butterscotch-flavored topping over Nestlé® Toll House® Semi-Sweet Chocolate Morsels, instead of melting caramels with $^1/_3$ cup evaporated milk.

Butterscotch Brownies

Candy Dandy Brownies

Rocky Road Brownies

¹/₂ cup butter or margarine
¹/₂ cup unsweetened cocoa
1 cup sugar
1 egg
¹/₂ cup all-purpose flour
¹/₄ cup buttermilk
1 teaspoon vanilla
1 cup miniature marshmallows
1 cup coarsely chopped walnuts
1 cup (6 ounces) semisweet chocolate chips

Preheat oven to 350°F. Lightly grease 8-inch square pan. Combine butter and cocoa in medium-sized heavy saucepan over low heat, stirring constantly until smooth. Remove from heat; stir in sugar, egg, flour, buttermilk and vanilla. Mix until smooth. Spread batter evenly in prepared pan.

Bake 25 minutes or until center feels dry. *Do not overbake or brownies will be dry.* Remove from oven; sprinkle marshmallows, walnuts and chocolate chips over top. Return to oven for 3 to 5 minutes or just until topping is melted. Cool in pan on wire rack. Cut into 2-inch squares.

Makes about 16 brownies

Candy Dandy Brownies

Brownies

1 package DUNCAN HINES® Chocolate Lovers' Peanut Butter Brownie Mix, separated
1 egg
¹/₃ cup water
¹/₃ cup CRISCO® Oil or CRISCO® PURITAN® Oil

Topping

¹/₃ cup sugar
¹/₃ cup light corn syrup
Peanut butter packet from Mix

Frosting

¹/₂ cup semi-sweet chocolate chips
2 tablespoons butter or margarine
1 tablespoon light corn syrup
¹/₄ cup sliced almonds, for garnish

1. Preheat oven to 350°F. Grease 13×9-inch pan.

2. For brownies, combine brownie mix, egg, water and oil in large bowl. Stir with spoon until well blended, about 50 strokes. Spread in prepared pan. Bake 25 to 28 minutes or until set. Cool in pan while preparing topping.

3. For topping, combine sugar and ¹/₃ cup corn syrup in heavy saucepan. Bring to a boil on moderate heat. Stir in peanut butter packet from Mix. Spread over warm brownies. Cool 10 to 15 minutes.

4. For frosting, combine chocolate chips, butter and 1 tablespoon corn syrup in small saucepan. Cook, stirring constantly, on low heat until melted. Spread frosting over peanut butter layer. Sprinkle with almonds. Cool completely. Refrigerate until chocolate is firm, about 15 minutes. Cut into bars.

Makes about 24 brownies

Black & White Cheesecake Brownies

Brownie Base

2 cups (12-ounce package) NESTLÉ® Toll House® Semi-Sweet Chocolate Mini Morsels, divided
¹/₂ cup sugar
¹/₄ cup butter, softened
2 eggs
1 teaspoon vanilla extract
¹/₂ teaspoon salt
²/₃ cup all-purpose flour

Cheesecake Topping

1 (8-ounce package) cream cheese, softened
¹/₂ cup sugar
2 tablespoons butter, softened
2 eggs
2 tablespoons milk
1 tablespoon all-purpose flour
¹/₂ teaspoon almond extract
³/₄ cup NESTLÉ® Toll House® Semi-Sweet Chocolate Mini Morsels, reserved from 12-ounce package

Brownie Base: Preheat oven to 350°F. Melt over hot (not boiling) water, 1¹/₄ cups Nestlé® Toll House® Semi-Sweet Chocolate Mini Morsels; stir until smooth. Set aside. In large bowl, combine sugar and butter; beat until creamy. Add eggs, vanilla extract and salt; mix well. Add melted morsels and flour; mix well. Spread into foil-lined 9-inch square baking pan.

Cheesecake Topping: In large bowl, combine cream cheese, sugar and butter; beat until creamy. Add eggs, milk, flour and almond extract; beat well. Stir in remaining ³/₄ cup Nestlé® Toll House® Semi-Sweet Chocolate Mini Morsels. Pour over Brownie Base. Bake at 350°F for 40 to 45 minutes. Cool completely on wire rack; cut into 2¹/₄-inch squares.

Makes about 16 brownies

Minty Fudge Brownies

¹/₄ cups all-purpose flour
¹/₂ teaspoon baking soda
¹/₂ teaspoon salt
1 cup sugar
¹/₂ cup butter
3 tablespoons water
1¹/₂ cups (10-ounce package) NESTLÉ® Toll House® Mint Flavored Semi-Sweet Chocolate Morsels
1¹/₂ teaspoons vanilla extract
3 eggs
1 cup chopped nuts
Walnut halves (optional)

Preheat oven to 325°F. In small bowl, combine flour, baking soda and salt; set aside. In medium saucepan, combine sugar, butter and water; bring just to a boil. Remove from heat. Add Nestlé® Toll House® Mint Flavored Semi-Sweet Chocolate Morsels and vanilla extract; stir until morsels are melted and mixture is smooth. Transfer to large bowl. Add eggs, 1 at a time, beating well after each addition. Gradually blend in flour mixture. Stir in nuts. Spread into greased 13×9-inch baking pan. Bake at 325°F for 30 to 35 minutes. Cool completely on wire rack; cut into 1¹/₂-inch squares. Garnish with walnut halves, if desired.

Makes about 48 brownies

Minty Fudge Brownies (top), Black & White Cheesecake Brownies (bottom)

Fudgy Cheesecake Swirl Brownies

Fudgy Cheesecake Swirl Brownies

Cream Cheese Batter
- 1 (8-ounce) package cream cheese, softened
- 1/2 cup sugar
- 1 egg
- 1 teaspoon vanilla extract

Chocolate Batter
- 3/4 cup (1 1/2 sticks) butter
- 2 foil-wrapped bars (4 ounces) NESTLÉ® Unsweetened Chocolate Baking Bars
- 1 3/4 cups sugar
- 3 eggs, well beaten
- 1 3/4 cups all-purpose flour

Cream Cheese Batter: Preheat oven to 350°F. In small mixer bowl, beat cream cheese and 1/2 cup sugar until smooth. Beat in 1 egg and vanilla extract; set aside.

Chocolate Batter: In heavy-gauge, medium saucepan over low heat, melt butter and Nestlé® Unsweetened Chocolate Baking Bars, stirring until smooth. Stir in 1 3/4 cups sugar. Blend in 3 eggs. Stir in flour.

Spread Chocolate Batter into greased 13×9-inch baking pan. Spoon Cream Cheese Batter over top. Swirl metal spatula through batters to marbleize.

Bake 30 to 35 minutes until edges begin to pull away from sides of pan. Cool completely; cut into 2-inch bars.

Makes about 2 dozen brownies

Vanilla Chip Orange Brownies

- 1 1/2 cups graham cracker crumbs
- 1/2 cup HERSHEY'S Cocoa
- 1 teaspoon grated orange rind
- 1 (14-ounce) can EAGLE® Brand Sweetened Condensed Milk (NOT evaporated milk)
- 3 tablespoons water
- 1 (10-ounce) package HERSHEY'S Vanilla Milk Chips

Preheat oven to 350°F. In medium bowl, combine crumbs, cocoa and rind. Stir in sweetened condensed milk, water and chips until well blended; spread into greased 9-inch square baking pan. Bake 25 to 30 minutes or until top springs back when lightly touched. Cool completely; cut into bars. Store tightly covered at room temperature.

Makes 20 to 24 brownies

Vanilla Chip Orange Brownie

Peanut Butter Brownie Cups

Brownie Cups

    1 package DUNCAN HINES®
       Chocolate Lovers' Double Fudge
       Brownie Mix
    2 eggs
    1/3 cup water
    1/4 cup CRISCO® Oil or CRISCO®
       PURITAN® Oil

Topping

    1/3 cup sugar
    1/3 cup light corn syrup
    1/2 cup peanut butter

Chocolate Glaze

    3/4 cup semi-sweet chocolate chips
    3 tablespoons butter or margarine
    1 tablespoon light corn syrup
    3 tablespoons chopped peanuts, for
      garnish

1. Preheat oven to 350°F. Place 24 (2-inch) foil liners on cookie sheets.

2. For brownie cups, combine brownie mix, fudge packet from Mix, eggs, water and oil in large bowl. Stir with spoon until well blended, about 50 strokes. Place 2 level measuring tablespoons batter in each foil liner. Bake at 350°F for 20 to 22 minutes or until set. Cool completely.

3. For topping, combine sugar and 1/3 cup corn syrup in small heavy saucepan. Bring to a boil on medium heat. Stir in peanut butter. Drop by rounded teaspoonfuls onto each brownie cup.

4. For chocolate glaze, combine chocolate chips, butter and 1 tablespoon corn syrup in small heavy saucepan. Cook, stirring constantly, on low heat until melted. Spoon 1 rounded teaspoonful chocolate glaze onto peanut butter topping. Sprinkle with chopped peanuts. Refrigerate 15 minutes or until chocolate is firm. *Makes 24 cups*

Peanut Butter Brownie Cups

Tex-Mex Brownies

    1/2 cup butter or margarine
    2 squares (1 ounce each)
      unsweetened chocolate
    1/2 to 1 teaspoon ground red pepper
    2 eggs
    1 cup sugar
    1/2 cup all-purpose flour
    1 teaspoon vanilla
    1 cup (6 ounces) semisweet chocolate
      chips

Preheat oven to 325°F. Grease and flour 8-inch square pan. Melt butter and unsweetened chocolate in small heavy saucepan over low heat. Remove from heat. Stir in pepper; cool.

Beat eggs in medium bowl until light. Add sugar; beat well. Blend in chocolate mixture. Stir in flour and vanilla. Spread batter evenly in prepared pan.

Bake 30 minutes or until firm in center. Remove from oven; sprinkle with chocolate chips. Let stand until chocolate is melted, then spread evenly over brownies. Cool completely in pan on wire rack. Cut into 2-inch squares.
Makes about 16 brownies

BOUNTIFUL BARS

Kahlúa® Pumpkin Squares with Praline Topping

1 cup flour
¹/₄ cup powdered sugar
¹/₂ cup cold unsalted butter
1 cup LIBBY'S® Solid Pack Pumpkin
1 (8-ounce) package cream cheese, cut up and softened
2 eggs
¹/₄ cup granulated sugar
¹/₄ cup KAHLÚA®
1 cup chopped walnuts or pecans
³/₄ cup firmly packed brown sugar
¹/₄ cup unsalted butter, melted

Preheat oven to 350°F. In medium bowl, combine flour and powdered sugar. Using 2 knives or pastry blender, cut in ¹/₂ cup butter until mixture forms fine crumbs. Press mixture into bottom of 8-inch square broilerproof baking dish. Bake 15 to 18 minutes or until golden.

Meanwhile, in food processor or blender, puree pumpkin, cream cheese, eggs, granulated sugar and Kahlúa® until smooth. Pour pumpkin mixture over warm baked crust; return to oven and bake about 20 minutes or until set. Cool in dish on rack. Cover; refrigerate.

In small bowl, combine nuts, brown sugar and melted butter. Just before serving, sprinkle topping over pumpkin filling. *Makes about 16 squares*

Raspberry Coconut Layer Bars

1²/₃ cups graham cracker crumbs
¹/₂ cup butter, melted
2²/₃ cups (7-ounce package) flaked coconut
1¹/₄ cups (14-ounce can) CARNATION® Sweetened Condensed Milk
1 cup red raspberry jam or preserves
¹/₃ cup finely chopped walnuts, toasted
¹/₂ cup semi-sweet chocolate pieces, melted
¹/₄ cup vanilla milk chocolate pieces, melted

Preheat oven to 350°F. In medium bowl, combine graham cracker crumbs and butter. Spread evenly over bottom of 13×9-inch baking pan, pressing firmly to make crust. Sprinkle coconut over crust. Pour sweetened condensed milk evenly over coconut. Bake 20 to 25 minutes or until lightly browned. Cool. Spread jam over coconut layer. Chill 3 to 4 hours. Sprinkle with walnuts. Drizzle melted chocolates over top layer, creating lacy effect. Chill. Cut into 3×1¹/₂-inch bars.

Makes about 24 bars

Raspberry Coconut Layer Bars (top), Kahlúa® Pumpkin Squares with Praline Topping (bottom)

Chocolate Raspberry Coconut Squares

Cookie Base: Preheat oven to 350°F. In medium bowl, combine flour and brown sugar. With pastry blender or 2 knives, cut in butter until mixture resembles fine crumbs. Press into greased 9-inch square baking pan. Bake 20 minutes.

Topping: In large bowl, combine sweetened condensed milk, flour, baking powder, salt and eggs; mix well. Stir in Nestlé® Toll House® Semi-Sweet Chocolate Morsels, 1 cup coconut and pecans. Pour over baked Cookie Base. Bake 25 minutes. Remove from oven. Spread preserves over top. Sprinkle with remaining ¹/₃ cup coconut. Cool completely on wire rack. Cut into 1¹/₂-inch squares.

Makes about 36 squares

Chocolate Raspberry Coconut Squares

Cookie Base

> 1 cup all-purpose flour
> ¹/₄ cup firmly packed brown sugar
> ¹/₂ cup cold butter

Topping

> 1 cup sweetened condensed milk
> ¹/₂ cup all-purpose flour
> ¹/₂ teaspoon baking powder
> ¹/₄ teaspoon salt
> 2 eggs
> 1 cup (6-ounce package) NESTLÉ®
>   Toll House® Semi-Sweet
>   Chocolate Morsels
> 1¹/₃ cups (3¹/₂-ounce can) flaked
>   coconut, divided
> ¹/₂ cup chopped pecans
> ¹/₂ cup raspberry preserves

Chippy Cheeseys

Base

> 1¹/₄ cups firmly packed brown sugar
> ³/₄ cup BUTTER FLAVOR CRISCO®
> 1 egg
> 2 tablespoons milk
> 1 tablespoon vanilla
> 2 cups all-purpose flour
> 1 teaspoon salt
> ³/₄ teaspoon baking soda
> 1 cup semi-sweet mini chocolate
>   chips
> 1 cup finely chopped walnuts

Filling

> 2 (8-ounce) packages cream cheese,
>   softened
> 2 eggs
> ³/₄ cup granulated sugar
> 1 teaspoon vanilla

1. Preheat oven to 375°F. Grease 13×9-inch pan with Butter Flavor Crisco®.

Chippy Cheeseys

2. For base, combine brown sugar and Butter Flavor Crisco® in large bowl. Beat at medium speed of electric mixer until creamy. Beat in 1 egg, milk and 1 tablespoon vanilla.

3. Combine flour, salt and baking soda. Add gradually to creamed mixture at low speed. Stir in chocolate chips and nuts with spoon. Spread half of dough in prepared pan.

4. Bake 8 minutes.

5. For filling, combine cream cheese, 2 eggs, granulated sugar and 1 teaspoon vanilla in medium bowl. Beat at medium speed of electric mixer until smooth. Pour over hot crust.

6. Roll remaining dough into 13×9-inch rectangle between sheets of waxed paper. Remove top sheet. Flip dough over onto filling. Remove waxed paper.

7. Bake 40 minutes or until top is set and light golden brown. Cool to room temperature. Cut into bars about 2×1³/₄ inches. Refrigerate.

Makes about 30 bars

Fudgy Walnut Cookie Wedges

1 (20-ounce) package refrigerated cookie dough, any flavor
1 (12-ounce) package HERSHEY'S Semi-Sweet Chocolate Chips
2 tablespoons margarine or butter
1 (14-ounce) can EAGLE® Brand Sweetened Condensed Milk (NOT evaporated milk)
1 teaspoon vanilla extract
¹/₂ cup chopped walnuts

Preheat oven to 350°F. Divide cookie dough into thirds. With floured hands, press on bottom of 3 aluminum foil-lined 9-inch round cake pans or press into 9-inch circles on ungreased cookie sheets. Bake 10 to 20 minutes or until golden. Cool. In heavy saucepan over medium heat, melt chips and margarine with sweetened condensed milk. Cook and stir until thickened, about 5 minutes; add vanilla. Spread over cookie circles. Top with walnuts. Chill. Cut into wedges. Store loosely covered at room temperature.

Makes about 36 wedges

Fudgy Walnut Cookie Wedges

Pumpkin Cheesecake Bars

Pecan Pie Bars

2 cups unsifted flour
$^1/_2$ cup confectioners' sugar
1 cup cold margarine or butter
1 (14-ounce) can EAGLE® Brand
    Sweetened Condensed Milk
    (NOT evaporated milk)
1 egg
1 teaspoon vanilla extract
1 (6-ounce) package almond brickle
    chips
1 cup chopped pecans

Preheat oven to 350°F (325°F for glass dish). In medium bowl, combine flour and sugar; cut in cold margarine until crumbly. Press firmly on bottom of 13×9-inch baking pan. Bake 15 minutes. Meanwhile, in large mixer bowl, beat sweetened condensed milk, egg and vanilla. Stir in chips and pecans. Spread evenly over baked crust. Bake 25 minutes or until golden brown. Cool. Cut into bars. Store covered in refrigerator. *Makes 24 to 36 bars*

Tip: If desired, omit almond brickle chips; increase pecans to 2 cups.

Pumpkin Cheesecake Bars

1 cup all-purpose flour
$^1/_3$ cup packed light brown sugar
5 tablespoons butter or margarine
$^1/_2$ cup pecans, finely chopped
1 (8-ounce) package cream cheese,
    softened
$^3/_4$ cup granulated sugar
$^1/_2$ cup LIBBY'S® Solid Pack Pumpkin
2 eggs, lightly beaten
$1^1/_2$ teaspoons ground cinnamon
1 teaspoon ground allspice
1 teaspoon vanilla extract
    Glazed Pecan Halves (recipe
    follows)

Preheat oven to 350°F. In medium bowl, combine flour and brown sugar. Cut in butter to make crumb mixture. Stir in nuts. Reserve $^3/_4$ cup mixture for topping. Press remaining mixture into bottom of 8-inch square baking pan. Bake 15 minutes. Cool slightly. In large mixer bowl, combine cream cheese, granulated sugar, pumpkin, eggs, cinnamon, allspice, and vanilla; blend until smooth. Pour over baked crust. Sprinkle with reserved topping. Bake an additional 35 to 40 minutes or until slightly firm. Cool on wire rack. Cut into 2×1-inch bars and then into triangles, if desired. Garnish each bar with a Glazed Pecan Half.
Makes 32 bars or 64 triangles

Glazed Pecan Halves: Place greased wire rack over cookie sheet. In small saucepan, bring $^1/_4$ cup dark corn syrup to a boil. Boil 1 minute, stirring constantly, until syrup slightly thickens. Remove from heat. Add 32 pecan halves, stirring until well coated. With slotted spoon, remove pecans from syrup. Transfer to wire rack; cool. Makes 32 pecan halves.

Almond Toffee Squares

1 cup (2 sticks) margarine or butter, softened
1 cup firmly packed brown sugar
1 egg
1 teaspoon vanilla
2 cups all-purpose flour
1/4 teaspoon salt
2 (4-ounce) packages BAKER'S® GERMAN'S® Sweet Chocolate, broken into squares
1/2 cup toasted slivered almonds
1/2 cup lightly toasted BAKER'S® ANGEL FLAKE® Coconut

Preheat oven to 350°F.

Beat margarine, sugar, egg and vanilla. Mix in flour and salt. Press into greased 13×9-inch pan.

Bake for 30 minutes or until edges are golden brown. Remove from oven. Immediately sprinkle with chocolate squares. Cover with foil; let stand 5 minutes or until chocolate is softened.

Spread chocolate evenly over entire surface; sprinkle with almonds and coconut. Cut into squares while still warm. Cool on wire rack.

Makes about 26 squares

Prep Time: 20 minutes
Bake Time: 30 minutes

Orange Chess Bars

Crust
1 package DUNCAN HINES® Moist Deluxe Orange Supreme Cake Mix
1/2 cup CRISCO® Oil or CRISCO® PURITAN Oil
1/3 cup chopped pecans

Topping
1 pound confectioners sugar (3 1/2 to 4 cups)
1 (8-ounce) package cream cheese, softened
2 eggs
2 teaspoons grated orange peel

1. Preheat oven to 350°F. Grease 13×9-inch baking pan.

2. For crust, combine cake mix, oil and pecans in large bowl. Stir until blended (mixture will be crumbly). Press in bottom of prepared pan.

3. For topping, combine confectioners sugar and cream cheese in large bowl. Beat at low speed with electric mixer until blended. Add eggs and orange peel. Beat at low speed until blended. Pour over crust. Bake 30 to 35 minutes or until topping is set. Cool. Refrigerate until ready to serve. Cut into bars.

Makes about 24 bars

Almond Toffee Squares

Almond Toffee Triangles

Bar Cookie Crust (recipe follows)
$1/3$ cup packed brown sugar
$1/3$ cup KARO® Light or Dark Corn
    Syrup
$1/4$ cup MAZOLA® margarine
$1/4$ cup heavy cream
$1^{1/2}$ cups sliced almonds
1 teaspoon vanilla

Preheat oven to 350°F. Prepare Bar
Cookie Crust according to recipe
directions. In medium saucepan,
combine brown sugar, corn syrup,
margarine and cream. Bring to boil over
medium heat; remove from heat. Stir in
almonds and vanilla. Pour over hot
crust; spread evenly. Bake 15 to 20
minutes or until set and golden. Cool
completely on wire rack. Cut into
$2^{1/2}$-inch squares; cut each in half
diagonally to create triangles.

Makes about 48 triangles

Prep Time: 30 minutes
Bake Time: 20 minutes, *plus* cooling

Bar Cookie Crust

MAZOLA® No Stick® cooking
    spray
$2^{1/2}$ cups flour
1 cup cold MAZOLA® Margarine,
    cut in pieces
$1/2$ cup confectioners sugar
$1/4$ teaspoon salt

Preheat oven to 350°F. Spray 15×10-inch
baking pan with cooking spray. In large
bowl with mixer at medium speed, beat
flour, margarine, sugar and salt until
mixture resembles coarse crumbs; press
firmly and evenly into prepared pan.
Bake 20 minutes or until golden brown.
Top with desired filling. Finish baking
according to individual recipe
directions.

Prep Time: 30 minutes
Bake Time: 25 minutes, *plus* cooling

Chocolate-Drizzled Peanut Bars

Bar Cookie Crust (this page)
$1/2$ cup packed brown sugar
$1/3$ cup KARO® Light Corn Syrup
$1/4$ cup MAZOLA® Margarine
$1/4$ cup heavy cream
1 teaspoon vanilla
$1/4$ teaspoon lemon juice
$1^{1/2}$ cups coarsely chopped roasted
    peanuts
Chocolate Glaze (recipe follows)

Preheat oven to 350°F. Prepare Bar
Cookie Crust according to recipe
directions. In medium saucepan
combine brown sugar, corn syrup,
margarine and cream. Bring to boil over
medium heat; remove from heat. Stir in
vanilla, lemon juice and peanuts. Pour
over hot crust; spread evenly. Bake 15 to
20 minutes or until set. Cool completely
on wire rack. Drizzle with Chocolate
Glaze; cool before cutting into bars.

Makes about 60 bars

Prep Time: 30 minutes
Bake Time: 20 minutes, *plus* cooling

Chocolate Glaze: In small heavy
saucepan over low heat, combine $2/3$ cup
semisweet chocolate chips and 1
tablespoon Mazola® Margarine; stir until
melted and smooth.

*Clockwise from top: Almond Toffee
Triangles, Chocolate Pecan Pie Squares
(page 58), Chocolate-Drizzled Peanut Bars*

Chewy Oatmeal-Apricot-Date Bars

Cookies

1¼ cups firmly packed brown sugar
¾ cup *plus* 4 teaspoons BUTTER FLAVOR CRISCO®
3 eggs
2 teaspoons vanilla
2 cups quick oats, uncooked, divided
½ cup all-purpose flour
2 teaspoons baking powder
1 teaspoon cinnamon
¼ teaspoon nutmeg
¼ teaspoon salt
1 cup finely grated carrots
1 cup finely minced dried apricots
1 cup minced dates
1 cup finely chopped walnuts
⅔ cup vanilla chips

Frosting

1 (3-ounce) package cream cheese, softened
¼ cup BUTTER FLAVOR CRISCO®
2½ cups confectioners sugar
1 to 2 teaspoons milk
¾ teaspoon lemon extract
½ teaspoon vanilla
½ teaspoon finely grated lemon peel
⅓ cup finely chopped walnuts

1. Preheat oven to 350°F. Grease 13×9-inch pan with Butter Flavor Crisco®. Flour lightly.

2. For cookies, combine brown sugar and ¾ cup *plus* 4 teaspoons Butter Flavor Crisco® in large bowl. Beat at medium speed of electric mixer until fluffy. Add eggs, 1 at a time, and 2 teaspoons vanilla. Beat until well blended and fluffy.

3. Process ½ cup oats in food processor or blender until finely ground. Combine with flour, baking powder, cinnamon, nutmeg and salt. Add gradually to creamed mixture at low speed. Add remaining 1½ cups oats, carrots, apricots, dates, 1 cup nuts and vanilla chips. Mix until partially blended. Finish mixing with spoon. Spread in prepared pan.

4. Bake 35 to 45 minutes or until center is set and cookie starts to pull away from sides of pan. Toothpick inserted in center should come out clean. *Do not overbake.* Cool completely.

5. For frosting, combine cream cheese, ¼ cup Butter Flavor Crisco®, confectioners sugar, milk, lemon extract, vanilla and lemon peel in medium bowl. Beat at low speed until blended. Increase speed to medium-high. Beat until fluffy. Stir in ⅓ cup nuts. Spread on baked surface. Cut into bars about 2¼×2 inches. Refrigerate.

Makes about 24 bars

Chewy Oatmeal-Apricot-Date Bars

Chocolate Mint Cheesecake Bars

1¹/₄ cups unsifted flour
1 cup confectioners' sugar
¹/₂ cup HERSHEY'S Cocoa
¹/₄ teaspoon baking soda
1 cup *cold* margarine or butter
1 (8-ounce) package cream cheese, softened
1 (14-ounce) can EAGLE® Brand Sweetened Condensed Milk (NOT evaporated milk)
2 eggs
1¹/₂ teaspoons peppermint extract
    Green or red food coloring, optional
    Chocolate Glaze

Preheat oven to 350°F. In large bowl, combine flour, sugar, cocoa and baking soda; cut in *cold* margarine until crumbly (mixture will be dry). Press firmly on bottom of 13×9-inch baking pan. Bake 15 minutes.

Meanwhile, in large mixer bowl, beat cheese until fluffy. Gradually beat in sweetened condensed milk until smooth. Add eggs, extract and food coloring if desired; mix well. Pour over baked crust. Bake 20 minutes or until lightly browned around edges. Cool. Drizzle with Chocolate Glaze. Chill. Cut into bars. Store covered in refrigerator.

Makes 24 to 36 bars

Chocolate Glaze: In small saucepan, over low heat, melt 2 (1-ounce) bars Hershey's Unsweetened Baking Chocolate with 2 tablespoons margarine or butter; stir until smooth. Remove from heat; stir in ¹/₂ teaspoon vanilla. Immediately drizzle over bars. Makes about ¹/₄ cup glaze.

Chocolate Mint Cheesecake Bar

Walnut Shortbread Bars

1 (8-ounce) package PHILADELPHIA BRAND® Cream Cheese, softened
1 cup PARKAY® Margarine
³/₄ cup granulated sugar
³/₄ cup packed brown sugar
1 egg
1 teaspoon vanilla
2¹/₂ cups flour
1 teaspoon CALUMET® Baking Powder
¹/₂ teaspoon salt
³/₄ cup chopped walnuts

• Preheat oven to 350°F.

• Beat cream cheese, margarine and sugars in large mixing bowl at medium speed with electric mixer until well blended. Blend in egg and vanilla.

• Add combined dry ingredients; mix well. Stir in walnuts. Spread into greased 15×10-inch jelly-roll pan.

• Bake 20 to 25 minutes or until lightly browned. Cool. Sprinkle with powdered sugar, if desired. Cut into bars.

Makes about 60 bars

Prep Time: 15 minutes
Cook Time: 25 minutes

Chocolate Caramel-Pecan Bars

2 cups butter, softened, divided
$1/2$ cup granulated sugar
1 large egg
$2^3/4$ cups all-purpose flour
$2/3$ cup packed light brown sugar
$1/4$ cup light corn syrup
$2^1/2$ cups coarsely chopped pecans
1 cup semisweet chocolate chips

Preheat oven to 375°F. Grease 15×10-inch jelly-roll pan; set aside. Beat 1 cup butter and granulated sugar in large bowl until light and fluffy. Beat in egg. Add flour. Beat until well combined. Spread dough with rubber spatula into prepared pan. Bake 20 minutes or until light golden brown.

While bars are baking, prepare topping. Combine remaining 1 cup butter, brown sugar and corn syrup in medium, heavy saucepan. Cook over medium heat until mixture boils, stirring frequently. Boil gently 2 minutes, without stirring. Quickly stir in pecans; spread evenly over base. Return to oven and bake 20 minutes or until dark golden brown and bubbling. Immediately sprinkle chocolate chips evenly over hot caramel. Gently press chips into caramel topping with spatula. Loosen caramel from edges of pan with a thin spatula or knife. Remove pan to wire rack; cool completely. Cut into 3×1$1/2$-inch bars.

Makes about 40 bars

Marble Squares

$1/2$ cup PARKAY® Margarine
$3/4$ cup water
$1^1/2$ (1-ounce) squares BAKER'S® Unsweetened Chocolate
2 cups flour
2 cups sugar
1 teaspoon baking soda
$1/2$ teaspoon salt
2 eggs
$1/2$ cup sour cream
1 (8-ounce) package PHILADELPHIA BRAND® Cream Cheese, softened
$1/3$ cup sugar
1 egg
1 cup BAKER'S® Semi-Sweet Real Chocolate Chips

• Preheat oven to 375°F.

• Melt margarine with water and chocolate in saucepan; bring to boil. Remove from heat. Stir in combined flour, 2 cups sugar, baking soda and salt.

• Add 2 eggs and sour cream; mix well. Pour into greased and floured 15×10-inch jelly-roll pan.

• Beat cream cheese, $1/3$ cup sugar and 1 egg in small mixing bowl at medium speed with electric mixer until well blended.

• Spoon cream cheese mixture over chocolate batter; cut through batter with knife several times to marbleize.

• Sprinkle with chocolate pieces. Bake 25 to 30 minutes or until toothpick inserted in center comes out clean.

Makes about 24 squares

Prep Time: 25 minutes
Cook Time: 30 minutes

Chocolate Caramel-Pecan Bars

Streusel Caramel Bars (left), Triple Layer Chocolate Bars (right)

Streusel Caramel Bars

2 cups unsifted flour
¾ cup firmly packed light brown
    sugar
1 egg, beaten
¾ cup cold margarine or butter
¾ cup chopped nuts
24 EAGLE™ Brand Caramels,
    unwrapped
1 (14-ounce) can EAGLE® Brand
    Sweetened Condensed Milk
    (NOT evaporated milk)

Preheat oven to 350°F. In large bowl, combine flour, sugar and egg; cut in ½ cup cold margarine until crumbly. Stir in nuts. Reserving 2 cups crumb mixture, press remainder firmly on bottom of greased 13×9-inch baking pan. Bake 15 minutes. Meanwhile, in heavy saucepan over low heat, melt caramels with sweetened condensed milk and remaining ¼ cup margarine. Pour over prepared crust. Top with reserved crumb mixture. Bake 20 minutes or until bubbly. Cool. Cut into bars. Store loosely covered at room temperature. *Makes 24 to 36 bars*

Chocolate Caramel Bars: Melt 2 (1-ounce) squares unsweetened chocolate with caramels, sweetened condensed milk and margarine. Proceed as above.

Triple Layer Chocolate Bars

1¹/₂ cups graham cracker crumbs
¹/₂ cup HERSHEY'S Cocoa
¹/₄ cup sugar
¹/₃ cup margarine or butter, melted
1 (14-ounce) can EAGLE® Brand
    Sweetened Condensed Milk
    (NOT evaporated milk)
¹/₄ cup unsifted flour
1 egg
1 teaspoon vanilla extract
¹/₂ teaspoon baking powder
³/₄ cup chopped nuts
1 (12-ounce) package HERSHEY'S
    Semi-Sweet Chocolate Chips

Preheat oven to 350°F. Combine crumbs, *¹/₄ cup* cocoa, sugar and margarine; press firmly on bottom of 13×9-inch baking pan. In large mixer bowl, beat sweetened condensed milk, flour, remaining *¹/₄ cup* cocoa, egg, vanilla and baking powder. Stir in nuts. Spread evenly over prepared crust. Top with chips. Bake 20 to 25 minutes or until set. Cool. Cut into bars. Store tightly covered at room temperature.

Makes 24 to 36 bars

Chocolate Filled Walnut-Oatmeal Bars

1 cup butter or margarine, softened
2 cups packed light brown sugar
2 eggs
1 teaspoon vanilla extract
¹/₂ teaspoon powdered instant coffee
    (optional)
3 cups quick-cooking rolled oats
2¹/₂ cups all-purpose flour
1 teaspoon baking soda
¹/₂ teaspoon salt
1¹/₂ cups chopped walnuts, divided
    Chocolate Filling

Preheat oven to 350°F. In large mixer bowl, cream butter and brown sugar until light and fluffy. Add eggs, vanilla and instant coffee, if desired; beat well. Combine oats, flour, baking soda, salt and 1 cup walnuts; gradually add to creamed mixture. (Batter will be stiff; stir in last part by hand.) Remove 2 cups dough; set aside. Press remaining dough evenly onto bottom of 15¹/₂×10¹/₂-inch jelly-roll pan. Spread Chocolate Filling evenly over oatmeal mixture in pan. Sprinkle remaining oatmeal mixture over chocolate. Sprinkle remaining ¹/₂ cup walnuts over top. Bake 25 minutes or until top is golden (chocolate will be soft). Cool completely. Cut into bars.

Makes about 48 bars

Chocolate Filling

1 cup butter or margarine
²/₃ cup HERSHEY'S Cocoa
¹/₄ cup sugar
1 can (14 ounces) sweetened
    condensed milk
1¹/₂ teaspoons vanilla extract

In medium saucepan, over low heat, melt butter. Stir in cocoa and sugar. Add sweetened condensed milk; cook, stirring constantly, until smooth and thick. Remove from heat. Stir in vanilla.

Chocolate Filled Walnut-Oatmeal Bars

Fudgy Almond Bars

Fudgy Almond Bars

³/₄ cup *plus* ¹/₃ cup margarine or
  butter, softened
³/₄ cup confectioners' sugar
1¹/₂ cups unsifted flour
¹/₂ cup HERSHEY'S Cocoa
1 (14-ounce) can EAGLE® Brand
  Sweetened Condensed Milk
  (NOT evaporated milk)
1¹/₄ cups almonds, toasted and
  coarsely chopped
¹/₂ cup hot water
2 eggs, well beaten
¹/₂ teaspoon almond extract
¹/₈ teaspoon salt

Preheat oven to 350°F. In large mixer
bowl, beat ³/₄ *cup* margarine and sugar
until well blended. Add flour; mix well.
Press on bottom of ungreased
13×9-inch baking pan. Bake 15 minutes
or until lightly browned.

Meanwhile, in medium saucepan, over
low heat, melt remaining ¹/₃ *cup*
margarine; stir in cocoa. Remove from
heat; stir in remaining ingredients. Pour
evenly over baked crust.

Bake 25 to 30 minutes or until center is
set. Cool. Chill thoroughly. Cut into
bars. Store covered in refrigerator.
Makes 24 to 36 bars

Lemon Raspberry Cheesecake Bars

Crust
³/₄ cup BUTTER FLAVOR CRISCO®
¹/₃ cup firmly packed brown sugar
1¹/₄ cups all-purpose flour
1 cup oats (quick or old fashioned),
  uncooked
¹/₄ teaspoon salt

Filling
¹/₂ cup seedless red raspberry jam
2 (8-ounce) packages cream cheese,
  softened
³/₄ cup granulated sugar
2 tablespoons all-purpose flour
2 eggs
2 teaspoons grated lemon peel
3 tablespoons lemon juice

1. Preheat oven to 350°F. Grease
13×9-inch baking pan with Butter
Flavor Crisco®.

2. For crust, combine Butter Flavor
Crisco® and brown sugar. Beat at
medium speed of electric mixer until
well blended. Add 1¹/₄ cups flour, oats
and salt gradually at low speed. Mix
until well blended. Press onto bottom of
prepared pan.

3. Bake 20 minutes or until lightly
browned.

4. For filling, spoon jam immediately on
hot crust. Spread carefully to cover.

5. Combine cream cheese, granulated
sugar and 2 tablespoons flour in large
bowl. Beat at low speed until well
blended. Add eggs. Mix well. Add
lemon peel and lemon juice. Beat until
smooth. Pour over raspberry layer.

6. Bake 25 minutes or until set. Cool to
room temperature. Cut into bars about
2×1¹/₂ inches. Cover. Refrigerate.
Makes about 36 bars

Magic Cookie Bars

¹/2 cup margarine or butter
1¹/2 cups graham cracker crumbs
1 (14-ounce) can EAGLE® Brand
    Sweetened Condensed Milk
    (NOT evaporated milk)
1 (6-ounce) package semi-sweet
    chocolate chips
1 (3¹/2-ounce) can flaked coconut
    (1¹/2 cups)
1 cup chopped nuts

Preheat oven to 350°F (325°F for glass dish). In 13×9-inch baking pan, melt margarine in oven. Sprinkle crumbs over margarine; pour sweetened condensed milk evenly over crumbs. Top with remaining ingredients; press down firmly. Bake 25 to 30 minutes or until lightly browned. Cool. Chill if desired. Cut into bars. Store loosely covered at room temperature.

Makes 24 to 36 bars

Seven Layer Magic Cookie Bars: Add 1 (6-ounce) package butterscotch flavored chips after chocolate chips.

Magic Peanut Cookie Bars: Omit chocolate chips and chopped nuts. Top sweetened condensed milk with 2 cups (about ³/4 pound) chocolate-covered peanuts, then coconut. Proceed as above.

Magic Cookie Bars

Pumpkin Jingle Bars

Pumpkin Jingle Bars

³/4 cup MIRACLE WHIP® Salad
    Dressing
1 package two-layer spice cake mix
1 (16-ounce) can pumpkin
3 eggs
    Confectioners' sugar
    Vanilla frosting
    Red and green gum drops, sliced

Preheat oven to 350°F. Mix first 4 ingredients in large bowl at medium speed of electric mixer until well blended. Pour into greased 15¹/2×10¹/2-inch jelly roll pan. Bake 18 to 20 minutes or until edges pull away from sides of pan. Cool. Sprinkle with sugar. Cut into bars. Decorate with frosting and gum drops.

Makes about 36 bars

Prep Time: 5 minutes
Cook Time: 20 minutes

Lemon Nut Bars

1^1/$_3$ cups flour
^{1}/$_2$ cup packed brown sugar
^{1}/$_4$ cup granulated sugar
^{3}/$_4$ cup PARKAY® Margarine
1 cup old fashioned or quick oats,
    uncooked
^{1}/$_2$ cup chopped nuts
1 (8-ounce) package
    PHILADELPHIA BRAND®
    Cream Cheese, softened
1 egg
3 tablespoons lemon juice
1 tablespoon grated lemon peel

Preheat oven to 350°F. Stir together
flour and sugars in medium bowl. Cut
in margarine until mixture resembles
coarse crumbs. Stir in oats and nuts.
Reserve 1 cup crumb mixture; press
remaining crumb mixture onto bottom
of greased 13×9-inch baking pan. Bake
15 minutes. Beat cream cheese, egg,
juice and peel in small mixing bowl at
medium speed with electric mixer until
well blended. Pour over crust; sprinkle
with reserved crumb mixture. Bake
25 minutes. Cool; cut into bars.

Makes about 36 bars

Prep Time: 30 minutes
Cook Time: 25 minutes

Marshmallow Krispie Bars

1 package DUNCAN HINES® Fudge
    Brownie Mix, Family Size
1 (10^1/$_2$-ounce) package miniature
    marshmallows
1^1/$_2$ cups semi-sweet chocolate chips
1 cup JIF® Creamy Peanut Butter
1 tablespoon butter or margarine
1^1/$_2$ cups crisp rice cereal

1. Preheat oven to 350°F. Grease bottom
of 13×9-inch pan.

2. Prepare and bake brownies following
package directions for original recipe.
Remove from oven. Sprinkle
marshmallows on hot brownies. Return
to oven. Bake for 3 minutes longer.

3. Place chocolate chips, peanut butter
and butter in medium saucepan. Cook
on low heat, stirring constantly, until
chips are melted. Add rice cereal; mix
well. Spread mixture over marshmallow
layer. Refrigerate until chilled. Cut into
bars. *Makes about 24 bars*

Chocolate 'n' Oat Bars

1 cup unsifted flour
1 cup quick-cooking oats
^{3}/$_4$ cup firmly packed light brown
    sugar
^{1}/$_2$ cup margarine or butter, softened
1 (14-ounce) can EAGLE® Brand
    Sweetened Condensed Milk
    (NOT evaporated milk)
1 cup chopped nuts
1 (6-ounce) package semi-sweet
    chocolate chips

Preheat oven to 350°F (325°F for glass
dish). In large bowl, combine flour,
oats, sugar and margarine; mix well.
Reserving ^{1}/$_2$ cup oat mixture, press
remainder on bottom of 13×9-inch
baking pan. Bake 10 minutes. Pour
sweetened condensed milk evenly over
crust. Sprinkle with nuts and chocolate
chips. Top with remaining oat mixture;
press down firmly. Bake 25 to 30
minutes or until lightly browned. Cool.
Cut into bars. Store covered at room
temperature. *Makes about 36 bars*

Chocolate Pecan Pie Squares

Bar Cookie Crust (see page 46)
1^1/$_2$ cups KARO® Light or Dark Corn
  Syrup
1 cup (6 ounces) semisweet chocolate
  chips
1 cup sugar
4 eggs, slightly beaten
1^1/$_2$ teaspoons vanilla
2^1/$_2$ cups coarsely chopped pecans

Preheat oven to 350°F. Prepare Bar
Cookie Crust according to recipe
directions. In large heavy saucepan,
combine corn syrup and chocolate
chips. Stir over low heat just until
chocolate melts. Remove from heat. Beat
in sugar, eggs and vanilla until blended.
Stir in pecans. Pour over hot crust;
spread evenly. Bake 30 minutes or until
filling is firm around edges and slightly
firm in center. Cool completely on wire
rack before cutting.

Makes about 24 squares

Prep Time: 30 minutes
Bake Time: 30 minutes, *plus* cooling

Norwegian Almond Bars

1^3/$_4$ cups all-purpose flour
1 cup sugar
^{1}/$_4$ cup ground almonds
1 cup butter or margarine, softened
1 egg
1 teaspoon ground cinnamon
^{1}/$_2$ teaspoon salt
1 egg white
^{3}/$_4$ cup sliced almonds

Preheat oven to 350°F. In large mixer
bowl combine flour, sugar, ground
almonds, butter, egg, cinnamon and
salt. Beat at low speed, scraping bowl
often, until well mixed, 2 to 3 minutes.
Divide dough in half. Press *each* half
onto a cookie sheet to ^{1}/$_{16}$-inch
thickness. In small bowl, beat egg white
with fork until foamy. Brush over
dough; sprinkle with almonds. Bake
12 to 15 minutes or until very lightly
browned. Immediately cut into 2-inch
squares and remove from pan. Cool;
store in tightly covered container.

Makes 36 to 48 bars

Norwegian Almond Bars

Peanut Butter Bars

Base

  ²/₃ cup JIF® Creamy Peanut Butter
  ¹/₂ cup BUTTER FLAVOR CRISCO®
  ³/₄ cup firmly packed brown sugar
  ¹/₂ cup granulated sugar
  2 eggs
  1 teaspoon vanilla
  1¹/₂ cups all-purpose flour
  ¹/₂ teaspoon baking soda
  ¹/₄ teaspoon salt
  1 cup quick oats, uncooked

Peanut Butter Layer

  1¹/₂ cups confectioners sugar
  2 tablespoons JIF® Creamy Peanut Butter
  1 tablespoon butter or margarine, softened
  3 tablespoons milk

Chocolate Glaze

  2 squares (1 ounce each) unsweetened baking chocolate
  2 tablespoons butter or margarine

Peanut Butter Bars

1. Preheat oven to 350°F. Grease 13×9-inch baking pan with Butter Flavor Crisco®.

2. For base, combine ²/₃ cup peanut butter and Butter Flavor Crisco® in large bowl. Beat at medium speed of electric mixer until blended. Add brown sugar and granulated sugar. Beat until well blended. Add eggs and vanilla. Beat until well blended.

3. Combine flour, baking soda and salt. Stir into creamed mixture with spoon. Stir in oats. Press into prepared pan.

4. Bake for 20 minutes or until golden brown. Cool to room temperature.

5. For peanut butter layer, combine confectioners sugar, 2 tablespoons peanut butter, 1 tablespoon butter and milk. Mix with spoon until smooth. Spread on base. Refrigerate 30 minutes.

6. For chocolate glaze, combine chocolate and 2 tablespoons butter in microwave-safe measuring cup. Microwave at 50% (MEDIUM). Stir after 1 minute. Repeat until smooth (or melt on rangetop in small saucepan on very low heat). Cool slightly. Spread over peanut butter layer. Cut into bars about 3×1¹/₂ inches. Refrigerate about 1 hour or until set. Let stand 15 to 20 minutes at room temperature before serving.

Makes about 24 bars

Chocolate Fruit Bar

Chocolate Fruit Bars

    2 cups vanilla wafer crumbs (about
        60 wafers)
    1/2 cup HERSHEY'S Cocoa
    3 tablespoons sugar
    2/3 cup *cold* margarine or butter
    1 cup REESE'S Peanut Butter Chips
    1/2 cup chopped dates
    1/2 cup candied green cherries, halved
    1/2 cup candied red cherries, halved
    1 (14-ounce) can EAGLE® Brand
        Sweetened Condensed Milk
        (NOT evaporated milk)
    3/4 cup coarsely chopped pecans

Preheat oven to 350°F. In medium bowl,
stir together crumbs, cocoa and sugar;
cut in *cold* margarine until crumbly.
Press evenly on bottom and 1/2 inch up
sides of 13×9-inch baking pan. Sprinkle
chips, dates and cherries over crust.
Pour sweetened condensed milk evenly
over fruit. Top with nuts; press down
lightly. Bake 25 to 30 minutes or until
lightly browned. Cool thoroughly. Chill.
Cut into bars. Store covered at room
temperature. *Makes 24 to 36 bars*

Cherry Butterscotch Squares

    2 cups *plus* 1 tablespoon all-purpose
        flour
    3/4 cup firmly packed brown sugar
    3/4 cup butter, softened
    2 eggs
    1/4 cup butterscotch chips, melted
    1 teaspoon baking powder
    1/4 teaspoon salt
    1 teaspoon vanilla
    1/2 cup chopped maraschino cherries,
        drained
    1/2 cup butterscotch chips
        Maraschino cherries
        Butterscotch chips
        Powdered sugar

Preheat oven to 350°F. In large mixer
bowl, combine 2 cups flour, brown
sugar, butter, eggs, melted chips, baking
powder, salt and vanilla. Beat at low
speed, scraping bowl often, until well
mixed, 1 to 2 minutes. In small bowl,
toss together drained maraschino
cherries and 1 tablespoon flour. Stir
cherries and 1/2 cup butterscotch chips
into batter. Spread into greased and
floured 13×9-inch baking pan. Bake 25
to 35 minutes or until edges are lightly
browned. Cool completely. Sprinkle
with additional cherries, chips and
powdered sugar. Cut into bars.
Makes about 36 bars

Cherry Butterscotch Squares

Fudge-wiches

Crust and Topping

    1 cup BUTTER FLAVOR CRISCO®
1½ cups firmly packed brown sugar
    1 egg
    1 teaspoon vanilla
    2 cups unsifted all-purpose flour
    1 teaspoon baking soda
    1 teaspoon salt
    1 tablespoon water
2½ cups rolled oats, quick or old-
      fashioned, uncooked

Filling

    1 package (12 ounces) semi-sweet
      chocolate pieces
    1 can (14 ounces) sweetened
      condensed milk
    2 tablespoons BUTTER FLAVOR
      CRISCO®
  ½ teaspoon almond extract
  ½ cup finely chopped blanched
      almonds

Preheat oven to 350°F. Grease 13×9-inch baking pan.

For crust and topping, cream Butter Flavor Crisco® and sugar in large bowl at medium speed of electric mixer until light and fluffy. Beat in egg and vanilla. Combine flour, soda and salt. Add to creamed mixture along with 1 tablespoon water. Stir in oats. Press half of mixture (about 3⅓ cups) into prepared pan.

For filling, stir chocolate, milk and Butter Flavor Crisco® in heavy 1-quart saucepan on low heat until melted and smooth. Stir in almond extract and almonds. Spread evenly over base. Work remaining oat mixture between fingers to form fine crumbs. Sprinkle evenly over chocolate mixture. Press down slightly. Bake 35 minutes. Cool to room temperature. Cut into 1-inch squares. Store in tightly covered container.   *Makes about 96 squares*

Cheese Crunchers

  2 cups (12-ounce package) NESTLÉ®
    Toll House® Butterscotch
    Flavored Morsels
  6 tablespoons butter
  2 cups graham cracker crumbs
  2 cups chopped walnuts
  2 (8-ounce) packages cream cheese,
    softened
 ½ cup sugar
  4 eggs
 ¼ cup all-purpose flour
  2 tablespoons lemon juice

Preheat oven to 350°F. Combine over hot (not boiling) water, Nestlé® Toll House® Butterscotch Flavored Morsels and butter, stir until morsels are melted and mixture is smooth. Transfer to large bowl; stir in graham cracker crumbs and walnuts with a fork until mixture resembles fine crumbs. Reserve 2 cups crumb mixture for topping. Press remaining mixture into ungreased 15½×10½-inch baking pan. Bake 12 minutes.

In large bowl, combine cream cheese and sugar; beat until creamy. Add eggs, 1 at a time, beating well after each addition. Blend in flour and lemon juice. Pour evenly over hot baked crust. Sprinkle reserved crumb mixture on top. Bake 25 minutes. Cool completely on wire rack; cut into 2×1-inch bars. Chill before serving.

Makes about 72 bars

Cheese Crunchers

Pecan Date Bars

Crust

>   1 package DUNCAN HINES® Moist
>   Deluxe White Cake Mix
> ⅓ cup butter or margarine
>   1 egg

Topping

>   1 (8-ounce) package chopped dates
> 1¼ cups chopped pecans
>   1 cup water
> ½ teaspoon vanilla extract
>   Confectioners sugar

1. Preheat oven to 350°F. Grease and flour 13×9-inch pan.

2. For crust, cut butter into cake mix with a pastry blender or 2 knives until mixture is crumbly. Add egg; stir well (mixture will be crumbly). Press mixture into bottom of prepared pan.

3. For topping, combine dates, pecans and water in medium saucepan. Bring to a boil. Reduce heat and simmer until mixture thickens, stirring constantly. Remove from heat. Stir in vanilla extract. Spread date mixture evenly over crust. Bake 25 to 30 minutes. Cool completely. Dust with confectioners sugar. *Makes about 32 bars*

Orange Shortbread Squares

> 2⅓ cups all-purpose flour, divided
> ¼ teaspoon DAVIS® Baking Powder
> ¼ teaspoon salt
>   1 cup BLUE BONNET® Spread,
>   softened
>   2 cups sugar, divided
>   4 eggs
> ⅓ cup orange juice
>   2 tablespoons grated orange peel
>   Confectioner's sugar

Preheat oven to 350°F. In small bowl, combine 2 cups flour, baking powder and salt. In large bowl, with electric mixer at medium speed, beat spread and ½ cup sugar until light and fluffy. At low speed, gradually stir in flour mixture until well blended. Chill 2 hours.

Press dough into 13×9-inch baking pan. Bake 20 minutes. In large bowl, beat eggs, remaining ⅓ cup flour and 1½ cups sugar, juice and peel until light and fluffy. Pour over baked layer; bake 30 minutes more. Cool. Sprinkle with confectioner's sugar; carefully cut into 1½-inch squares.

Makes about 36 squares

Butter Pecan Squares

> ½ cup butter, softened
> ½ cup packed light brown sugar
>   1 egg
>   1 teaspoon vanilla extract
> ¾ cup all-purpose flour
>   2 cups HERSHEY¡S Milk Chocolate
>   Chips, divided
> ¾ cup chopped pecans, divided

Heat oven to 350°F. In small mixer bowl, cream butter, sugar, egg and vanilla until light and fluffy. Blend in flour. Stir in 1 cup chocolate chips and ½ cup pecans. Spread into greased 8- or 9-inch square baking pan. Bake 25 to 30 minutes or until lightly browned. Remove from oven. Immediately sprinkle remaining 1 cup chips over surface. Let stand 5 to 10 minutes or until chips soften; spread evenly. Immediately sprinkle remaining ¼ cup pecans over top; press gently onto chocolate. Cool completely. Cut into squares. *Makes about 16 squares*

Pecan Date Bars

Peanut Butter Chips and Jelly Bars

Peanut Butter Chips and Jelly Bars

1¹/₂ cups all-purpose flour
¹/₂ cup sugar
³/₄ teaspoon baking powder
¹/₂ cup butter or margarine
1 egg, beaten
³/₄ cup grape jelly
1 cup REESE'S® Peanut Butter Chips, divided

Preheat oven to 375°F. Grease 9-inch square baking pan. In medium bowl, combine flour, sugar and baking powder; cut in butter with pastry blender or fork to form coarse crumbs. Add egg; blend well. Reserve half of mixture; press remaining mixture onto bottom of prepared pan. Spread jelly evenly over crust. Sprinkle ¹/₂ cup peanut butter chips over jelly. Combine remaining crumb mixture with remaining ¹/₂ cup chips; sprinkle over top. Bake 25 to 30 minutes or until lightly browned. Cool completely. Cut into bars.   *Makes about 18 bars*

Almond Fudge Topped Shortbread

1 cup margarine or butter, softened
¹/₂ cup confectioners' sugar
¹/₄ teaspoon salt
1¹/₄ cups unsifted flour
1 (12-ounce) package HERSHEY'S Semi-Sweet Chocolate Chips
1 (14-ounce) can EAGLE® Brand Sweetened Condensed Milk (NOT evaporated milk)
¹/₂ teaspoon almond extract
Sliced almonds, toasted

Preheat oven to 350°F. In large mixer bowl, beat margarine, sugar and salt until fluffy. Add flour; mix well. With floured hands, press evenly into greased 13×9-inch baking pan. Bake 20 to 25 minutes or until lightly browned. In heavy saucepan, over low heat, melt chips and sweetened condensed milk, stirring constantly. Remove from heat; stir in extract. Spread evenly over baked shortbread. Garnish with almonds; press down firmly. Cool. Chill 3 hours or until firm. Cut into bars. Store covered at room temperature.
Makes 24 to 36 bars

Almond Fudge Topped Shortbread

Four-Layer Oatmeal Bars

Oat Layer

   1/2 cup BUTTER FLAVOR CRISCO®
   1 egg
1 1/2 cups quick oats, uncooked
   1 cup firmly packed brown sugar
   3/4 cup *plus* 2 tablespoons all-purpose
      flour
   1 teaspoon cinnamon
   3/4 teaspoon baking soda
   1/4 teaspoon salt

Fruit Layer

1 1/2 cups sliced, peeled fresh peaches*
      (cut slices in half crosswise)
   3/4 cup crushed pineapple, undrained
   3/4 cup sliced, peeled Granny Smith
      apple (cut slices in half
      crosswise)
   1/2 cup chopped walnuts or pecans
   1/4 cup granulated sugar
   2 tablespoons cornstarch
   1/2 teaspoon nutmeg

Cream Cheese Layer

   1 (8-ounce) package cream cheese,
      softened
   1 egg
   1/4 cup granulated sugar
   1/2 teaspoon fresh lemon juice
   1/2 teaspoon vanilla

1. Preheat oven to 350°F. Grease 11×7-inch glass baking dish with Butter Flavor Crisco®.

2. For oat layer, combine Butter Flavor Crisco® and egg in large bowl. Stir with fork until blended. Add oats, brown sugar, flour, cinnamon, baking soda and salt. Stir until well blended and crumbs form. Press 1 3/4 cups crumbs lightly into bottom of prepared dish. Reserve remaining crumbs.

3. Bake 10 minutes. Cool completely.

4. For fruit layer, combine peaches, pineapple, apple, nuts, granulated sugar, cornstarch and nutmeg in medium saucepan. Cook and stir on medium heat until mixture comes to a boil and thickens. Cool completely.

5. *Increase oven temperature to 375°F.*

6. For cream cheese layer, combine cream cheese, egg, granulated sugar, lemon juice and vanilla in medium bowl. Beat at medium speed of electric mixer until well blended. Spread over cooled oat layer. Spoon cooled fruit mixture over cheese layer. Spread gently to cover cream cheese. Sprinkle reserved crumbs over fruit.

7. Bake 30 minutes. Cool to room temperature. Refrigerate. Cut into bars about 2×1 3/4 inches.

Makes about 20 bars

* Diced canned peaches, well drained, can be used in place of fresh peaches.

Four-Layer Oatmeal Bars

Chocolate Cheesecake Bars

Chocolate Cheesecake Bars

Crust

    1 cup graham cracker crumbs
    ¼ cup firmly packed brown sugar
    ⅓ cup BUTTER FLAVOR CRISCO®, melted

Filling

    1 (8-ounce) package cream cheese, softened
    ½ cup granulated sugar
    3 tablespoons unsweetened cocoa powder
    2 eggs
    1 tablespoon all-purpose flour
    ½ teaspoon vanilla

Topping

    2 tablespoons BUTTER FLAVOR CRISCO®
    1 (3-ounce) package cream cheese, softened
    1 cup confectioners sugar
    ½ teaspoon vanilla

1. Preheat oven to 350°F.

2. For crust, combine graham cracker crumbs and brown sugar. Stir in melted Butter Flavor Crisco®. Press into ungreased 8-inch square pan.

3. Bake 10 minutes.

4. For filling, beat 8-ounce package cream cheese in small bowl at medium speed of electric mixer until smooth. Add, 1 at a time, granulated sugar, cocoa, eggs, flour and vanilla. Mix well after each addition. Pour over crust.

5. Bake for 30 minutes. Cool to room temperature.

6. For topping, combine 2 tablespoons Butter Flavor Crisco® and 3-ounce package cream cheese in small bowl. Beat at medium speed until well blended. Add confectioners sugar and vanilla. Beat until smooth. Spread over filling. Cut into 2×1½-inch bars. Refrigerate. *Makes about 20 bars*

English Toffee Bars

    2 cups all-purpose flour
    1 cup packed light brown sugar
    ½ cup butter
    1 cup pecan halves
    Toffee Topping (recipe follows)
    1 cup HERSHEY₅'S Milk Chocolate Chips

Preheat oven to 350°F. In large mixer bowl, combine flour, brown sugar and butter; mix until fine crumbs form (a few large crumbs may remain). Press into ungreased 13×9-inch baking pan. Sprinkle pecans over crust. Drizzle Toffee Topping evenly over pecans and crust. Bake 20 to 22 minutes or until topping is bubbly and golden. Remove from oven. Immediately sprinkle chocolate chips over top; press gently onto surface. Cool completely. Cut into bars. *Makes about 36 bars*

Toffee Topping: In small saucepan, combine ⅔ cup butter and ⅓ cup packed light brown sugar. Cook over medium heat, stirring constantly, until mixture comes to boil; boil and stir 30 seconds. Use immediately.

Chocolate Apple Crisp

Chocolate Apple Crisp

1¹/₂ cups all-purpose flour
  1 cup firmly packed brown sugar
 ¹/₂ teaspoon baking soda
 ¹/₄ teaspoon salt
 ³/₄ cup (1¹/₂ sticks) butter
1¹/₂ cups quick oats, uncooked
  2 cups (12-ounce) package NESTLÉ®
    Toll House® Semi-Sweet
    Chocolate Mini Morsels, divided
  3 apples, unpeeled if desired,
    chopped
  1 cup pecans or walnuts, chopped
    Ice cream

Preheat oven to 375°F. In large bowl, combine flour, brown sugar, baking soda and salt. With pastry blender or two knives, cut in butter until mixture resembles fine crumbs. Stir in oats; press half of oat mixture into greased 13×9-inch baking pan.

To remaining oat mixture, add Nestlé® Toll House® Semi-Sweet Chocolate Mini Morsels, apples and nuts; stir to combine. Sprinkle over base.

Bake 35 to 40 minutes until lightly browned. Cool slightly; cut into squares. Serve warm with ice cream.
Makes about 15 servings

Cranberry Jewel Bars

  2 cups unsifted flour
1¹/₂ cups quick-cooking or old-
    fashioned oats
 ³/₄ cup *plus* 1 tablespoon firmly
    packed brown sugar
  1 cup *cold* margarine or butter
  1 (14-ounce) can EAGLE® Brand
    Sweetened Condensed Milk
    (NOT evaporated milk)
  1 cup ricotta cheese
  2 eggs
1¹/₂ teaspoons vanilla extract
  1 teaspoon grated orange rind
  2 tablespoons cornstarch
  1 (16-ounce) can whole berry
    cranberry sauce

Preheat oven to 350°F. In large bowl, combine flour, oats and ³/₄ *cup* sugar. Cut in *cold* margarine until crumbly. Reserving 2 cups crumb mixture, press remainder firmly on bottom of 13×9-inch baking pan. Bake 15 minutes.

Meanwhile, in small mixer bowl, beat sweetened condensed milk, cheese, eggs, vanilla and rind until smooth. Spread evenly over baked crust. In small bowl, combine remaining 1 tablespoon sugar and cornstarch; stir in cranberry sauce. Spoon over cheese layer. Top with reserved crumb mixture. Bake 40 minutes or until lightly browned. Cool. Chill. Garnish as desired. Cut into bars. Store covered in refrigerator.   *Makes 36 to 40 bars*

Cranberry Jewel Bars

Choco Cheesecake Squares

1/3 cup butter or margarine, softened
1/3 cup packed light brown sugar
1 cup *plus* 1 tablespoon all-purpose
  flour, divided
1/2 cup chopped pecans (optional)
1 cup semisweet chocolate chips
1 (8-ounce) package cream cheese,
  softened
1/4 cup granulated sugar
1 large egg
1 teaspoon vanilla

Preheat oven to 350°F. Grease 8-inch square baking pan; set aside. Beat butter and brown sugar in large bowl until light and fluffy. Add 1 cup flour. Beat until well combined. Stir in nuts. (Mixture will be crumbly.) Press evenly into prepared pan. Bake 15 minutes.

Place chocolate chips in 1 cup glass measuring cup. Melt in microwave oven at HIGH (100% power) 2½ to 3 minutes, stirring after 2 minutes. Beat cream cheese and granulated sugar in medium bowl until light and fluffy. Add remaining 1 tablespoon flour, egg and vanilla; beat until smooth. Gradually stir in melted chocolate, mixing well. Pour cream cheese mixture over partially baked crust. Return to oven; bake 15 minutes or until set. Remove pan to wire rack; cool completely. Cut into 2-inch squares.

Makes about 16 squares

Candy Bar Cookies

Cookie Crust

1 package DUNCAN HINES®
  Chocolate Chip Cookie Mix
1/4 cup unsweetened cocoa
1 egg

Caramel Layer

1 package (14 ounces) caramels,
  unwrapped
1/3 cup evaporated milk
1/3 cup butter or margarine
1²/3 cups confectioners sugar
1 cup chopped pecans

Chocolate Drizzle

1/2 cup semi-sweet chocolate chips
2 teaspoons CRISCO® shortening

1. Preheat oven to 375°F.

2. For cookie crust, combine cookie mix and cocoa in large bowl. Stir until blended. Add buttery flavor packet from Mix and egg. Stir until well blended. Press into bottom of ungreased 13×9-inch pan. Bake 14 to 16 minutes or until set.

3. For caramel layer, place caramels, evaporated milk and butter in medium saucepan. Melt on low heat, stirring occasionally until smooth. Remove from heat. Stir in confectioners sugar until smooth. Stir in pecans. Pour over warm cookie crust.

4. For chocolate drizzle, melt chocolate chips and shortening in small bowl over hot water. Stir until blended. Drizzle over caramel layer. Refrigerate until chocolate is firm. Cut into bars.

Makes about 48 bars

Choco Cheesecake Squares

Banana Split Bars

Creamy Vanilla Frosting

¹/₄ cup margarine
3 to 4 tablespoons milk
3 cups powdered sugar
1 teaspoon vanilla extract

In small saucepan, heat margarine and milk until margarine melts. Remove from heat. Stir in powdered sugar and vanilla. Beat until smooth.

Banana Split Bars

2 extra-ripe, medium DOLE®
Bananas, peeled
2 cups all-purpose flour
1 cup granulated sugar
³/₄ teaspoon baking soda
¹/₂ teaspoon salt
¹/₂ teaspoon ground cinnamon
1 can (8 ounces) DOLE® Crushed
Pineapple, undrained
2 eggs
¹/₂ cup vegetable oil
1 teaspoon vanilla extract
¹/₄ cup maraschino cherries, drained,
halved
Creamy Vanilla Frosting (recipe
follows)

Preheat oven to 350°F. In food processor or blender container, process bananas until puréed (1 cup). In large bowl, combine flour, granulated sugar, baking soda, salt and cinnamon. Add puréed bananas, pineapple with juice, eggs, oil and vanilla. Mix until well blended. Stir in cherries. Pour into greased and floured 13×9-inch baking pan. Bake 30 to 35 minutes. Cool in pan on wire rack 30 minutes. Spread with Creamy Vanilla Frosting, if desired. Cut into bars.

Makes about 36 bars

Gorp Bars

2 cups bite-size crispy corn cereal
squares
2¹/₂ cups thin pretzel sticks, broken in
half
1¹/₂ cups "M&M's"® Plain or Peanut
Chocolate Candies
1 cup banana chips
³/₄ cup golden raisins
¹/₂ cup butter or margarine
¹/₃ cup creamy peanut butter
1 (10-ounce) bag marshmallows

In large bowl, combine cereal, pretzels, candies, banana chips and raisins. In medium saucepan, melt together butter, peanut butter and marshmallows. Stir over low heat until mixture is smooth. Immediately pour over cereal mixture, mixing until all ingredients are thoroughly coated. Press lightly into greased 13×9-inch pan. Let stand until firm. Cut into 2-inch squares.

Makes about 36 bars

Gorp Bars

Streusel Peanut Butter Bars

Base

1/2 cup BUTTER FLAVOR CRISCO®
1 1/2 cups firmly packed brown sugar
2/3 cup JIF® Creamy or Extra Crunchy
   Peanut Butter
2 eggs
1 teaspoon vanilla
1 1/2 cups all-purpose flour
1/2 teaspoon salt
1/4 cup milk

Streusel Topping

3 tablespoons BUTTER FLAVOR
   CRISCO®
1/3 cup all-purpose flour
1/3 cup firmly packed brown sugar
1 tablespoon JIF® Creamy or Extra
   Crunchy Peanut Butter
1/4 cup finely chopped peanuts

1. Preheat oven to 350°F. Grease 13×9-inch baking pan with Butter Flavor Crisco®.

2. For Base, combine Butter Flavor Crisco®, sugar and peanut butter in large bowl. Beat at medium speed of electric mixer until well blended. Beat in eggs and vanilla.

3. Combine flour and salt. Add alternately with milk to creamed mixture at low speed. Beat until well blended. Spread in prepared pan.

4. For Topping, combine Butter Flavor Crisco®, flour, sugar and peanut butter. Mix with spoon until well blended and coarse crumbs form. Sprinkle over unbaked Base. Sprinkle nuts over top.

5. Bake 30 to 33 minutes, or until golden brown and center is set. Cool in pan on cooling rack. Cut into 2 1/4×1 1/2-inch bars.

Makes about 32 bars

Caramel Apple Oat Square

Caramel Apple Oat Squares

1 3/4 cups unsifted flour
1 cup quick-cooking oats
1/2 cup firmly packed brown sugar
1/2 teaspoon baking soda
1/2 teaspoon salt
1 cup cold margarine or butter
1 cup chopped California Walnuts
20 caramels, unwrapped
1 (14-ounce) can EAGLE® Brand
   Sweetened Condensed Milk
   (NOT evaporated milk)
1 (21-ounce) can COMSTOCK®
   Brand Apple Filling or Topping

Preheat oven to 375°F. In large bowl, combine flour, oats, sugar, baking soda and salt; cut in margarine until crumbly. Reserving 1 1/2 cups crumb mixture, press remainder on bottom of 13×9-inch baking pan. Bake 15 minutes. Add walnuts to reserved crumb mixture. In heavy saucepan over low heat, melt caramels and sweetened condensed milk, stirring until smooth. Spoon apple filling over prepared crust; top with caramel mixture, then reserved crumb mixture. Bake 20 minutes or until set. Cool. Serve warm with ice cream.

Makes 10 to 12 servings

Chocolate Streusel Bars

1³/₄ cups unsifted flour
1¹/₂ cups confectioners' sugar
¹/₂ cup HERSHEY'S Cocoa
1 cup cold margarine or butter
1 (8-ounce) package cream cheese, softened
1 (14-ounce) can EAGLE® Brand Sweetened Condensed Milk (NOT evaporated milk)
1 egg
2 teaspoons vanilla extract
¹/₂ cup chopped nuts

Preheat oven to 350°F. In large bowl, combine flour, sugar and cocoa. Cut in cold margarine until crumbly (mixture will be dry). Reserving 2 cups crumb mixture, press remainder firmly on bottom of 13×9-inch baking pan. Bake 15 minutes. In large mixer bowl, beat cream cheese until fluffy. Gradually beat in sweetened condensed milk until smooth. Add egg and vanilla; mix well. Pour over baked crust. Combine nuts with reserved crumb mixture; sprinkle over cheese mixture. Bake 25 minutes or until bubbly. Cool. Chill. Cut into bars. Store covered in refrigerator.

Makes 24 to 36 bars

Chocolate Peanut Butter Streusel Bars: Beat ³/₄ cup peanut butter with cream cheese; use ¹/₂ cup chopped peanuts for nuts. Proceed as above.

Chocolate Streusel Bar

Pineapple Almond Shortbread Bars

Pineapple Almond Shortbread Bars

Crust

1¹/₂ cups all-purpose flour
¹/₂ cup DOLE® Almonds, toasted, ground
¹/₄ cup sugar
¹/₂ cup cold margarine

Topping

1 can (20 ounces) DOLE® Crushed Pineapple, drained
3 eggs
¹/₄ cup honey
¹/₄ cup sugar
1 tablespoon grated lemon peel
1¹/₂ cups DOLE® Slivered Almonds, toasted

For Crust, preheat oven to 350°F. In large bowl, combine flour, almonds and sugar. Cut in margarine until crumbly. Form dough into a ball; press into ungreased 13×9-inch baking pan. Bake 10 minutes. Cool slightly.

For Topping, in medium bowl, combine pineapple, eggs, honey, sugar and lemon peel. Stir in almonds. Pour topping over partially baked crust. Bake an additional 30 to 35 minutes. Cool completely in pan on wire rack. Cut into bars.

Makes about 2 dozen bars

Walnut Toffee Bars

1½ cups unsifted flour
½ cup firmly packed brown sugar
¾ cup *cold* margarine or butter
1 (14-ounce) can EAGLE® Brand Sweetened Condensed Milk (NOT evaporated milk)
1 egg, beaten
1 teaspoon vanilla extract
1 (7.20-ounce) package milk chocolate-covered English toffee candy bars, cut into small pieces (6 bars)
1 cup chopped walnuts

Preheat oven to 350°F (325°F for glass dish). In medium bowl, combine flour and sugar; cut in *cold* margarine until crumbly. Press firmly on bottom of 13×9-inch baking pan. Bake 15 minutes.

Meanwhile, in large bowl, combine sweetened condensed milk, egg and vanilla; mix well. Stir in candy pieces and walnuts. Spread evenly over baked crust.

Bake 25 minutes or until golden brown. Cool. Cut into bars. Store loosely covered in refrigerator.

Makes 24 to 36 bars

Caramel Marshmallow Bars

Crumb Mixture

1¼ cups all-purpose flour
¼ cup graham cracker crumbs
½ cup sugar
½ cup butter or margarine, softened
¼ teaspoon salt
½ cup chopped salted peanuts

Filling

¾ cup caramel ice cream topping
½ cup salted peanuts
½ cups miniature marshmallows
½ cup milk chocolate chips

Caramel Marshmallow Bars

Preheat oven to 350°F. For crumb mixture, in small mixer bowl combine flour, graham cracker crumbs, sugar, butter and salt. Beat at low speed, scraping bowl often, until mixture is crumbly, 1 to 2 minutes. Stir in nuts. Reserve ¾ cup crumb mixture. Press remaining crumb mixture on bottom of greased and floured 9-inch square baking pan. Bake 10 to 12 minutes or until lightly browned.

For filling, spread caramel topping evenly over hot crust. Sprinkle nuts, marshmallows and chocolate chips over top. Crumble ¾ cup reserved crumb mixture over top. Continue baking 10 to 12 minutes or until marshmallows just start to brown. Cool on rack about 30 minutes. Cover; refrigerate 1 to 2 hours or until firm. Cut into bars.

Makes about 30 bars

Peachy Oatmeal Bars

Crumb Mixture

1$\frac{1}{2}$ cups all-purpose flour
1 cup quick cooking oats
$\frac{1}{2}$ cup sugar
$\frac{3}{4}$ cup margarine, melted
$\frac{1}{2}$ teaspoon baking soda
$\frac{1}{4}$ teaspoon salt
2 teaspoons almond extract

Filling

$\frac{3}{4}$ cup peach preserves
$\frac{1}{3}$ cup flaked coconut

Preheat oven to 350°F. For crumb mixture, in large mixer bowl combine all crumb mixture ingredients. Beat at low speed, scraping bowl often, until mixture is crumbly, 1 to 2 minutes. Reserve $\frac{3}{4}$ cup crumb mixture; press remaining crumb mixture onto bottom of greased 9-inch square baking pan.

For filling, spread peach preserves to within $\frac{1}{2}$ inch of edge of crumb mixture; sprinkle reserved crumb mixture and coconut over top. Bake for 22 to 27 minutes or until edges are lightly browned. Cool completely. Cut into bars. *Makes 24 to 30 bars*

Strawberry Streusel Bars

Crumb Mixture

2 cups all-purpose flour
1 cup sugar
$\frac{3}{4}$ cup pecans, coarsely chopped
1 cup butter or margarine, softened
1 egg

Filling

1 jar (10 ounces) strawberry
    preserves

Preheat oven to 350°F. For crumb mixture, in large mixer bowl combine all crumb mixture ingredients. Beat at low speed, scraping bowl often, until mixture is crumbly, 2 to 3 minutes. Reserve 1 cup crumb mixture; press remaining crumb mixture onto bottom of greased 9-inch square baking pan. Spread preserves to within $\frac{1}{2}$ inch of edge of unbaked crumb mixture. Crumble remaining crumb mixture over preserves. Bake for 42 to 50 minutes or until lightly browned. Cool completely. Cut into bars. *Makes about 24 bars*

Apple Crumb Squares

2 cups QUAKER® Oats (Quick or
    Old Fashioned), uncooked
1$\frac{1}{2}$ cups all-purpose flour
1 cup packed brown sugar
$\frac{3}{4}$ cup butter or margarine, melted
1 teaspoon ground cinnamon
$\frac{1}{2}$ teaspoon baking soda
$\frac{1}{2}$ teaspoon salt (optional)
$\frac{1}{4}$ teaspoon ground nutmeg
1 cup applesauce
$\frac{1}{2}$ cup chopped nuts

Preheat oven to 350°F. In large bowl, combine all ingredients except applesauce and nuts; mix until crumbly. Reserve 1 cup oats mixture. Press remaining mixture on bottom of greased 13×9-inch pan. Bake 13 to 15 minutes; cool. Spread applesauce over partially baked crust; sprinkle with nuts. Sprinkle reserved 1 cup oats mixture over top. Bake 13 to 15 minutes or until golden brown. Cool in pan on wire rack; cut into 2-inch squares.
Makes about 24 squares

Top to bottom: Peachy Oatmeal Bars, Strawberry Streusel Bars

Blueberry Cheesecake Bars

Blueberry Cheesecake Bars

  1 package DUNCAN HINES®
    Bakery Style Blueberry Muffin
    Mix
¹/₄ cup butter or margarine, softened
¹/₃ cup finely chopped pecans
  1 (8-ounce) package cream cheese,
    softened
¹/₂ cup sugar
  1 egg
  3 tablespoons lemon juice
  1 teaspoon grated lemon peel

1. Preheat oven to 350°F. Grease 9-inch square pan.

2. Rinse blueberries from Mix with cold water and drain.

3. Place muffin mix in medium bowl. Cut in butter with pastry blender or two knives. Stir in pecans. Press into bottom of prepared pan. Bake 15 minutes or until set.

4. Combine cream cheese and sugar in medium bowl. Beat until smooth. Add egg, lemon juice and lemon peel. Beat well. Spread over baked crust. Sprinkle with blueberries. Sprinkle topping packet from Mix over blueberries. Return to oven. Bake 35 to 40 minutes or until filling is set. Cool completely. Refrigerate until ready to serve. Cut into bars.   *Makes about 16 bars*

Banana Gingerbread Bars

  1 extra-ripe, medium DOLE®
    Banana, peeled
  1 package (14.5 ounce) gingerbread
    cake mix
¹/₂ cup lukewarm water
  1 egg
  1 small DOLE® Banana, peeled and
    chopped
¹/₂ cup DOLE® Raisins
¹/₂ cup DOLE® Slivered Almonds
1¹/₂ cups powdered sugar
    Juice from 1 DOLE® Lemon

• Preheat oven to 350°F.

• Purée medium banana in blender to measure ¹/₂ cup.

• In bowl, combine gingerbread mix, water, banana purée and egg. Beat on low speed 1 minute.

• Stir in chopped banana (¹/₂ cup), raisins and almonds.

• Spread batter in greased 13×9-inch baking pan. Bake 20 to 25 minutes until springy to touch.

• In bowl, mix powdered sugar and 3 tablespoons lemon juice to make thin glaze. Spread over warm gingerbread. Cool before cutting into bars. Sprinkle with powdered sugar if desired.
          Makes about 32 bars

Prep Time: 20 minutes
Bake Time: 25 minutes

Banana Gingerbread Bars

Tropical Sun Bars

Tropical Sun Bars

Crust

    1 cup all-purpose flour
    ¹/₄ cup sugar
    ¹/₃ cup butter, softened
    1 tablespoon grated tangerine or
      orange peel

Filling

    ¹/₂ cup sugar
    ¹/₂ cup flaked coconut
    2 eggs
    2 tablespoons all-purpose flour
    ¹/₂ teaspoon baking powder
    ¹/₈ teaspoon salt
  1¹/₂ tablespoons grated tangerine or
      orange peel
    1 tablespoon orange juice
    1 tablespoon orange liqueur
      Fine strips of orange peel

Preheat oven to 350°F. For crust, in small mixer bowl, combine all crust ingredients. Beat at low speed, scraping bowl often, until particles are fine, 1 to 2 minutes. Press on bottom of 9-inch square baking pan. Bake 10 to 12 minutes or until edges are lightly browned.

For filling, in small mixer bowl, combine all filling ingredients. Beat at medium speed, scraping bowl often, until well mixed, 1 to 2 minutes. Pour over hot crust. Continue baking for 20 to 25 minutes or until edges are lightly brown. Immediately sprinkle with orange peel. Cool completely. Cut into bars. *Makes about 24 bars*

CHAMPION CHIPPERS

Ultimate Chippers

2¹/₂ cups all-purpose flour
1 teaspoon baking soda
¹/₂ teaspoon salt
1 cup butter or margarine, softened
1 cup packed light brown sugar
¹/₂ cup granulated sugar
2 large eggs
1 tablespoon vanilla
1 cup semisweet chocolate chips
1 cup milk chocolate chips
1 cup vanilla milk chips
¹/₂ cup coarsely chopped pecans
   (optional)

Preheat oven to 375°F. Place flour, baking soda and salt in medium bowl; stir to combine. Beat butter, brown sugar and granulated sugar in large bowl until light and fluffy. Beat in eggs and vanilla. Add flour mixture. Beat until well blended. Stir in chips and pecans. Drop dough by heaping teaspoonfuls 2 inches apart onto ungreased cookie sheets. Bake 10 to 12 minutes or until edges are golden brown. Let cookies stand on cookie sheets 2 minutes. Remove cookies to wire racks; cool completely.

Makes about 6 dozen cookies

Reese's® Cookies

1 cup shortening or ³/₄ cup butter or
   margarine, softened
1 cup sugar
¹/₂ cup packed light brown sugar
1 teaspoon vanilla
2 eggs
2 cups unsifted all-purpose flour
1 teaspoon baking soda
1 cup REESE'S® Peanut Butter Chips
1 cup HERSHEY'S Semi-Sweet
   Chocolate Chips

Preheat oven to 350°F. Cream shortening, sugar, brown sugar and vanilla in large mixer bowl until light and fluffy. Add eggs; beat well. Combine flour and baking soda; add to creamed mixture. Stir in peanut butter chips and chocolate chips.

Drop by teaspoonfuls onto ungreased cookie sheet. Bake 10 to 12 minutes or until lightly browned. Cool slightly. Remove from cookie sheet; cool completely on wire rack.

Makes about 5 dozen cookies

Brian's Buffalo Cookies

1 cup **BUTTER FLAVOR CRISCO®**,
  melted
1 cup **granulated sugar**
1 cup **firmly packed brown sugar**
2 tablespoons **milk**
1 teaspoon **vanilla**
2 **eggs**
2 cups **all-purpose flour**
1 teaspoon **baking powder**
1 teaspoon **baking soda**
$\frac{1}{2}$ teaspoon **salt**
1 cup **oats (quick or old fashioned),
  uncooked**
1 cup **corn flakes, crushed to about**
  $\frac{1}{2}$ **cup**
1 cup **semi-sweet chocolate chips**
$\frac{1}{2}$ cup **chopped pecans**
$\frac{1}{2}$ cup **flake coconut**

1. Preheat oven to 350°F. Grease cookie sheet with Butter Flavor Crisco®.

2. Combine Butter Flavor Crisco®, granulated sugar, brown sugar, milk and vanilla in large bowl. Beat at low speed of electric mixer until well blended. Add eggs. Beat at medium speed until well blended.

3. Combine flour, baking powder, baking soda and salt. Add gradually to creamed mixture at low speed. Stir in oats, corn flakes, chocolate chips, nuts and coconut. Fill ice cream scoop that holds $\frac{1}{4}$ cup with dough (or use $\frac{1}{4}$ cup measuring cup). Level with knife. Drop 3 inches apart onto prepared cookie sheet.

4. Bake at 350°F for 13 to 15 minutes or until lightly browned around edges but still slightly soft in center. Cool 3 minutes on cookie sheet before removing to cooling rack with wide, thin pancake turner.

Makes 2 to 2$\frac{1}{2}$ dozen cookies

Brian's Buffalo Cookies

Fruit and Nut Chippers

1 cup butter or margarine, softened
3/4 cup granulated sugar
3/4 cup packed light brown sugar
2 large eggs
1 teaspoon vanilla
2 1/4 cups all-purpose flour
1 teaspoon baking soda
1/2 teaspoon salt
1 (11 1/2-ounce) package milk
   chocolate chips
1 cup chopped dried apricots
1 cup chopped pecans or walnuts

Preheat oven to 375°F. Beat butter, granulated sugar and brown sugar in large bowl until light and fluffy. Beat in eggs and vanilla. Add combined flour, baking soda and salt. Beat until well blended. Stir in chips, apricots and pecans. Drop dough by heaping teaspoonfuls 2 inches apart onto cookie sheets. Bake 9 to 10 minutes or until edges are golden brown. Let cookies stand on cookie sheets 2 minutes. Remove cookies to wire racks; cool completely.

Makes about 5 dozen cookies

Anise Cookie Cordials

2 3/4 cups all-purpose flour
1 1/2 teaspoons baking powder
1 cup sugar
1/2 cup butter, softened
3 eggs
2 tablespoons anise flavored liqueur
2 tablespoons water
1 tablespoon anise seed
1 cup (1/2 of 12-ounce package)
   NESTLÉ® Toll House® Semi-
   Sweet Chocolate Mini Morsels
1 cup coarsely chopped toasted
   almonds

Anise Cookie Cordials

In medium bowl, combine flour and baking powder; set aside. In large bowl, combine sugar and butter; beat until creamy. Add eggs, anise flavored liqueur, water and anise seed; beat until well blended. Gradually beat in flour mixture. Stir in Nestlé® Toll House® Semi-Sweet Chocolate Mini Morsels and almonds. Cover; chill several hours. Preheat oven to 375°F. Divide dough into 4 pieces. With floured hands, shape each piece into 15 1/2×2×1/2-inch loaf. Place loaves 4 inches apart on greased cookie sheets. Bake at 375°F for 15 minutes. Remove from oven. Cut into 1-inch slices. Place slices on cookie sheets. Bake at 375°F for 7 minutes. Turn cookies over. Bake at 375°F for 7 minutes. Cool completely on wire racks. *Makes about 4 1/2 dozen cookies*

Chocolate-Dipped Sandwich Macaroons

Almond Delightful Cookies

¹/₄ cup (¹/₂ stick) margarine or butter, softened
¹/₄ cup vegetable shortening
¹/₂ cup packed brown sugar
¹/₄ cup sugar
 1 egg, beaten
 1 teaspoon vanilla extract
 1 cup all-purpose flour
 1 teaspoon baking powder
 3 cups HONEY ALMOND DELIGHT® cereal, crushed to 1¹/₂ cups
¹/₂ cup semi-sweet chocolate pieces or raisins

Preheat oven to 350°F. Lightly grease cookie sheet. In large bowl, cream margarine, shortening and sugars. Add egg and vanilla; mix well. Stir in flour and baking powder until well combined. Add cereal and chocolate pieces; mix well. Drop by level tablespoonfuls onto prepared cookie sheet. Bake 10 to 12 minutes or until lightly browned. Let stand 1 minute before removing from cookie sheet. Cool on wire rack.

Makes about 2¹/₂ dozen cookies

Chocolate-Dipped Sandwich Macaroons

2 cups (12-ounce package) NESTLÉ® Toll House® Semi-Sweet Chocolate Morsels, divided
1¹/₂ cups whole blanched almonds, finely ground
1¹/₂ cups sifted confectioners' sugar
 3 egg whites, at room temperature
¹/₃ cup jam or jelly
 2 tablespoons vegetable shortening

Preheat oven to 350°F. Line 4 large cookie sheets with parchment paper. In small bowl, combine 1 cup Nestlé® Toll House® Semi-Sweet Chocolate Morsels, almonds and confectioners' sugar; set aside. In large mixer bowl, beat egg whites until stiff peaks form. Fold in almond mixture. Drop by level measuring teaspoonfuls onto prepared cookie sheets. Bake 8 to 10 minutes until set. Let stand 5 minutes. Remove from paper; cool completely. Spread ¹/₄ teaspoon jam on flat side of one cookie; top with flat side of second cookie. Repeat with remaining cookies and jam. Line same cookie sheets with waxed paper. In small saucepan over low heat, melt remaining 1 cup Nestlé® Toll House® Semi-Sweet Chocolate Morsels and shortening, stirring until smooth. Dip half of each sandwich cookie into chocolate. Place on prepared cookie sheets. Refrigerate 5 to 10 minutes to set chocolate.

Makes about 4 dozen cookies

Variation: Omit jam; do not "sandwich" cookies. Dip each cookie halfway into melted chocolate. Place on prepared cookie sheets. Refrigerate 5 to 10 minutes to set chocolate. Makes about 8 dozen cookies.

Chocolate Chip Crispers

1 package DUNCAN HINES®
  Chocolate Chip Cookie Mix
1 egg
1 tablespoon water
3 cups cocoa- or fruit-flavored crisp
  rice cereal

1. Preheat oven to 375°F.

2. Combine cookie mix, buttery flavor packet from Mix, egg and water in large bowl. Stir until thoroughly blended. Shape dough into 36 (1-inch) balls. Place cereal in large resealable plastic bag. Seal bag and crush cereal with rolling pin. Drop several dough balls at a time into bag and shake until well coated. Place balls 2 inches apart on ungreased cookie sheets. Bake at 375°F for 8 to 9 minutes or until light golden brown. Cool 1 minute on cookie sheets. Remove to cooling racks. Cool completely. Store in airtight container.

Makes 3 dozen cookies

Dreamy Chocolate Chip Cookies

1¼ cups firmly packed brown sugar
  ¾ cup BUTTER FLAVOR CRISCO®
  3 eggs, lightly beaten
  2 teaspoons vanilla
  1 (4-ounce) package German sweet
    chocolate, melted, cooled
  3 cups all-purpose flour
  1 teaspoon baking soda
  ½ teaspoon salt
  1 (11½-ounce) package milk
    chocolate chips
  1 (10-ounce) package premium semi-
    sweet chocolate chunks
  1 cup coarsely chopped macadamia
    nuts

1. Preheat oven to 375°F.

2. Combine brown sugar, Butter Flavor Crisco®, eggs and vanilla in large bowl. Beat at low speed of electric mixer until blended. Increase speed to high. Beat 2 minutes. Add melted chocolate. Mix until well blended.

3. Combine flour, baking soda and salt. Add gradually to creamed mixture at low speed.

4. Stir in chocolate chips, chocolate chunks and nuts with spoon. Drop by rounded tablespoonfuls 3 inches apart onto ungreased cookie sheet.

5. Bake at 375°F for 9 to 11 minutes or until set. Cool 2 minutes on cookie sheet before removing to cooling rack.

Makes about 3 dozen cookies

Dreamy Chocolate Chip Cookies

Kids' Favorite Jumbo Chippers

1 cup butter or margarine, softened
³/₄ cup granulated sugar
³/₄ cup packed brown sugar
2 large eggs
1 teaspoon vanilla
2¹/₄ cups all-purpose flour
1 teaspoon baking soda
³/₄ teaspoon salt
1 (9-ounce) package sprinkle candy-coated chocolate chips
1 cup peanut butter flavored chips

Preheat oven to 375°F. Beat butter, granulated sugar and brown sugar in large bowl until light and fluffy. Beat in eggs and vanilla. Add combined flour, baking soda and salt. Beat until well blended. Stir in chips. Drop dough by heaping tablespoonfuls 3 inches apart onto ungreased cookie sheets. Bake 10 to 12 minutes or until edges are golden brown. Let cookies stand on cookie sheets 2 minutes. Remove cookies to wire racks; cool completely.
Makes 3 dozen jumbo cookies

Butterscotch Walnut Crisps

2 cups (12 ounce package) NESTLÉ® Toll House® Butterscotch Flavored Morsels, divided
³/₄ cup (1¹/₂ sticks) butter
³/₄ cup sugar
1 egg
2 cups quick oats, uncooked
1 cup all-purpose flour
1 teaspoon baking soda
¹/₄ teaspoon salt
1 cup chopped walnuts

Preheat oven to 350°F. In medium saucepan, combine 1 cup Nestlé® Toll House® Butterscotch Flavored Morsels and butter. Cook over low heat until morsels melt and mixture is smooth. Remove from heat; cool 5 minutes. Transfer to large mixer bowl. Add sugar and egg; beat until creamy. Gradually add oats, flour, baking soda and salt. Stir in remaining Nestlé® Toll House® Butterscotch Flavored Morsels and walnuts. Drop by slightly rounded measuring tablespoonfuls onto ungreased cookie sheets. Bake 10 to 12 minutes, until edges are golden brown. Cool on wire racks.
Makes about 3¹/₂ dozen cookies

Gold Mine Nuggets

¹/₂ cup margarine
³/₄ cup brown sugar, packed
¹/₂ teaspoon vanilla extract
1 egg
1 (8¹/₄-ounce) can DOLE® Crushed Pineapple in syrup*
1 cup rolled oats
1 cup all-purpose flour
1 teaspoon baking soda
1 teaspoon salt
¹/₂ teaspoon ground cinnamon
¹/₂ cup chopped walnuts
1 (6-ounce) package chocolate chips

Preheat oven to 350°F. Beat margarine, sugar and vanilla until fluffy. Beat in egg and undrained pineapple. Combine oats, flour, soda, salt and cinnamon; stir into pineapple mixture with nuts and chocolate chips. Drop by teaspoonful onto ungreased cookie sheets. Bake in 350°F oven 12 to 15 minutes.
Makes about 3 dozen cookies

* Use pineapple packed in juice, if desired.

Kids' Favorite Jumbo Chippers

Oatmeal Scotchies™

1 cup all-purpose flour
1 teaspoon baking soda
¹/₂ teaspoon salt
¹/₂ teaspoon cinnamon
1 cup butter, softened
³/₄ cup sugar
³/₄ cup firmly packed brown sugar
2 eggs
1 teaspoon vanilla extract
3 cups oats, uncooked (quick or old
    fashioned)
2 cups (12-ounce package) NESTLÉ®
    Toll House® Butterscotch
    Flavored Morsels

Preheat oven to 375°F. In small bowl, combine flour, baking soda, salt and cinnamon; set aside. In large bowl, combine butter, sugar, brown sugar, eggs and vanilla extract; beat until creamy. Gradually add flour mixture.

Clockwise from top: Oatmeal Scotchies, Butterscotch Lemon Cookies

Stir in oats and Nestlé® Toll House® Butterscotch Flavored Morsels. Drop by level tablespoonfuls onto ungreased cookie sheets. Bake at 375°F for 7 to 8 minutes for chewy cookies, 9 to 10 minutes for crispy cookies.
Makes about 4 dozen 3-inch cookies

Oatmeal Scotchie Pan Cookie: Spread dough into greased 15¹/₂×10¹/₂-inch baking pan. Bake at 375°F for 20 to 25 minutes. Cool completely. Cut into 2-inch squares. Makes about 35 cookies.

Butterscotch Lemon Cookies

1¹/₂ cups all-purpose flour
2 teaspoons baking powder
¹/₂ teaspoon salt
³/₄ cup sugar
¹/₂ cup butter, softened
1 egg
2 tablespoons milk
1 tablespoon lemon juice
1 teaspoon grated lemon rind
1¹/₂ cups (³/₄ of 12-ounce package)
    NESTLÉ® Toll House®
    Butterscotch Flavored Morsels

Preheat oven to 375°F. In small bowl, combine flour, baking powder and salt; set aside. In large bowl, combine sugar and butter; beat well. Add egg, milk, lemon juice and lemon rind; beat well.* Gradually beat in flour mixture. Stir in Nestlé® Toll House® Butterscotch Flavored Morsels. Drop by rounded tablespoonfuls onto greased cookie sheets. Bake at 375°F for 8 to 10 minutes. Allow to stand 2 minutes before removing from cookie sheets. Cool completely on wire racks.
Makes about 1¹/₂ dozen 3-inch cookies

* Mixture will appear curdled.

Almond-Milk Chocolate Chippers

Almond-Milk Chocolate Chippers

½ cup butter or margarine, softened
½ cup packed light brown sugar
⅓ cup granulated sugar
1 large egg
2 tablespoons almond-flavored liqueur
1¼ cups all-purpose flour
½ teaspoon baking soda
½ teaspoon salt
1 cup milk chocolate chips
½ cup slivered almonds, toasted

Preheat oven to 375°F. Beat butter, brown sugar and granulated sugar in large bowl until light and fluffy. Beat in egg until well blended. Beat in liqueur. Gradually add combined flour, baking soda and salt. Beat until well blended. Stir in chips and almonds. Drop dough by rounded teaspoonfuls 2 inches apart onto ungreased cookie sheets. Bake 9 to 10 minutes or until edges are golden brown. Let cookies stand on cookie sheets 2 minutes. Remove cookies with spatula to wire racks; cool completely.

Makes about 3 dozen cookies

Baker's® Chocolate Chip Cookies

    1 cup (2 sticks) margarine or butter, softened
    ³/₄ cup firmly packed brown sugar
    ³/₄ cup granulated sugar
    1 teaspoon vanilla
    2 eggs
 2¹/₄ cups all-purpose flour
    1 teaspoon baking soda
    ¹/₄ teaspoon salt
    1 package (12 ounces) BAKER'S® Semi-Sweet Real Chocolate Chips
    1 cup chopped nuts (optional)

Preheat oven to 375°F.

Beat margarine, sugars, vanilla and eggs until light and fluffy. Mix in flour, baking soda and salt. Stir in chips and nuts. Drop by rounded teaspoonfuls, 2 inches apart, onto ungreased cookie sheets.

Bake for 8 to 10 minutes or until golden brown. Remove from cookie sheets to cool on wire racks.

Makes about 6 dozen cookies

Prep Time: 15 minutes
Bake Time: 8 to 10 minutes

Baker's® Chocolate Chip Cookies

Double Chocolate Dream Cookies

 2¹/₄ cups all-purpose flour
    ¹/₂ cup NESTLÉ® Cocoa
    1 teaspoon baking soda
    ¹/₂ teaspoon salt
    1 cup (2 sticks) butter or margarine, softened
    1 cup firmly packed brown sugar
    ³/₄ cup granulated sugar
    2 eggs
    1 teaspoon vanilla extract
    2 cups (12-ounce package) NESTLÉ® Toll House® semi-sweet chocolate morsels

Preheat oven to 375°F. In small bowl, combine flour, cocoa, baking soda and salt; set aside.

In large mixer bowl, beat butter, brown sugar and granulated sugar until creamy. Add eggs, 1 at a time, beating well after each addition. Blend in vanilla extract. Gradually beat in flour mixture. Stir in Nestlé® Toll House® semi-sweet chocolate morsels. Drop by rounded measuring tablespoonfuls onto ungreased cookie sheets.

Bake 8 to 10 minutes until cookies are set. Let stand 2 minutes. Remove from cookie sheets; cool.

Makes about 3¹/₂ dozen cookies

Heavenly Oatmeal Hearts

Heavenly Oatmeal Heart

Cookies

    1 cup *plus* 2 tablespoons BUTTER
        FLAVOR CRISCO®
    1 cup firmly packed brown sugar
    1/2 cup granulated sugar
    2 eggs
    1 teaspoon vanilla
    1 1/2 cups *plus* 1/3 cup all-purpose flour
    1 1/2 teaspoons baking soda
    3/4 teaspoon salt
    3 cups oats (quick or old fashioned),
        uncooked
    1 cup milk chocolate chips
    1 cup vanilla milk chips
    1 cup *plus* 2 tablespoons cinnamon
        roasted peanuts,* chopped

Drizzle

    1/2 cup milk chocolate chips
    1/2 cup vanilla milk chips
    1 teaspoon BUTTER FLAVOR
        CRISCO®, divided

1. Preheat oven to 375°F.

2. For cookies, combine 1 cup *plus* 2 tablespoons Butter Flavor Crisco®, brown sugar and granulated sugar in large bowl. Beat at medium speed of electric mixer until light and fluffy. Beat in eggs and vanilla.

3. Combine flour, baking soda and salt. Add gradually to creamed mixture at low speed. Mix until well blended. Stir in oats, 1 cup chocolate chips, 1 cup vanilla milk chips and nuts with spoon.

4. Place 3-inch heart-shaped cookie cutter on ungreased cookie sheet. Place 1/3 cup dough inside cutter. Press to edges and level. Remove cutter. Repeat to form remaining cookies. Space 2 1/2 inches apart.

5. Bake at 375°F for 9 minutes or until light golden brown. Cool on cookie sheet until slightly warm before removing to cooling rack. Cool completely.

6. For drizzle, place 1/2 cup chocolate chips and 1/2 cup vanilla milk chips in separate heavy resealable plastic bags. Add 1/2 teaspoon Butter Flavor Crisco® to each bag. Seal. Microwave at 50% (MEDIUM). Knead bag after 1 minute. Repeat with each bag until smooth (or melt by placing each in bowl of hot water). Cut tiny tip off corner of each bag. Squeeze out and drizzle over cookies. To serve, cut in half, if desired.

Makes about 22 heart cookies

* Substitute honey roasted peanuts and 1 1/2 teaspoons cinnamon if cinnamon roasted peanuts are unavailable.

Chocolate Chip Shortbread

1/2 cup butter, softened
1/2 cup sugar
1 teaspoon vanilla
1 cup all-purpose flour
1/4 teaspoon salt
1 cup mini semisweet chocolate
    chips

Preheat oven to 375°F. Beat butter and sugar in large bowl until light and fluffy. Beat in vanilla. Add flour and salt. Beat until well combined. Stir in chocolate chips. Divide dough in half. Press each half into ungreased 8-inch round cake pan. Bake 12 minutes or until edges are golden brown. Score shortbread with sharp knife, taking care not to cut completely through shortbread, into 8 wedges per pan. Let pans stand on wire rack 10 minutes. Invert shortbread onto wire racks; cool completely. Break into triangles.

Makes 16 cookies

Double Chocolate Banana Cookies

3 to 4 extra-ripe, medium DOLE®
    Bananas, peeled
2 cups rolled oats
2 cups sugar
1 3/4 cups all-purpose flour
1/2 cup unsweetened cocoa powder
1 teaspoon baking soda
1/2 teaspoon salt
2 eggs, slightly beaten
1 1/4 cups margarine, melted
1 cup DOLE® Chopped Natural
    Almonds, toasted
2 cups semisweet chocolate chips

• Purée bananas in blender; measure 2 cups for recipe.

• Combine oats, sugar, flour, cocoa, baking soda and salt until well mixed. Stir in bananas, eggs and margarine until blended. Stir in almonds and chocolate chips.

• Refrigerate batter 1 hour or until mixture becomes partially firm (batter runs during baking if too soft).

• Measure 1/4 cup batter; drop onto greased cookie sheet. Flatten slightly with spatula.

• Bake in 350°F oven 15 to 17 minutes until cookies are golden brown. Remove to wire rack to cool.

Makes about 2 1/2 dozen (3-inch) cookies

Prep Time: 15 minutes
Chill Time: 1 hour
Bake Time: 17 minutes/batch

Coconut Chocolate Chip Cookies

1 package DUNCAN HINES®
    Chocolate Chip Cookie Mix
1 egg
2 teaspoons water
2 cups flaked coconut

1. Preheat oven to 375°F.

2. Combine cookie mix, buttery flavor packet from Mix, egg and water in large bowl. Stir until thoroughly blended. Drop by rounded teaspoonfuls into coconut. Roll to cover. Place 2 inches apart on ungreased cookie sheets. Bake at 375°F for 10 to 11 minutes or until light golden brown. Cool 1 minute on cookie sheets. Remove to cooling racks. Cool completely. Store in airtight container. *Makes about 3 dozen cookies*

Chocolate Chip Shortbread

Jumbo Chunky Cookies

Chocolate Chip Pretzel Cookies

1 package DUNCAN HINES®
   Chocolate Chip Cookie Mix
1 egg
2 teaspoons water
³/₄ cup coarsely broken thin pretzel
   sticks

1. Preheat oven to 375°F.

2. Combine cookie mix, buttery flavor packet from Mix, egg and water in large bowl. Stir until thoroughly blended. Stir in pretzels. Drop by rounded teaspoonfuls 2 inches apart onto ungreased cookie sheets. Bake at 375°F for 8 to 10 minutes or until light golden brown. Cool 1 minute on cookie sheets. Remove to cooling racks. Cool completely. Store in airtight container.

Makes about 3 dozen cookies

Jumbo Chunky Cookies

1 cup (2 sticks) margarine or butter,
   softened
³/₄ cup firmly packed brown sugar
³/₄ cup granulated sugar
2 eggs
1 teaspoon vanilla
1³/₄ cups all-purpose flour
¹/₂ cup quick oats
1 teaspoon baking soda
¹/₂ teaspoon cinnamon
¹/₄ teaspoon salt
1 (8-ounce) package BAKER'S®
   Semi-Sweet Chocolate, cut into
   chunks, *or* 1 (12-ounce) package
   BAKER'S® Semi-Sweet Real
   Chocolate Chips
1 cup BAKER'S® ANGEL FLAKE®
   Coconut
²/₃ cup chopped nuts
¹/₂ cup raisins (optional)

Preheat oven to 375°F.

Beat margarine, sugars, eggs and vanilla until light and fluffy. Mix in flour, oats, baking soda, cinnamon and salt.

Stir in chocolate, coconut, nuts and raisins. Drop by rounded tablespoonfuls, 2¹/₂ inches apart, onto ungreased cookie sheets.

Bake for 15 minutes or until golden brown. Remove from cookie sheets to cool on wire racks.

Makes about 2¹/₂ dozen cookies

Prep Time: 20 minutes
Bake Time: 15 minutes

Orange-Walnut Chippers

¹/₂ cup butter or margarine, softened
1 cup packed light brown sugar
1 large egg
1 tablespoon grated orange peel
¹/₂ cup all-purpose flour
¹/₄ teaspoon baking soda
¹/₄ teaspoon salt
1¹/₂ cups uncooked quick-cooking or old-fashioned oats
1 cup semisweet chocolate chips
¹/₂ cup coarsely chopped walnuts

Preheat oven to 375°F. Lightly grease cookie sheets; set aside. Beat butter and sugar in large bowl until light and fluffy. Beat in egg and orange peel. Add combined flour, baking soda and salt. Beat until well combined. Stir in oats. Stir in chips and nuts. Drop dough by rounded teaspoonfuls 2 inches apart onto prepared cookie sheets. Bake 10 to 12 minutes or until golden brown. Let cookies stand on cookie sheets 2 minutes. Remove cookies to wire racks; cool completely.

Makes about 3 dozen cookies

Orange-Walnut Chippers

Double Chocolate Cookies

2¼ cups all-purpose flour
1 teaspoon baking soda
1 teaspoon salt
1 cup butter, softened
¾ cup sugar
¾ cup firmly packed brown sugar
1 teaspoon vanilla extract
2 eggs
2 (2-ounce) envelopes NESTLÉ®
   Choco-Bake® unsweetened
   baking chocolate flavor
2 cups (12-ounce package) NESTLÉ®
   Toll House® Semi-Sweet
   Chocolate Morsels
1 cup chopped walnuts

Preheat oven to 375°F. In medium bowl, combine flour, baking soda and salt; set aside. In large bowl, combine butter, sugar, brown sugar and vanilla extract;

Clockwise from top: Chocolate Orange Granola Cookies, Double Chocolate Cookies

beat until creamy. Beat in eggs and Nestlé® Choco-Bake® unsweetened baking chocolate flavor. Gradually beat in flour mixture. Stir in Nestlé® Toll House® Semi-Sweet Chocolate Morsels and nuts. Drop by rounded teaspoonfuls onto ungreased cookie sheets. Bake at 375°F for 8 to 10 minutes. Cool completely on wire racks.

Makes about 6 dozen 2½-inch cookies

Chocolate Orange Granola Cookies

1 cup all-purpose flour
½ teaspoon baking powder
½ teaspoon allspice
½ teaspoon salt
⅔ cup firmly packed brown sugar
½ cup butter, softened
1 egg
1 teaspoon vanilla extract
½ teaspoon grated orange rind
1¼ cups granola cereal
1 cup (6-ounce package) NESTLÉ®
   Toll House® Semi-Sweet
   Chocolate Morsels
½ cup flaked coconut
¼ cup chopped nuts

Preheat oven to 350°F. In small bowl, combine flour, baking powder, allspice and salt; set aside. In large bowl, combine brown sugar and butter; beat until creamy. Add egg, vanilla extract and orange rind; beat well. Gradually beat in flour mixture. Stir in granola cereal, Nestlé® Toll House® Semi-Sweet Chocolate Morsels, coconut and nuts. Drop by rounded tablespoonfuls onto ungreased cookie sheets. Sprinkle with additional coconut, if desired. Bake at 350°F for 9 to 11 minutes. Cool completely on wire racks.

Makes about 1½ dozen 2-inch cookies

Dandy Candy Oatmeal Cookies

1 cup granulated sugar
1 cup firmly packed brown sugar
1 (12-ounce) jar JIF® Creamy Peanut Butter
$^1/_2$ cup BUTTER FLAVOR CRISCO®
3 eggs
$^3/_4$ teaspoon vanilla
$^3/_4$ teaspoon maple (or maple-blend) syrup
2 teaspoons baking soda
$4^1/_2$ cups quick oats, uncooked, divided
1 (8-ounce) package candy coated chocolate pieces

1. Heat oven to 350°F. Grease cookie sheet with Butter Flavor Crisco®.

2. Combine granulated sugar, brown sugar, peanut butter and Butter Flavor Crisco® in large bowl. Beat at medium speed of electric mixer until well blended and fluffy. Add eggs, vanilla and maple syrup. Beat at high speed 3 to 4 minutes. Add baking soda and $2^1/_4$ cups oats. Stir with spoon. Stir in candy. Stir in remaining $2^1/_4$ cups oats. Shape dough into $1^1/_2$-inch balls. Flatten slightly. Place 2 inches apart on prepared cookie sheet.

3. Bake at 350°F for 9 to 10 minutes for chewy cookies or 11 to 12 minutes for crispy cookies. Cool 2 minutes on cookie sheet before removing to cooling rack.   *Makes about $3^1/_2$ dozen cookies*

Dandy Candy Oatmeal Cookies

Chocolate Chip Chocolate Cookies

$^1/_2$ cup butter or margarine, softened
1 cup sugar
1 egg
1 teaspoon vanilla
$1^1/_2$ cups unsifted all-purpose flour
$^1/_3$ cup HERSHEY'S Cocoa
$^1/_2$ teaspoon baking soda
$^1/_2$ teaspoon salt
$^1/_4$ cup milk
1 cup HERSHEY'S Semi-Sweet Chocolate Chips

Cream butter, sugar, egg and vanilla in large mixer bowl until light and fluffy. Combine flour, cocoa, baking soda and salt; add alternately with milk to creamed mixture, blending well. Stir in chocolate chips.

Drop by teaspoonfuls onto ungreased cookie sheet. Bake at 375°F for 10 to 12 minutes or until almost set *(do not overbake)*. Cool 1 minute. Remove from cookie sheet; cool completely on wire rack.   *Makes about $3^1/_2$ dozen cookies*

Oatmeal Candied Chippers

³/₄ **cup butter or margarine, softened**
³/₄ **cup granulated sugar**
³/₄ **cup packed light brown sugar**
 3 **tablespoons milk**
 1 **large egg**
 2 **teaspoons vanilla**
³/₄ **cup all-purpose flour**
³/₄ **teaspoon salt**
¹/₂ **teaspoon baking soda**
 3 **cups uncooked quick-cooking or**
   old-fashioned oats
1¹/₃ **cups (10-ounce package) candy**
   coated semisweet chocolate chips

Preheat oven to 375°F. Grease cookie
sheets; set aside. Beat butter, granulated
sugar and brown sugar in large bowl
until light and fluffy. Add milk, egg and
vanilla; beat well. Add combined flour,
salt and baking soda. Beat until well
combined. Stir in oats. Stir in chocolate
chips. Drop dough by tablespoonfuls
2 inches apart on prepared cookie
sheets. Bake 10 to 11 minutes until
edges are golden brown. Let cookies
stand 2 minutes on cookie sheets.
Remove cookies to wire racks; cool
completely.   *Makes about 4 dozen cookies*

Ultimate Chocolate Chip Cookies

³/₄ **cup BUTTER FLAVOR CRISCO®**
1¹/₄ **cups firmly packed brown sugar**
 2 **tablespoons milk**
 1 **tablespoon vanilla**
 1 **egg**
1³/₄ **cups all-purpose flour**
 1 **teaspoon salt**
³/₄ **teaspoon baking soda**
 1 **cup semi-sweet chocolate chips**
 1 **cup coarsely chopped pecans***

1. Preheat oven to 375°F.
2. Combine Butter Flavor Crisco®, sugar,
milk and vanilla in large bowl. Beat at
medium speed of electric mixer until
well blended. Beat in egg.

3. Combine flour, salt and baking soda.
Mix into creamed mixture at low speed
just until blended. Stir in chocolate
chips and nuts.

4. Drop rounded tablespoonfuls of
dough 3 inches apart onto ungreased
cookie sheet.

5. Bake at 375°F for 8 to 10 minutes for
chewy cookies (they will look light and
moist—do not overbake) or 11 to
13 minutes for crisp cookies. Cool
2 minutes on cookie sheet. Remove to
cooling rack.

Makes about 3 dozen cookies

* You may substitute an additional
¹/₂ cup semi-sweet chocolate chips for
pecans.

Variations

Drizzle: Combine 1 teaspoon BUTTER
FLAVOR CRISCO® and 1 cup
semi-sweet chocolate chips or 1 cup
white melting chocolate, cut into small
pieces, in microwave-safe measuring
cup. Microwave at 50% (MEDIUM). Stir
after 1 minute. Repeat until smooth (or
melt on rangetop in small saucepan on
very low heat). To thin, add more
Butter Flavor Crisco®. Drizzle back and
forth over cookie. Sprinkle with nuts
before chocolate hardens, if desired. To
quickly harden chocolate, place cookies
in refrigerator to set.

Chocolate Dipped: Melt chocolate as
directed for Drizzle. Dip half of cooled
cookie in chocolate. Sprinkle with finely
chopped nuts before chocolate hardens.
Place on waxed paper until chocolate is
firm. To quickly harden chocolate, place
cookies in refrigerator to set.

Oatmeal Candied Chippers

Chocolate Oatmeal Chippers

Chocolate Oatmeal Chippers

1¼ cups all-purpose flour
½ cup NESTLÉ® Cocoa
1 teaspoon baking soda
½ teaspoon salt
1 cup (2 sticks) butter or margarine, softened
1 cup firmly packed brown sugar
½ cup granulated sugar
1 teaspoon vanilla extract
2 eggs
2 cups (11½-ounce package) NESTLÉ® Toll House® Milk Chocolate Morsels
2 cups quick or old-fashioned oats, uncooked
1 cup walnuts, chopped

Preheat oven to 350°F. In small bowl, combine flour, Nestlé® Cocoa, baking soda and salt; set aside. In large mixer bowl, beat butter, brown sugar, granulated sugar and vanilla extract until creamy. Add eggs, 1 at a time, beating well after each addition. Gradually beat in flour mixture. Stir in Nestlé® Toll House® Milk Chocolate Morsels, oats and walnuts. Drop by slightly rounded measuring tablespoonfuls onto ungreased cookie sheets. Bake 9 to 10 minutes until edges are firm. Let stand on cookie sheets 2 minutes. Remove from cookie sheets; cool. *Makes about 4 dozen cookies*

Chocolate Crunch Cookies

1 cup butter or margarine
1½ cups firmly packed light brown sugar
2 eggs
1½ teaspoons vanilla
2½ cups flour
1 teaspoon salt
¾ teaspoon baking soda
1½ cups "M&M's"® Plain Chocolate Candies
½ cup chopped nuts, if desired

Preheat oven to 375°F. Beat together butter and sugar until light and fluffy, blend in eggs and vanilla. Add combined dry ingredients; mix well. Add "M&M's"® and nuts; mix well. Drop by rounded teaspoonfuls onto greased cookie sheet. Bake 9 to 11 minutes or until golden brown. Immediately press about 3 additional candies firmly on top of each cookie. Cool thoroughly on wire rack.
Makes about 5 dozen cookies

Chocolate Scotcheroos

1 cup light corn syrup
1 cup sugar
1 cup peanut butter
6 cups KELLOGG'S® RICE
    KRISPIES® cereal
1 cup (6-ounce package) semi-sweet
    chocolate morsels
1 cup (6-ounce package) butterscotch
    morsels

Combine corn syrup and sugar in large saucepan. Cook over medium heat, stirring frequently, until sugar dissolves and mixture begins to boil. Remove from heat. Stir in peanut butter. Mix well. Add Kellogg's® Rice Krispies® cereal. Stir until well coated. Press mixture into 13×9-inch pan coated with cooking spray. Set aside.

Melt chocolate and butterscotch morsels together in small saucepan over low heat, stirring constantly. Spread evenly over cereal mixture. Let stand until firm. Cut into 2×1-inch bars to serve.

Makes about 48 bars

Kate's Chocolate Chip Cookies

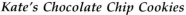

  1 cup BUTTER FLAVOR CRISCO®
  1 cup granulated sugar
  1 cup firmly packed brown sugar
  3 eggs
  2 teaspoons vanilla
3½ cups all-purpose flour
  1 teaspoon baking soda
  1 teaspoon salt
  1 cup quick oats, uncooked
  2 cups (12-ounce package) semi-
    sweet chocolate chips
  1 cup chopped pecans, walnuts or
    peanuts

1. Preheat oven to 375°F. Grease cookie sheet with Butter Flavor Crisco®.

2. Combine Butter Flavor Crisco®, granulated sugar, brown sugar, eggs and vanilla in large bowl. Beat at high speed of electric mixer until fluffy (about 5 minutes).

3. Combine flour, baking soda and salt. Add gradually to creamed mixture at low speed. Mix until well blended. Add oats. Mix until well blended. Stir in chocolate chips and nuts. Drop by rounded teaspoonfuls 2 inches apart onto greased cookie sheet.

4. Bake at 375°F for 10 to 12 minutes or until light golden brown. Cool 3 to 4 minutes on cookie sheet before removing to flat surface.

Makes about 3½ dozen cookies

Kate's Chocolate Chip Cookies

Double Chocolate Chip Cookies

2 cups all-purpose flour
1 teaspoon baking soda
$^1/_2$ teaspoon salt
4 cups (24-ounce package)
    HERSHEY'S Semi-Sweet
    Chocolate Chips, divided
$^3/_4$ cup ($1^1/_2$ sticks) butter or
    margarine, softened
$^3/_4$ cup sugar
2 eggs

Preheat oven to 350°F. In small bowl, stir together flour, baking soda and salt. In medium microwave-safe bowl, place 2 cups chocolate chips. Microwave at HIGH (100% power) $1^1/_2$ minutes; stir. Microwave at HIGH (100% power) an additional 30 seconds or until chips are melted and smooth when stirred: cool slightly. In large mixer bowl, beat butter and sugar until light and fluffy. Add eggs; beat well. Blend in melted chocolate. Gradually add flour mixture, beating well. Stir in remaining 2 cups chips. Drop dough by rounded teaspoonfuls onto ungreased cookie sheets.

Bake 8 to 9 minutes. *Do not overbake.* Cookies should be soft. Cool slightly: remove from cookie sheet to wire rack. Cool completely.

Makes about 5 dozen cookies

Forgotten Chips Cookies (left), Double Chocolate Chip Cookies (right)

Forgotten Chips Cookies

2 egg whites
1/8 teaspoon cream of tartar
1/8 teaspoon salt
2/3 cup sugar
1 teaspoon vanilla extract
1 cup HERSHEY'S Semi-Sweet
    Chocolate Chips or Milk
    Chocolate Chips

Preheat oven to 375°F. Lightly grease cookie sheet. In small mixer bowl, beat egg whites with cream of tartar and salt until soft peaks form. Gradually add sugar, beating until stiff peaks form. Carefully fold in vanilla extract and chocolate chips. Drop by teaspoonfuls onto prepared cookie sheet. Place cookie sheet in preheated oven; immediately turn off oven and allow cookies to remain in oven six hours or overnight without opening door. Remove cookies from cookie sheet. Store in airtight container in cool, dry place. *Makes about 2 1/2 dozen cookies*

Child's Choice

2 1/3 cups all-purpose flour
1 cup BUTTER FLAVOR CRISCO®
1 teaspoon baking soda
1/2 teaspoon baking powder
1 cup granulated sugar
1 cup firmly packed brown sugar
2 eggs
1 teaspoon maple flavor
2 cups oats (quick or old fashioned),
    uncooked
3/4 cup semi-sweet chocolate chips
3/4 cup peanut butter chips
3/4 cup miniature marshmallows

Child's Choice

1. Preheat oven to 350°F. Grease cookie sheet with Butter Flavor Crisco®.

2. Combine flour, Butter Flavor Crisco®, baking soda and baking powder in large bowl. Beat at low speed of electric mixer until blended. Increase speed to medium. Mix thoroughly. Beat in granulated sugar, brown sugar, eggs and maple flavor. Add oats. Stir in chocolate chips, peanut butter chips and marshmallows with spoon until well blended.

3. Shape dough into 1 1/2-inch balls. Flatten slightly. Place 2 inches apart on greased cookie sheet.

4. Bake at 350°F for 9 to 10 minutes or until light golden brown. Cool 1 minute on cookie sheet before removing to cooling rack.

Makes about 3 1/2 dozen cookies

Banana Chocolate Chip Softies

1/3 cup butter or margarine, softened
1/3 cup granulated sugar
1/3 cup packed light brown sugar
1 ripe, medium banana, mashed to measure 1/2 cup
1 large egg
1 teaspoon vanilla
1 1/4 cups all-purpose flour
1 teaspoon baking powder
1/2 teaspoon salt
1 cup milk chocolate chips
1/2 cup coarsely chopped walnuts (optional)

Preheat oven to 375°F. Beat butter, granulated sugar and brown sugar in large bowl until light and fluffy. Beat in banana, egg and vanilla. Add combined flour, baking powder and salt. Beat until well blended. Stir in chips and walnuts. (Dough will be soft.) Drop dough by rounded teaspoonfuls 2 inches apart onto greased cookie sheets. Bake 9 to 11 minutes or until edges are golden brown. Let cookies stand on cookie sheets 2 minutes. Remove cookies with spatula to wire racks; cool completely.

Makes about 3 dozen cookies

Peanut Butter Chocolate Chip Cookies

1 cup sugar
1/2 cup SKIPPY® Creamy or Super Chunk Peanut Butter
1/2 cup *undiluted* evaporated milk
1 (6-ounce) package semisweet chocolate chips
1 cup coarsely chopped nuts

Preheat oven to 325°F. In medium bowl, mix sugar and peanut butter until well blended. Stir in evaporated milk, chips and nuts until well mixed. Drop batter by heaping teaspoonfuls 1 1/2 inches apart onto foil-lined cookie sheets. Spread batter evenly into 2-inch rounds. Bake 18 to 20 minutes or until golden. Cool completely on foil on wire racks. Peel foil from cookies.

Makes about 3 1/2 dozen cookies

Pudding Drop Cookies

3/4 cup sugar
2 eggs
1/4 cup BLUE BONNET® Spread, melted
1 cup all-purpose flour
1 (3 3/8-ounce) package ROYAL® Instant Butterscotch Pudding & Pie Filling*
1/2 cup chopped walnuts
1/2 cup semisweet chocolate chips

Preheat oven to 375°F. In medium bowl, with electric mixer at high speed, beat sugar and eggs until thick and pale yellow. Beat in spread until smooth. Stir in flour and pudding mix until blended. Stir in walnuts and chocolate chips. Drop batter by tablespoonfuls, 2 inches apart, onto greased and floured cookie sheets. Bake for 10 to 12 minutes or until lightly browned. Cool slightly on cookie sheets. Remove from sheets; cool completely on wire racks. Store in airtight container.

Makes about 2 dozen cookies

* 1 (3 3/8-ounce) package ROYAL® Instant Chocolate or Vanilla Pudding and Pie Filling may be substituted.

Banana Chocolate Chip Softies

Choco-Scutterbotch

²/₃ cup BUTTER FLAVOR CRISCO®
¹/₂ cup firmly packed brown sugar
2 eggs
1 package DUNCAN HINES® Moist
　　Deluxe Yellow Cake Mix
1 cup toasted rice cereal
¹/₂ cup milk chocolate chunks
¹/₂ cup butterscotch chips
¹/₂ cup semi-sweet chocolate chips
¹/₂ cup coarsely chopped walnuts or
　　pecans

1. Preheat oven to 375°F.

2. Combine Butter Flavor Crisco® and brown sugar in large bowl. Beat at medium speed of electric mixer until well blended. Beat in eggs.

3. Add Duncan Hines® Moist Deluxe Yellow Cake Mix gradually at low speed. Mix until well blended. Stir in cereal, chocolate chunks, butterscotch chips, chocolate chips and nuts with

Choco-Scutterbotch

spoon. Stir until well blended. Shape dough into 1¹/₄-inch balls. Place 2 inches apart on ungreased cookie sheet. Flatten slightly. Shape sides to form circle, if necessary.

4. Bake at 375°F for 7 to 9 minutes or until lightly browned around edges. Cool 2 minutes before removing to paper towels.

Makes about 3 dozen cookies

Jumbo Corn Flake Cookies

1³/₄ cups all-purpose flour
1 teaspoon baking powder
¹/₂ teaspoon baking soda
¹/₄ teaspoon salt
1 cup margarine or butter
1 cup sugar
2 eggs
¹/₂ teaspoon vanilla flavoring
6 cups KELLOGG'S® CORN
　　FLAKES® cereal, crushed to
　　4 cups, divided
¹/₂ cup milk chocolate morsels
¹/₂ cup peanut butter morsels

1. Stir together flour, baking powder, soda and salt. Set aside.

2. In large mixing bowl, cream margarine and sugar until light and fluffy. Add eggs and beat well. Blend in vanilla. Add flour mixture, mixing until combined.

3. Fold in 2 cups crushed Kellogg's® Corn Flakes® cereal, chocolate morsels and peanut butter morsels. Drop batter from ¹/₄-cup measure; roll in remaining cereal and flatten to 3-inch diameter. Place on lightly greased cookie sheets.

4. Bake at 350°F for 15 to 18 minutes or until lightly golden brown. Remove immediately from cookie sheets. Cool on wire racks. *Makes about 16 cookies*

Chocolate Mint Sugar Cookie Drops

2¹/₂ cups all-purpose flour
1¹/₂ teaspoons baking powder
³/₄ teaspoon salt
1 cup granulated sugar
³/₄ cup vegetable oil
2 eggs
1 teaspoon vanilla extract
1¹/₂ cups (10 ounce package) NESTLÉ®
    Toll House® Mint Flavored Semi-
    Sweet Chocolate Morsels
    Assorted colored sugars

Preheat oven to 350°F. In small bowl, combine flour, baking powder and salt; set aside.

In large mixer bowl, combine granulated sugar and oil. Add eggs, 1 at a time, beating well after each addition. Blend in vanilla extract. Gradually beat in flour mixture. Stir in Nestlé® Toll House® Mint Flavored Chocolate Morsels. Shape rounded measuring teaspoonfuls of dough into balls; roll in colored sugar or additional granulated sugar. Place on ungreased cookie sheets.

Bake 8 to 10 minutes until set. Let stand 2 minutes. Remove from cookie sheets; cool. *Makes about 5¹/₂ dozen cookies*

Double Chocolate Mint Chip Cookies

1¹/₂ cups (10-ounce package) NESTLÉ®
    Toll House® Mint Flavored
    Semi-Sweet Chocolate Morsels,
    divided
1¹/₄ cups all-purpose flour
³/₄ teaspoon baking soda
¹/₂ teaspoon salt
¹/₂ cup butter, softened
¹/₂ cup firmly packed brown sugar
¹/₄ cup sugar
¹/₂ teaspoon vanilla extract
1 egg
¹/₂ cup chopped nuts

Chocolate Mint Chip Cookies (top), Chocolate Mint Sugar Cookie Drops (bottom)

Preheat oven to 375°F. Melt over hot (not boiling) water, ³/₄ cup Nestlé® Toll House® Mint Flavored Semi-Sweet Chocolate Morsels; stir until smooth. Remove from heat; cool to room temperature. In small bowl, combine flour, baking soda and salt; set aside. In large bowl, combine butter, brown sugar, sugar and vanilla extract; beat until creamy. Add melted morsels and egg; beat well. Gradually blend in flour mixture. Stir in remaining ³/₄ cup Nestlé® Toll House® Mint Flavored Semi-Sweet Chocolate Morsels and nuts. Drop by rounded tablespoonfuls onto ungreased cookie sheets. Bake at 375°F for 8 to 9 minutes. Allow to stand 2 to 3 minutes; remove from cookie sheets. Cool completely on wire racks.
Makes about 1¹/₂ dozen 2-inch cookies

Butterscotch Granola Cookies

Chocolate Chip Cookies

1¼ cups all-purpose flour
½ teaspoon baking soda
¼ teaspoon salt
½ cup margarine or butter, softened
1 cup sugar
1 egg
1 teaspoon vanilla
2 cups KELLOGG'S® RICE KRISPIES® cereal
1 cup (6-ounce package) semi-sweet chocolate morsels

Stir together flour, baking soda and salt. Set aside.

In large mixing bowl, beat margarine and sugar until well combined. Add egg and vanilla. Beat well. Add flour mixture. Mix thoroughly. Stir in Kellogg's® Rice Krispies® cereal and chocolate morsels. Drop by level measuring tablespoonfuls onto greased cookie sheets.

Bake at 350°F about 12 minutes or until lightly browned. Remove immediately from cookie sheets. Cool on wire racks.
Makes about 3½ dozen cookies

Butterscotch Granola Cookies

1½ cups all-purpose flour
1 teaspoon cinnamon
½ teaspoon salt
½ teaspoon baking powder
½ teaspoon baking soda
½ cup butter, softened
½ cup honey
½ cup firmly packed brown sugar
1 egg
1 teaspoon vanilla extract
¼ cup milk
2 cups (12-ounce package) NESTLÉ® Toll House® Butterscotch Flavored Morsels
1 cup quick oats, uncooked
1 cup chopped walnuts
¾ cup raisins
¼ cup wheat germ

Preheat oven to 350°F. In small bowl, combine flour, cinnamon, salt, baking powder and baking soda; set aside. In large bowl, combine butter, honey and brown sugar; beat until creamy. Beat in egg and vanilla extract. Blend in flour mixture alternately with milk. Stir in Nestlé® Toll House® Butterscotch Flavored Morsels, oats, walnuts, raisins and wheat germ. Drop by rounded teaspoonfuls onto greased cookie sheets. Bake at 350°F for 8 to 10 minutes. Allow to stand 2 minutes; remove from cookie sheets. Cool completely on wire racks.
Makes about 5 dozen 2¼-inch cookies

Grandpa Would Have Loved These Cookies

   1 cup BUTTER FLAVOR CRISCO®
   1 cup firmly packed brown sugar
  ²/₃ cup granulated sugar
   2 eggs
  ¹/₄ cup milk
   1 tablespoon vanilla
   1 package (4-serving size) vanilla
     flavor instant pudding and pie
     filling mix (not sugar-free)
 1³/₄ cups whole wheat flour
  ¹/₂ cup quick oats, uncooked
  ¹/₂ cup flake coconut
   1 teaspoon baking soda
  ¹/₂ teaspoon salt
   1 cup oats (quick or old fashioned),
     uncooked
   1 cup semi-sweet chocolate chips
  ¹/₂ cup mini semi-sweet chocolate
     chips*
   1 cup butterscotch chips
   1 cup chopped pecans

1. Preheat oven to 325°F.

2. Combine Butter Flavor Crisco®, brown sugar and granulated sugar in large bowl. Beat at low speed of electric mixer until well blended. Add, 1 at a time, eggs, milk and vanilla. Mix well after each addition. Beat in pudding mix just until blended. Add flour, ¹/₂ cup quick oats, coconut, baking soda and salt. Mix until blended. Stir in 1 cup oats, regular and mini semi-sweet chocolate chips, butterscotch chips and nuts with spoon. Drop by rounded teaspoonfuls onto ungreased cookie sheet.

3. Bake at 325°F for 7 to 9 minutes or until golden brown around edges and slightly moist in center. Cool 3 to 5 minutes before removing to paper towels. *Makes about 8 dozen cookies*

* Substitute regular semi-sweet chips for mini chips, if desired.

Chocolate Chip Oatmeal Raisin Cookies

   1 package DUNCAN HINES®
     Oatmeal Raisin Cookie Mix
   1 egg
   1 tablespoon water
  ¹/₂ cup chopped walnuts
  ¹/₂ cup semi-sweet chocolate chips
   2 tablespoons sugar
  ³/₄ teaspoon ground cinnamon

1. Preheat oven to 375°F.

2. Combine cookie mix, buttery flavor packet from Mix, egg and water in large bowl. Stir until thoroughly blended. Stir in walnuts and chocolate chips. Shape dough into 1-inch balls. Place balls 2 inches apart on ungreased cookie sheet.

3. Combine sugar and cinnamon in small bowl. Flatten cookies with glass dipped in sugar-cinnamon mixture. Bake at 375°F for 8 to 10 minutes or until lightly browned. Cool 1 minute on cookie sheet. Remove to cooling rack.
Makes about 3 dozen cookies

Chocolate Chip Oatmeal Raisin Cookies

SURPRISINGLY SIMPLE

Quick Chocolate Softies

**1 package (18.25 ounces) devil's
food cake mix**
¹/₃ cup water
¹/₄ cup butter or margarine, softened
1 large egg
1 cup white chocolate baking chips
¹/₂ cup coarsely chopped walnuts

Preheat oven to 350°F. Combine cake
mix, water, butter and egg in large
bowl. Beat with electric mixer at low
speed until moistened, scraping down
side of bowl once. Increase speed to
medium; beat 1 minute, scraping down
side of bowl once. (Dough will be
thick.) Stir in chips and nuts; mix until
well blended. Drop dough by heaping
teaspoonfuls 2 inches apart onto
greased cookie sheets. Bake 10 to
12 minutes or until set. Let cookies
stand on cookie sheets 1 minute.
Remove cookies to wire racks; cool
completely.

Makes about 4 dozen cookies

Pecan Drops

³/₄ cup sugar
**¹/₂ cup FLEISCHMANN'S®
Margarine, softened**
**¹/₄ cup EGG BEATERS® 99% Egg
Product**
1 teaspoon vanilla extract
2 cups all-purpose flour
**²/₃ cup PLANTERS® Pecans, finely
chopped**
**3 tablespoons jam, jelly or
preserves, any flavor**

In small bowl, with electric mixer at
medium speed, cream sugar and
margarine. Add egg product and
vanilla; beat for 1 minute. Stir in flour
until blended. Chill dough for 1 hour.

Preheat oven to 350°F. Form dough into
36 (1¹/₄-inch) balls; roll in pecans,
pressing into dough. Place 2 inches
apart on greased cookie sheets. Indent
center of each ball with thumb or back
of wooden spoon. Bake for 10 minutes;
remove from oven. Spoon ¹/₄ teaspoon
jam into each cookie indentation. Bake
for 2 to 5 more minutes or until lightly
browned. Remove from sheets; cool on
wire racks. *Makes 3 dozen cookies*

Quick Chocolate Softies

Chocolate Mint Snow-Top Cookies

1½ cups all-purpose flour
1½ teaspoons baking powder
¼ teaspoon salt
1½ cups (10-ounce package) NESTLÉ® Toll House® Mint Flavored Semi-Sweet Chocolate Morsels, divided
6 tablespoons butter, softened
1 cup granulated sugar
1½ teaspoons vanilla extract
2 eggs
⅔ cup confectioners' sugar

In small bowl, combine flour, baking powder and salt. In small saucepan over low heat, melt 1 cup Nestlé® Toll House® Mint Flavored Semi-Sweet Chocolate Morsels. In large bowl, cream butter and granulated sugar. Beat in melted Nestlé® Toll House® Mint Flavored Semi-Sweet Chocolate Morsels and vanilla; beat in eggs. Gradually beat in dry ingredients. Stir in remaining ½ cup Nestlé® Toll House® Mint Flavored Semi-Sweet Chocolate Morsels. Wrap in plastic wrap; freeze for 30 minutes or until firm.

Chocolate Mint Snow-Top Cookies

Preheat oven to 350°F. Shape dough into 1-inch balls; roll in confectioners' sugar. Place on ungreased cookie sheets. Bake for 10 to 12 minutes or until sides are set but centers are still slightly soft. Let stand for 2 minutes; cool on wire racks.

Note: Nestlé® Toll House® Mint Flavored Semi-Sweet Chocolate Morsels may be melted in microwave on HIGH (100% power) for 1½ minutes, stirring once.

Makes about 3 dozen cookies

Baked Truffle Treasures

¼ cup (½ stick) butter, melted
1 cup granulated sugar
2 eggs, beaten
3 tablespoons cherry brandy or amaretto *or* ½ teaspoon almond extract
2 tablespoons honey
1 teaspoon vanilla extract
2 cups HONEY ALMOND DELIGHT® brand cereal, crushed to 1 cup
½ cup unsweetened cocoa
½ cup flaked coconut
½ cup powdered sugar

Preheat oven to 350°F. In medium bowl, beat butter and granulated sugar. Add eggs, brandy, honey and vanilla, stirring until well combined. Stir in cereal, cocoa and coconut. Pour into ungreased 2-quart casserole. Bake 30 minutes. Remove from oven and stir immediately until well blended. Let cool to room temperature. Shape level tablespoons into 1½-inch balls. Roll each ball in powdered sugar. Store in airtight container. *Makes about 30 cookies*

Nerds® Sprinkle Cookies

Nerds® Sprinkle Cookies

3 cups unsifted flour
1 tablespoon baking powder
$^1/_2$ teaspoon salt
1 (14-ounce) can sweetened
    condensed milk (not evaporated
    milk)
$^3/_4$ cup margarine or butter, softened
2 eggs
$1^1/_2$ teaspoons vanilla
1 (7-ounce) box Rainbow NERDS®

Preheat oven to 350°F. Combine flour, baking powder and salt; set aside. In large bowl, beat sweetened condensed milk, margarine, eggs and vanilla until well blended. Add flour mixture; mix well. On floured surface, lightly knead dough to form a smooth ball. Divide dough into 1-inch balls and place 1 inch apart on greased cookie sheet. Flatten slightly. Cover tops of cookies with Nerds® Candy. Bake 7 to 9 minutes or until lightly browned around edges. Cool thoroughly. Store loosely covered at room temperature.

Makes about 5$^1/_2$ dozen cookies

Lemon Wafers

$^3/_4$ cup ($1^1/_2$ sticks) margarine,
    softened
$^1/_2$ cup sugar
1 egg
1 tablespoon grated lemon peel
    (about 1 medium lemon)
2 cups QUAKER® or AUNT
    JEMIMA® Enriched Corn Meal
$1^1/_2$ cups all-purpose flour
$^1/_2$ teaspoon salt (optional)
$^1/_4$ cup milk

Preheat oven to 375°F. Beat margarine and sugar until fluffy. Blend in egg and lemon peel. Add combined dry ingredients alternately with milk, mixing well after each addition. Shape dough into 1-inch balls. Place on ungreased cookie sheet. Using bottom of glass dipped in sugar, press into $^1/_8$-inch thick circles. Bake 13 to 15 minutes or until bottoms are lightly browned. Cool 2 minutes on cookie sheet; remove to wire rack. Cool completely. Store tightly covered.

Makes about 3 dozen cookies

No-Fuss Bar Cookies

2 cups graham cracker crumbs
  (about 24 graham cracker
  squares)
1 cup semisweet chocolate chips
1 cup flaked coconut
³/₄ cup coarsely chopped walnuts
1 can (14 ounces) sweetened
  condensed milk

Preheat oven to 350°F. Combine crumbs, chips, coconut and walnuts in medium bowl; toss to blend. Add milk; mix until blended. Spread batter into greased 13×9-inch baking pan. Bake 15 to 18 minutes or until edges are golden brown. Let pan stand on wire rack until completely cooled. Cut into 2¹/₄-inch squares. *Makes about 20 bars*

Cream Cheese Cookies

¹/₂ cup BUTTER FLAVOR CRISCO®
1 package (3 ounces) cream cheese,
  softened
1 tablespoon milk
1 cup sugar
¹/₂ teaspoon vanilla
1 cup all-purpose flour
¹/₂ cup chopped pecans

1. Preheat oven to 375°F.
2. Combine Butter Flavor Crisco®, cream cheese and milk in medium bowl. Beat at medium speed of electric mixer until well blended. Beat in sugar and vanilla. Mix in flour. Add nuts. Drop by level measuring tablespoonfuls 2 inches apart onto ungreased cookie sheet.
3. Bake at 375°F for 10 minutes. Remove to cooling rack.
Makes about 3 dozen cookies

Chocolate Butter-Pecan Crescents

4 foil-wrapped bars (8-ounce
  package) NESTLÉ® Semi-Sweet
  Chocolate Baking Bars, divided
³/₄ cup (1¹/₂ sticks) butter or
  margarine, softened
³/₄ cup confectioners' sugar
1 teaspoon vanilla extract
2 cups all-purpose flour
1¹/₂ cups pecans, ground

Preheat oven to 350°F. In small saucepan over low heat, melt 2 (2-ounce) Nestlé® Semi-Sweet Chocolate Baking Bars; set aside.

In large mixer bowl, beat butter and confectioners' sugar until creamy. Blend in melted chocolate and vanilla extract. Gradually beat in flour and pecans. Knead gently to form smooth dough.

Drop by rounded measuring teaspoonfuls onto ungreased cookie sheets. Shape into crescents.

Bake 8 to 10 minutes until set. Let stand 2 minutes. Remove from cookie sheets; cool completely. (Keep remaining dough covered with plastic wrap while baking cookies. If dough becomes dry, knead gently.)

In small saucepan over low heat, melt remaining 2 (2-ounce) Nestlé® Semi-Sweet Chocolate Baking Bars. Dip half of each crescent into melted chocolate. Refrigerate 10 to 15 minutes to set chocolate.
Makes about 4 dozen cookies

Variation: Decrease Nestlé® Semi-Sweet Chocolate Baking Bars to 2 foil-wrapped bars (4 ounces). Prepare, bake and cool cookies as directed. Sift combined confectioners' sugar and Nestlé® Cocoa over crescents.

No-Fuss Bar Cookies

Cheery Chocolate Teddy Bear Cookies

Cheery Chocolate Teddy Bear Cookies

1 (10-ounce) package REESE'S®
  Peanut Butter Chips
1 cup (6 ounces) HERSHEY'S® Semi-
  Sweet Chocolate Chips
2 tablespoons shortening (*do not* use
  butter, margarine or oil)
1 (20-ounce) package chocolate
  sandwich cookies
1 (10-ounce) package teddy bear
  shaped graham snack crackers

Line tray or cookie sheet with waxed
paper. In 2-quart glass measuring cup
with handle, combine chips and
shortening. Microwave on HIGH (100%
power) 1¹/₂ to 2 minutes or until chips
are melted and mixture is smooth when
stirred. With fork, dip each cookie into
chip mixture; gently tap fork on side of
cup to remove excess chocolate. Place
coated cookies on prepared tray; top
each cookie with a graham snack
cracker. Chill until chocolate is set,
about 30 minutes. Store in airtight
container in cool, dry place.

Makes about 4 dozen cookies

Oatmeal Honey Cookies

1 cup BUTTER FLAVOR CRISCO®
1 cup firmly packed dark brown
  sugar
1 egg
¹/₂ cup honey
¹/₄ cup granulated sugar
¹/₄ cup water
1¹/₂ teaspoons vanilla
1¹/₂ cups all-purpose flour
1 teaspoon cinnamon
¹/₂ teaspoon baking soda
¹/₂ teaspoon salt
3 cups oats (quick or old fashioned),
  uncooked
1 cup raisins
¹/₂ cup coarsely chopped pecans

1. Preheat oven to 350°F. Grease cookie
sheet with Butter Flavor Crisco®.

2. Combine Butter Flavor Crisco®,
brown sugar, egg, honey, granulated
sugar, water and vanilla in large bowl.
Beat at low speed of electric mixer until
blended. Increase speed to medium.
Beat until light and creamy.

3. Combine flour, cinnamon, baking
soda and salt. Add gradually to
creamed mixture at low speed. Increase
speed to medium. Beat until well
blended. Stir in oats with spoon. Mix
until well blended. Stir in raisins and
nuts. Drop by heaping tablespoonfuls
onto greased cookie sheet.

4. Bake at 350°F for 11 to 12 minutes or
until golden brown. Cool 3 to 5 minutes
on cookie sheet before removing to flat
surface.   *Makes about 3 dozen cookies*

Note: For small cookies, drop dough by
heaping teaspoonfuls onto greased
cookie sheet. Bake at 350°F for
9 to 11 minutes. Makes 4 to 5 dozen
small cookies.

Peanut Butter Brickle Cookies

1½ cups all-purpose flour
1 cup granulated sugar
2 tablespoons firmly packed light brown sugar
1 cup butter or margarine, softened
½ cup peanut butter
1 egg
½ teaspoon baking soda
1 teaspoon vanilla
1 package (6 ounces) almond brickle bits

Preheat oven to 350°F. In large mixer bowl, combine flour, granulated sugar, brown sugar, butter, peanut butter, egg, baking soda and vanilla. Beat at medium speed, scraping bowl often until well mixed, 2 to 3 minutes. Stir in almond brickle bits. Shape rounded teaspoonfuls of dough into 1-inch balls. Place 2 inches apart on greased cookie sheets. Flatten cookies to ⅛-inch thickness with bottom of glass covered with waxed paper. Bake 7 to 9 minutes or until edges are very lightly browned.   *Makes about 4 dozen cookies*

Peanut Butter Brickle Cookies

Chocolate-Pecan Angels

Chocolate-Pecan Angels

1 cup mini semisweet chocolate chips
1 cup chopped pecans, toasted
1 cup sifted powdered sugar
1 large egg white

Preheat oven to 350°F. Combine chips, pecans and powdered sugar in medium bowl. Add egg white; mix well. Drop batter by teaspoonfuls 2 inches apart onto greased cookie sheets. Bake 11 to 12 minutes until edges are light golden brown. Let cookies stand on cookie sheets 1 minute. Remove cookies to wire racks; cool completely.
     Makes about 3 dozen cookies

Chunky Chocolate Cookies

Chunky Chocolate Cookies

    ³/₄ cup granulated sugar
    ³/₄ cup firmly packed light brown
        sugar
    1 cup margarine, softened
    2 eggs
1¹/₂ teaspoons vanilla
2¹/₄ cups all-purpose flour
    1 teaspoon baking soda
    ¹/₂ teaspoon salt
    1 cup coarsely chopped walnuts
    1 (8-ounce) milk chocolate candy
        bar, cut into ¹/₂-inch pieces

Preheat oven to 375°F. In large mixer
bowl, combine granulated sugar, brown
sugar, margarine, eggs and vanilla. Beat
at medium speed, scraping bowl often,
until well mixed, 1 to 2 minutes. Add
flour, baking soda and salt. Continue
beating until well mixed, 1 to 2 minutes.
Stir in nuts and chocolate. Drop
rounded tablespoonfuls of dough
2 inches apart onto ungreased cookie
sheets. Bake 9 to 11 minutes or until
lightly browned. Cool 1 minute on
cookie sheet; remove immediately.
Makes about 3 dozen cookies

Mocha Cookies

    1 cup all-purpose flour
    1 cup whole wheat flour
¹/₄ cup cocoa powder
    2 teaspoons baking powder
¹/₂ teaspoon salt
    1 cup KELLOGG'S® ALL-BRAN®
        cereal
¹/₂ cup *plus* 1 tablespoon skim milk
    2 teaspoons instant coffee crystals
¹/₂ cup margarine, softened
    1 cup firmly packed brown sugar
    3 egg whites
    2 teaspoons vanilla flavoring
³/₄ cup confectioners' sugar

1. Preheat oven to 350°F. Combine
flours, cocoa, baking powder and salt.
Set aside.

2. Measure Kellogg's® All-Bran® cereal,
¹/₂ cup milk and coffee crystals into
small bowl. Stir to combine. Let stand
3 minutes or until milk is absorbed.

3. Beat margarine, brown sugar, egg
whites and vanilla until smooth. Mix in
cereal mixture. Add flour mixture and
mix until combined. Drop by level
measuring tablespoons onto cookie
sheets coated with cooking spray.

4. Bake about 10 minutes or until almost
firm to touch. Cool.

5. In small bowl, combine confectioners'
sugar and 1 tablespoon milk until
smooth. Drizzle over cooled cookies.
Store in airtight container.
Makes about 4 dozen cookies

Old-Fashioned Ice Cream Sandwiches

2 squares (1 ounce each) semisweet baking chocolate, coarsely chopped
¹/₂ cup butter or margarine, softened
¹/₂ cup sugar
1 large egg
1 teaspoon vanilla
1¹/₂ cups all-purpose flour
¹/₄ teaspoon baking soda
¹/₄ teaspoon salt
Softened vanilla *or* mint chocolate chip ice cream*

Place chocolate in 1 cup glass measuring cup. Cook, uncovered, on HIGH (100% power) 3 to 4 minutes or until chocolate is melted, stirring after 2 minutes; set aside.

Beat butter and sugar in large bowl until light and fluffy. Beat in egg and vanilla. Gradually beat in chocolate. Stir in combined flour, baking soda and salt. Form dough into two discs; wrap in plastic wrap and refrigerate until firm, at least 2 hours. (Dough may be refrigerated up to 3 days before baking.)

Preheat oven to 350°F. Roll each piece of dough between two sheets of waxed paper to ¹/₄- to ¹/₈-inch thickness. Remove top sheet of waxed paper; invert dough onto greased cookie sheet. Cut through dough with paring knife, forming 3×2-inch rectangles. Remove excess scraps of dough from edges. Add to second disc of dough and repeat rolling and scoring until all of dough is cut. Prick each rectangle with fork.

Bake 10 minutes or until set. Let cookies stand on cookie sheets 1 minute. Cut through score marks with paring knife while cookies are still warm. Remove cookies to wire racks; cool completely. Spread half of cookies with softened ice cream; top with remaining cookies.
Makes about 8 ice cream sandwiches

*One quart of ice cream can be softened in the microwave oven at HIGH (100% power) about 20 seconds.

Old-Fashioned Ice Cream Sandwiches

Special Treat No-Bake Squares

¹/₂ cup *plus* 1 teaspoon butter or
    margarine
¹/₄ cup granulated sugar
¹/₄ cup unsweetened cocoa
  1 large egg
¹/₄ teaspoon salt
1¹/₂ cups graham cracker crumbs
³/₄ cup flaked coconut
¹/₂ cup chopped pecans
¹/₃ cup butter or margarine, softened
  1 package (3 ounces) cream cheese,
    softened
  1 teaspoon vanilla
  1 cup powdered sugar
  1 (2-ounce) dark sweet or bittersweet
    candy bar, broken into ¹/₂-inch
    pieces

Line 9-inch square pan with foil, shiny side up, allowing a 2-inch overhang on sides. Set aside.

For crust, combine ¹/₂ cup butter, granulated sugar, cocoa, egg and salt in medium saucepan. Cook over medium heat, stirring constantly, until mixture thickens, about 2 minutes. Remove from heat; stir in graham cracker crumbs, coconut and pecans. Press evenly into prepared baking pan.

For filling, beat ¹/₃ cup softened butter, cream cheese and vanilla in small bowl until smooth. Gradually beat in powdered sugar. Spread over crust; refrigerate 30 minutes.

For glaze, combine candy bar and 1 teaspoon butter in small resealable plastic bag; seal. Microwave at HIGH (100% power) 50 seconds. Turn bag over; heat at HIGH (100% power) 40 to 50 seconds or until melted. Knead bag until candy bar is smooth. Cut off

very tiny corner of bag; drizzle chocolate over filling. Refrigerate until firm, about 20 minutes. Remove foil from pan. Cut into 1¹/₂-inch squares.
Makes about 25 squares

Oatmeal Supremes

1¹/₂ cups sugar
  1 cup BUTTER FLAVOR CRISCO®
¹/₄ cup molasses
  1 egg
  2 tablespoons whipping cream
¹/₂ cup applesauce
  1 teaspoon vanilla
  1 teaspoon cinnamon
  1 teaspoon salt
  1 teaspoon baking soda
2¹/₂ cups quick oats (not instant or old
    fashioned), uncooked
2¹/₃ cups all-purpose flour
  1 cup chopped walnuts

1. Preheat oven to 350°F.

2. Combine sugar and Butter Flavor Crisco® in large bowl. Beat at medium speed of electric mixer until well blended. Add molasses, egg and whipping cream. Beat well. Mix in applesauce and vanilla. Add cinnamon, salt and baking soda. Mix well. Add, 1 at a time, oats, flour and nuts, mixing well after each addition. Cover. Allow to stand 30 minutes to absorb moisture and flavor. Drop by heaping teaspoonfuls 2 inches apart onto ungreased cookie sheet.

3. Bake at 350°F for 11 to 13 minutes or until lightly browned around edges and top is set. Cool 1 minute on cookie sheet before removing to cooling rack.
Makes about 5 dozen cookies

Special Treat No-Bake Squares

Peanut Butter Chewies

1 cup BUTTER FLAVOR CRISCO®
1½ cups JIF® Creamy Peanut Butter
1½ cups firmly packed brown sugar
2 eggs
1 can (14 ounces) sweetened
   condensed milk
2 teaspoons vanilla
2 cups all-purpose flour
1 teaspoon baking soda
1 teaspoon salt
1½ cups chopped pecans

1. Preheat oven to 350°F.

2. Combine Butter Flavor Crisco®, peanut butter and sugar in large bowl. Beat at medium speed of electric mixer until well blended. Beat in eggs, sweetened condensed milk and vanilla.

3. Combine flour, baking soda and salt. Mix into creamed mixture at low speed until just blended. Stir in nuts.

4. Drop rounded tablespoonfuls of dough 2 inches apart onto ungreased cookie sheet.

5. Bake at 350°F for 10 to 11 minutes or until lightly browned on bottom. Cool 2 minutes on cookie sheet. Remove to cooling rack.

Makes about 4 dozen cookies

Peanut Butter Chewies

Chocolate Almond Cookie Bites

4 foil-wrapped bars (8-ounce
   package) NESTLÉ® Semi-Sweet
   Chocolate Baking Bars
2 eggs
¼ teaspoon salt
¾ cup firmly packed brown sugar
1 teaspoon vanilla extract
1 cup almonds, chopped, toasted
   Sliced or slivered almonds

Preheat oven to 325°F. Grease 2 large cookie sheets. In small saucepan over low heat, melt Nestlé® Semi-Sweet Chocolate Baking Bars; set aside to cool.

In small mixer bowl, beat eggs and salt until thick. Beat in brown sugar. Blend in cooled chocolate and vanilla extract. Stir in chopped almonds. Drop mixture by rounded measuring teaspoonfuls onto prepared cookie sheets; insert one almond slice into each mound of dough.

Bake 8 to 10 minutes until set. Let stand 2 minutes. Remove from cookie sheets; cool on wire racks.

Makes about 4 dozen cookies

Chocolate Walnut Cookie Bites:
Substitute 1 cup chopped toasted walnuts for almonds. Top mounds of dough with small walnut pieces before baking.

Marshmallow Sandwich Cookies

Marshmallow Sandwich Cookies

²/₃ cup butter or margarine
1¹/₄ cups sugar
¹/₄ cup light corn syrup
1 large egg
1 teaspoon vanilla
2 cups all-purpose flour
¹/₂ cup unsweetened cocoa
2 teaspoons baking soda
¹/₄ teaspoon salt
Sugar
24 large marshmallows

Preheat oven to 350°F. Beat butter and 1¹/₄ cups sugar in large bowl until light and fluffy. Beat in corn syrup, egg and vanilla. Gradually add combined flour, cocoa, baking soda and salt. Beat until well blended. Cover and refrigerate dough 15 minutes or until firm enough to roll into balls.

Place sugar in shallow dish. Roll tablespoonfuls of dough into 1-inch balls; roll in sugar to coat. Place 3 inches apart on cookie sheets. Bake 10 to 11 minutes or until set. Remove cookies to wire rack; cool completely.

To assemble sandwiches, place one marshmallow on flat side of one cookie on paper plate. Microwave at HIGH (100% power) 12 seconds or until marshmallow is hot. Immediately place another cookie, flat side down, over marshmallow; press together slightly.

Makes about 2 dozen sandwich cookies

Preheat oven to 325°F. In large mixer bowl, combine sugar and butter. Beat well. Add eggs, honey and vanilla. Beat until well mixed. Combine flour, baking soda, nutmeg and salt. Stir dry ingredients into butter mixture; mix well. Stir in carrot. Using well floured hands, shape rounded teaspoonfuls of dough into 1-inch balls. Place 2 inches apart on ungreased cookie sheets. Bake 13 to 18 minutes or until edges are lightly browned. Remove immediately to wire racks to cool.

Makes about 3 dozen cookies

Honey Carrot Cookies (top), Soft Spicy Molasses Cookies (bottom)

Soft Spicy Molasses Cookies

2 cups all-purpose flour
1 cup sugar
³/₄ cup butter, softened
¹/₃ cup light molasses
3 tablespoons milk
1 egg
¹/₂ teaspoon baking soda
¹/₂ teaspoon ground ginger
¹/₂ teaspoon ground cinnamon
¹/₂ teaspoon ground cloves
¹/₈ teaspoon salt
Sugar for rolling

In large mixer bowl, combine flour, 1 cup sugar, butter, molasses, milk, egg, baking soda, ginger, cinnamon, cloves and salt. Beat at low speed, scraping bowl often until well mixed, 2 to 3 minutes. Cover; refrigerate until firm, at least 4 hours or overnight.

Preheat oven to 350°F. Shape rounded teaspoonfuls of dough into 1-inch balls. Roll in sugar. Place 2 inches apart on ungreased cookie sheets. Bake 10 to 12 minutes or until slightly firm to the touch. Remove immediately.

Makes about 4 dozen cookies

Honey Carrot Cookies

1 cup sugar
¹/₂ cup butter
2 eggs
3 tablespoons honey
1 teaspoon vanilla
2¹/₄ cups all-purpose flour
2 teaspoons baking soda
¹/₂ teaspoon nutmeg
¹/₄ teaspoon salt
¹/₂ cup shredded carrot (about 1 medium)

Fudgy Raisin Pixies

Old-Fashioned Oatmeal Cookies

³/₄ cup **BUTTER FLAVOR CRISCO®**
1¹/₄ **cups firmly packed brown sugar**
　1 **egg**
¹/₃ **cup milk**
1¹/₂ **teaspoons vanilla**
　1 **cup all-purpose flour**
¹/₂ **teaspoon baking soda**
¹/₂ **teaspoon salt**
¹/₄ **teaspoon cinnamon**
　3 **cups quick oats (not instant or old fashioned)**
　1 **cup raisins**
　1 **cup coarsely chopped walnuts**

1. Preheat oven to 375°F. Grease cookie sheet with Butter Flavor Crisco®.

2. Combine Butter Flavor Crisco®, sugar, egg, milk and vanilla in large bowl. Beat at medium speed of electric mixer until well blended.

3. Combine flour, baking soda, salt and cinnamon. Mix into creamed mixture at low speed until just blended. Stir in oats, raisins and nuts with spoon.

4. Drop rounded tablespoonfuls of dough 2 inches apart onto cookie sheet.

5. Bake at 375°F for 10 to 12 minutes or until lightly browned. Cool 2 minutes on cookie sheet. Remove to cooling rack. 　　*Makes about 2¹/₂ dozen cookies*

Fudgy Raisin Pixies

¹/₂ **cup butter**
　2 **cups granulated sugar**
　4 **eggs**
　2 **cups all-purpose flour, divided**
³/₄ **cup unsweetened cocoa powder**
　2 **teaspoons baking powder**
¹/₂ **teaspoon salt**
¹/₂ **cup chocolate-covered raisins**
　　Powdered sugar

Cream butter and sugar until light and fluffy. Add eggs; mix until well blended. Add combined 1 cup flour, cocoa, baking powder and salt. Mix until well blended. Stir in remaining 1 cup flour and chocolate-covered raisins. Cover; refrigerate until firm, 2 hours or overnight.

Preheat oven to 350°F. Coat hands with powdered sugar. Shape rounded teaspoonfuls of dough into 1-inch balls; roll in powdered sugar. Place 2 inches apart on greased cookie sheets. Bake for 14 to 17 minutes or until firm to the touch. Remove immediately. Cool completely.

Makes about 4 dozen cookies

Old-Fashioned Oatmeal Cookies

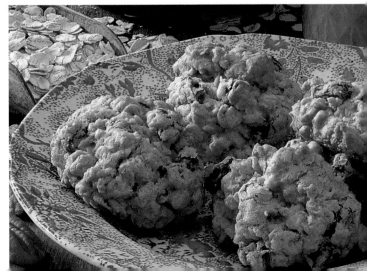

Peanut Butter Chocolate Chippers

1 cup creamy or chunky peanut
   butter
1 cup packed light brown sugar
1 large egg
1 cup milk chocolate chips

Preheat oven to 350°F. Combine peanut butter, sugar and egg in medium bowl; mix until well blended. Add chips; mix well. Roll heaping teaspoonfuls of dough into 1¹/₂-inch balls. Place balls 2 inches apart on cookie sheets. Dip fork in sugar; press criss-cross indentation on each ball, flattening to ¹/₂-inch thickness. Bake 12 minutes or until set. Let cookies stand on cookie sheets 2 minutes. Remove cookies to wire racks; cool completely.

Makes about 2 dozen cookies

Date-Nut Macaroons

1 (8-ounce) package pitted dates,
   chopped
1¹/₂ cups flaked coconut
1 cup PLANTERS® Pecan Halves,
   chopped
³/₄ cup sweetened condensed milk
¹/₂ teaspoon vanilla extract

Preheat oven to 350°F.

In medium bowl, combine dates, coconut and nuts; blend in milk and vanilla. Drop by rounded tablespoonfuls onto greased and floured cookie sheets. Bake for 10 to 12 minutes or until light golden brown. Carefully remove from cookie sheets; cool completely on wire racks. Store in airtight container.

Makes about 2 dozen cookies

Circus Cookies

2 cups all-purpose flour
¹/₂ teaspoon baking powder
¹/₄ teaspoon salt
1 cup margarine, softened
¹/₂ cup granulated sugar
2 eggs
¹/₂ cup orange juice
2 cups KELLOGG'S® FROOT
   LOOPS® cereal, crushed to fine
   crumbs

Orange Icing

2 cups confectioners sugar
3 tablespoons margarine, softened
2 tablespoons orange juice

1. Preheat oven to 350°F. Stir together flour, baking powder and salt. Set aside.

2. In large mixing bowl, beat 1 cup margarine and granulated sugar until light and fluffy. Add eggs and ¹/₂ cup orange juice. Beat well. Add flour mixture. Mix until well combined. Stir in Kellogg's® Froot Loops® cereal. Drop by level measuring tablespoonfuls, about two inches apart, onto ungreased cookie sheets.

3. Bake about 12 minutes or until lightly browned. Remove immediately from cookie sheets. Cool on wire racks.

4. To make Orange Icing, measure confectioners sugar, margarine and orange juice in small mixing bowl. Beat until smooth. When cookies are completely cooled, frost and decorate with additional cereal, whole or crushed.   *Makes about 4 dozen cookies*

Peanut Butter Chocolate Chippers

Orange Pecan Gems

Orange Pecan Gems

1 package DUNCAN HINES® Moist
  Deluxe Orange Supreme Cake
  Mix
1 container (8 ounces) vanilla lowfat
  yogurt
1 egg
2 tablespoons butter or margarine,
  softened
1 cup finely chopped pecans
1 cup pecan halves

1. Preheat oven to 350°F. Grease cookie
sheets.

2. Combine Duncan Hines® Moist
Deluxe Orange Supreme Cake Mix,
yogurt, egg, butter and chopped pecans
in large bowl. Beat at low speed with
electric mixer until blended. Drop by
rounded teaspoonfuls 2 inches apart
onto greased cookie sheets. Press pecan
half onto center of each cookie. Bake at
350°F for 11 to 13 minutes or until
golden brown. Cool 1 minute on cookie
sheets. Remove to cooling racks. Cool
completely. Store in airtight container.
Makes about 4¹/₂ to 5 dozen cookies

Pineapple Carrot Cookies

2 cans (8 ounces *each*) DOLE®
  Crushed Pineapple in Juice
³/₄ cup margarine, softened
¹/₂ cup granulated sugar
¹/₂ cup brown sugar, packed
1 egg
1 teaspoon vanilla extract
1 cup shredded DOLE® Carrots
1 cup chopped walnuts
1 cup DOLE® Raisins
1¹/₂ cups all-purpose flour
1 teaspoon ground cinnamon
¹/₂ teaspoon ground ginger
¹/₂ teaspoon baking powder
¹/₄ teaspoon salt

• Preheat oven to 375°F.

• Drain pineapple well; reserve juice for
beverage.

• Beat margarine and sugars until light
and fluffy. Beat in egg and vanilla. Beat
in pineapple, carrots, nuts and raisins.

• Combine remaining ingredients; beat
into pineapple mixture until well
blended.

• Drop batter by heaping tablespoonfuls
onto greased cookie sheets. Flatten tops
with spoon. Bake 15 to 20 minutes.
Makes about 3 dozen cookies

Prep Time: 20 minutes
Bake Time: 20 minutes per batch

Pineapple Carrot Cookies

Chocolate Chip Macaroons

Chocolate Chip Macaroons

2¹/₂ cups flaked coconut
²/₃ cup mini semisweet chocolate
    chips
²/₃ cup sweetened condensed milk
    (not evaporated milk)
1 teaspoon vanilla

Preheat oven to 350°F. Combine
coconut, chips, milk and vanilla in
medium bowl; mix until well blended.
Drop dough by rounded teaspoonfuls 2
inches apart onto greased cookie sheets.
Press dough gently with back of spoon
to flatten slightly. Bake 10 to 12 minutes
or until light golden brown. Let cookies
stand on cookie sheets 1 minute.
Remove cookies to wire racks; cool
completely.

Makes about 3¹/₂ dozen cookies

No-Bake Peanutty Cookies

2 cups Roasted Honey Nut SKIPPY®
    Creamy or Super Chunk® Peanut
    Butter
2 cups graham cracker crumbs
1 cup confectioners' sugar
¹/₂ cup KARO® Light or Dark Corn
    Syrup
¹/₄ cup semisweet chocolate chips,
    melted
Colored sprinkles (optional)

In large bowl, combine peanut butter,
graham cracker crumbs, confectioners'
sugar and corn syrup. Mix until
smooth. Shape into 1-inch balls. Place
on waxed paper-lined cookie sheet.
Drizzle melted chocolate over balls; roll
in colored sprinkles if desired. Store
covered in refrigerator.

Makes about 5 dozen cookies

KIDS' CREATIONS

Peanut Butter and Chocolate Cookie Sandwich Cookies

$^{1}/_{2}$ cup REESE'S® Peanut Butter Chips
3 tablespoons *plus* $^{1}/_{2}$ cup butter or
    margarine, softened and divided
$1^{1}/_{4}$ cups sugar, divided
$^{1}/_{4}$ cup light corn syrup
1 egg
1 teaspoon vanilla extract
2 cups *plus* 2 tablespoons
    all-purpose flour, divided
2 teaspoons baking soda
$^{1}/_{4}$ teaspoon salt
$^{1}/_{2}$ cup HERSHEY'S Cocoa
5 tablespoons butter or margarine,
    melted
Sugar
About 2 dozen large
    marshmallows

Preheat oven to 350°F. In small saucepan over very low heat, melt peanut butter chips and 3 tablespoons softened butter. Remove from heat; cool slightly.

In large mixer bowl, beat remaining $^{1}/_{2}$ cup softened butter and 1 cup sugar until light and fluffy. Add corn syrup, egg and vanilla; blend thoroughly. Stir together 2 cups flour, baking soda and salt; add to butter mixture, blending well. Remove $1^{1}/_{4}$ cups batter and place in small bowl; stir in remaining 2 tablespoons flour and peanut butter chip mixture. Blend cocoa, remaining $^{1}/_{4}$ cup sugar and 5 tablespoons melted butter into remaining batter. Refrigerate both batters 5 to 10 minutes or until firm enough to handle.

Roll dough into 1-inch balls; roll in sugar. Place on ungreased cookie sheet. Bake 10 to 11 minutes or until set. Cool slightly; remove from cookie sheet to wire rack. Cool completely.

Place 1 marshmallow on flat side of 1 chocolate cookie. Microwave at MEDIUM (50%) 10 seconds or until marshmallow is softened; place a peanut butter cookie over marshmallow, pressing down slightly. Repeat for remaining cookies. Serve immediately.
Makes 2 dozen cookie sandwiches

*Peanut Butter and Chocolate Cookie
Sandwich Cookies*

128

Pinwheels and Checkerboards

2 cups flour
1 teaspoon CALUMET® Baking
  Powder
¹/₂ teaspoon salt
²/₃ cup butter or margarine, softened
1 cup sugar
1 egg
1 teaspoon vanilla
2 squares BAKER'S® Unsweetened
  Chocolate, melted

Mix flour, baking powder and salt; set aside. Cream butter. Gradually add sugar and continue beating until light and fluffy. Add egg and vanilla; beat well. Gradually add flour mixture, mixing well after each addition. Divide dough in half; blend chocolate into one half. Use prepared doughs to make Pinwheels or Checkerboards.

Pinwheels: Roll chocolate and vanilla doughs separately between sheets of waxed paper into 12×8-inch rectangles. Remove top sheets of paper and invert vanilla dough onto chocolate dough. Remove remaining papers. Roll up as a jelly-roll; then wrap in waxed paper. Chill until firm, at least 3 hours (or freeze 1 hour).

Preheat oven to 375°F. Cut roll into ¹/₄-inch slices and place on cookie sheets. Bake about 10 minutes or until cookies just begin to brown around edges. Cool on racks.

Checkerboards: Set out small amount of milk. Roll chocolate and vanilla doughs separately on lightly floured board into 9×4¹/₂-inch rectangles. Brush chocolate dough lightly with milk and top with vanilla dough. Using a long sharp knife, cut lengthwise into 3 strips, 1¹/₂ inches wide. Stack strips, alternating colors and brushing each layer with milk. Cut lengthwise again into 3 strips, each ¹/₂ inch wide. Invert middle section so that colors are alternated; brush sides with milk. Press strips together lightly to form a rectangle. Wrap in waxed paper. Chill overnight.

Preheat oven to 375°F. Cut roll into ¹/₈-inch slices using a very sharp knife. Place on cookie sheets. Bake at 375°F for about 8 minutes, or just until white portions begin to brown. Cool on racks.
Makes about 5 dozen cookies

Corn Flake Macaroons

4 egg whites
¹/₄ teaspoon cream of tartar
1 teaspoon vanilla
1¹/₃ cups sugar
1 cup chopped pecans
1 cup shredded coconut
3 cups KELLOGG'S® CORN
  FLAKES® cereal

1. Preheat oven to 325°F. In large mixing bowl, beat egg whites until foamy. Stir in cream of tartar and vanilla. Gradually add sugar, beating until stiff and glossy. Fold in pecans, coconut and Kellogg's® Corn Flakes® cereal. Drop by rounded measuring tablespoonfuls onto cookie sheets sprayed with vegetable cooking spray.

2. Bake about 15 minutes or until lightly browned. Remove immediately from cookie sheets. Cool on wire racks.
Makes about 3 dozen cookies

Variation: Fold in ¹/₂ cup crushed peppermint candy with pecans and coconut.

Snow Covered Almond Crescents

1 cup (2 sticks) margarine or butter, softened
3/4 cup powdered sugar
1/2 teaspoon almond extract *or*
   2 teaspoons vanilla
2 cups all-purpose flour
1/4 teaspoon salt (optional)
1 cup QUAKER® Oats (quick or old fashioned, uncooked)
1/2 cup finely chopped almonds
   Powdered sugar

Preheat oven to 325°F. Beat margarine, sugar and almond extract until fluffy. Add flour and salt; mix until well blended. Stir in oats and almonds. Using level measuring tablespoonfuls, shape dough into crescents. Bake on ungreased cookie sheet 14 to 17 minutes or until bottoms are light golden brown. Remove to wire rack. Sift additional powdered sugar generously over warm cookies. Cool completely. Store tightly covered.   *Makes about 4 dozen cookies*

Peanut Butter Stars

1 package DUNCAN HINES® Peanut Butter Cookie Mix
1 egg
2 packages (3¹/₂ ounces each) chocolate sprinkles
2 packages (7 ounces each) milk chocolate candy stars

1. Preheat oven to 375°F.

2. Combine cookie mix, peanut butter packet from Mix and egg in large bowl. Stir until thoroughly blended. Shape dough into ³/₄-inch balls. Roll in

Peanut Butter Stars

chocolate sprinkles. Place 2 inches apart onto ungreased cookie sheets. Bake at 375°F for 8 to 9 minutes or until set. Immediately place milk chocolate candy stars on top of hot cookies. Cool 1 minute on cookie sheets. Remove to cooling racks. Cool completely. Store in airtight containers.

Makes 7¹/₂ to 8 dozen cookies

Chocolate Mint Meltaways (left),
Chocolate Mint Cookie (right)

Chocolate Mint Cookies

Cookies
  1/2 cup (from 10-ounce package) NESTLÉ® Toll House® Mint Flavored Semi-Sweet Chocolate Morsels, divided
  1 cup all-purpose flour
  3/4 teaspoon baking powder
  1/4 teaspoon baking soda
  1/4 teaspoon salt
  1/4 cup butter, softened
  6 tablespoons sugar
  1/2 teaspoon vanilla extract
  1 egg

Glaze
  1 cup NESTLÉ® Toll House® Mint Flavored Semi-Sweet Chocolate Morsels (reserved from 10-ounce package)
  1/4 cup vegetable shortening
  3 tablespoons corn syrup
  2 1/4 teaspoons water

Cookies: Melt over hot (not boiling) water, 1/2 cup Nestlé® Toll House® Mint Flavored Semi-Sweet Chocolate Morsels; stir until smooth. Set aside. In small bowl, combine flour, baking powder, baking soda and salt; set aside. In large bowl, combine butter, sugar and vanilla extract; beat until creamy. Beat in egg; blend in melted morsels. Gradually beat in flour mixture. Shape dough into ball and wrap in waxed paper. Chill about 1 hour.

Preheat oven to 350°F. On lightly floured board, roll dough to 3/16-inch thickness. Cut with 2-inch cookie cutter. Reroll remaining dough and cut out cookies. Place on ungreased cookie sheets. Bake at 350°F for 8 to 10 minutes. Cool completely on wire racks.

Glaze: Combine over hot (not boiling) water, remaining 1 cup Nestlé® Toll House® Mint Flavored Semi-Sweet Chocolate Morsels, vegetable shortening, corn syrup and water; stir until morsels are melted and mixture is smooth. Remove from heat, but keep mixture over hot water.

Dip 1/2 of each cookie into Glaze; shake off any excess Glaze. Place cookies on waxed paper-lined cookie sheets. Chill until Glaze sets (about 10 minutes).
  Makes about 3 1/2 dozen 2-inch cookies

Note: Keep refrigerated until ready to serve.

Chocolate Mint Meltaways

Cookies

1½ cups (10-ounce package) NESTLÉ® Toll House® Mint Flavored Semi-Sweet Chocolate Morsels, divided

¾ cup butter, softened

½ cup sifted confectioners' sugar

1 egg yolk

1¼ cups all-purpose flour

Glaze

½ cup NESTLÉ® Toll House® Mint Flavored Semi-Sweet Chocolate Morsels (reserved from 10-ounce package)

1½ tablespoons vegetable shortening

2 tablespoons chopped toasted almonds

Cookies: Preheat oven to 350°F. Melt over hot (not boiling) water, 1 cup Nestlé® Toll House® Mint Flavored Semi-Sweet Chocolate Morsels; stir until smooth. Set aside. In large bowl, combine butter, confectioners' sugar and egg yolk; beat until creamy. Add melted morsels and flour; beat until well blended. Drop by heaping teaspoonfuls onto ungreased cookie sheets. Bake at 350°F for 8 to 10 minutes. Allow to stand 3 minutes before removing from cookie sheets. Cool completely on wire racks.

Glaze: Combine over hot (not boiling) water, remaining ½ cup Nestlé® Toll House® Mint Flavored Semi-Sweet Chocolate Morsels and vegetable shortening. Stir until morsels are melted and mixture is smooth.

Drizzle each cookie with ½ teaspoon Glaze; sprinkle with almonds. Chill until set. Store in airtight container in refrigerator.

Makes about 4 dozen 1¾-inch cookies

Orange Drop Cookies

Cookies

1 package DUNCAN HINES® Golden Sugar Cookie Mix

1 egg

1 tablespoon orange juice

½ teaspoon grated orange peel

¾ cup flaked coconut

½ cup chopped pecans

Glaze

1 cup confectioners sugar

2 teaspoons lemon juice

2 teaspoons orange juice

1 teaspoon grated orange peel

1. Preheat oven to 375°F.

2. For cookies, combine cookie mix, buttery flavor packet from Mix, egg, 1 tablespoon orange juice and ½ teaspoon orange peel in large bowl. Stir with spoon until well blended. Stir in coconut and pecans. Drop by rounded teaspoonfuls 2 inches apart onto ungreased cookie sheets. Bake at 375°F for 7 to 8 minutes or until set. Cool 1 minute on cookie sheets. Remove to cooling racks. Cool completely.

3. For glaze, combine confectioners sugar, lemon juice, 2 teaspoons orange juice and 1 teaspoon orange peel in small bowl. Stir until blended. Drizzle over top of cooled cookies. Allow glaze to set before storing between layers of waxed paper in airtight container.

Makes about 3 dozen cookies

Orange Drop Cookies

Chewy Choco-Peanut Pudgies

Cookie

  ½ cup BUTTER FLAVOR CRISCO®
  1¼ cups firmly packed brown sugar
  ¾ cup JIF® Creamy Peanut Butter
  1 tablespoon light corn syrup
  1 egg
  1 tablespoon milk
  1 teaspoon vanilla
  1½ cups all-purpose flour
  ½ teaspoon baking soda
  ½ teaspoon salt
  1½ cups coarsely chopped unsalted peanuts (raw or dry roasted)
  ½ cup granulated sugar

Frosting

  ½ teaspoon BUTTER FLAVOR CRISCO®
  ½ cup semi-sweet chocolate chips
  ½ teaspoon granulated sugar

1. Preheat oven to 375°F. Grease cookie sheet with Butter Flavor Crisco®.

2. For Cookie, combine Butter Flavor Crisco®, brown sugar, peanut butter and syrup in large bowl. Beat at medium speed of electric mixer until well blended. Beat in egg, milk and vanilla.

3. Combine flour, baking soda and salt. Mix into creamed mixture at low speed until just blended. Stir in nuts.

4. Form dough into 1¼-inch balls. Roll in granulated sugar. Place 2 inches apart on cookie sheet.

5. Bake at 375°F for 8 to 9 minutes, or until set. Cool 2 minutes on cookie sheet. Remove to cooling rack.

6. For Frosting, combine Butter Flavor Crisco®, chocolate chips and granulated sugar in microwave-safe measuring cup. Microwave at 50% (MEDIUM). Stir after

1 minute. Repeat until smooth (or melt on rangetop in small saucepan on very low heat). Generously drizzle over cooled cookies.

Makes about 4 dozen cookies

Almond Shortbread Cookies

  2½ cups unsifted flour
  1 teaspoon baking soda
  1 teaspoon cream of tartar
  1 cup margarine or butter, softened
  1½ cups confectioners' sugar
  1 egg
  1 (9-ounce) package NONE SUCH® Condensed Mincemeat, crumbled
  ½ cup sliced almonds
  ½ teaspoon almond extract
    Almond Frosting (recipe follows)
    Additional sliced almonds

Preheat oven to 375°F. Stir together flour, baking soda and cream of tartar; set aside. In large mixer bowl, beat margarine and sugar until fluffy. Add egg; mix well. Stir in mincemeat, *½ cup* almonds and extract. Add flour mixture; mix well (dough will be stiff). Roll into 1¼-inch balls. Place on ungreased cookie sheets; flatten slightly. Bake 10 to 12 minutes or until lightly browned. Cool. Frost with Almond Frosting and garnish with additional almonds if desired.   *Makes about 3 dozen cookies*

Almond Frosting: In small mixer bowl, combine 2¼ cups confectioners' sugar, 3 tablespoons margarine or butter, softened, 3 tablespoons water and ½ teaspoon almond extract; beat well. Makes about 1 cup.

Chewy Choco-Peanut Pudgies

Macadamia Bites

1 package DUNCAN HINES®
    Golden Sugar Cookie Mix
1 egg
1 container (16 ounces) DUNCAN
    HINES® Creamy Homestyle
    Chocolate Frosting
1 jar (3¹/₂ ounces) macadamia nuts
1¹/₂ cups flaked coconut, toasted

1. Preheat oven to 375°F.

2. Combine cookie mix, buttery flavor packet from Mix and egg in large bowl. Stir until thoroughly blended. Shape measuring teaspoonful dough around each macadamia nut to form ball. Place 2 inches apart on ungreased cookie sheets. Bake at 375°F for 7 to 8 minutes or until set but not browned. Cool 1 minute on cookie sheets. Remove to cooling racks. Cool completely.

3. Spread chocolate frosting on top of 1 cookie. Sprinkle with toasted coconut. Repeat with remaining cookies. Allow frosting to set. Store between layers of waxed paper in airtight container.

Makes about 5 dozen cookies

Oatmeal Shaggies Cookies

Oatmeal Shaggies Cookies

Cookies

    2 cups quick oats, uncooked
    1 cup finely shredded carrots
    1 cup firmly packed brown sugar
    1 cup raisins
    1 cup all-purpose flour
    1 teaspoon baking powder
    1 teaspoon baking soda
    1 teaspoon salt
    ¹/₂ teaspoon cinnamon
    ¹/₂ teaspoon cloves
    2 eggs, beaten
    ¹/₂ cup BUTTER FLAVOR CRISCO®,
        melted and cooled
    ¹/₃ cup milk
    1 cup shredded coconut
    ¹/₂ cup finely chopped walnuts

Frosting

    1 cup confectioners sugar
    2 tablespoons butter or margarine,
        softened
    2 teaspoons grated orange peel
    1 tablespoon *plus* 1 teaspoon orange
        juice

1. Preheat oven to 350°F. Grease cookie sheet with Butter Flavor Crisco®.

2. For cookies, combine oats, carrots, brown sugar and raisins in large bowl.

3. Combine flour, baking powder, baking soda, salt, cinnamon and cloves. Stir into oat mixture with spoon.

4. Combine eggs, Butter Flavor Crisco® and milk. Stir into carrot mixture. Stir in coconut and nuts. Drop by rounded tablespoonfuls 2¹/₂ inches apart onto greased cookie sheet.

5. Bake at 350°F for 10 to 12 minutes or until lightly browned. Remove to cooling rack. Cool completely.

6. For frosting, combine confectioners sugar, butter, orange peel and orange juice in small bowl. Stir until smooth and of good spreading consistency. Frost cookies.

Makes 2¹/₂ to 3 dozen cookies

Brownie Sandwich Cookies

Brownie Cookies

    1 package DUNCAN HINES®
       Chocolate Lovers' Double Fudge
       Brownie Mix
    1 egg
    3 tablespoons water
    Sugar

Filling

    1 container (16 ounces) DUNCAN
       HINES® Creamy Homestyle
       Cream Cheese Frosting
       Red food coloring (optional)
    1/2 cup semi-sweet mini chocolate
       chips

1. Preheat oven to 375°F. Grease cookie sheets.

2. For brownie cookies, combine brownie mix, fudge packet from Mix, egg and water in large bowl. Stir until well blended, about 50 strokes. Shape dough into 50 (1-inch) balls. Place 2 inches apart on prepared cookie sheets. Grease bottom of drinking glass; dip in sugar. Press gently to flatten 1 cookie to 3/8-inch thickness. Repeat with remaining cookies. Bake at 375°F for 6 to 7 minutes or until set. Cool 1 minute on cookie sheets. Remove to cooling racks. Cool completely.

3. For filling, tint frosting with red food coloring, if desired. Stir in chocolate chips.

4. To assemble, spread 1 tablespoon frosting on bottom of one cookie; top with second cookie. Press together to make sandwich cookie. Repeat with remaining cookies.

Makes 25 sandwich cookies

Brownie Sandwich Cookies

"Philly" Apricot Cookies

    1 1/2 cups PARKAY® Margarine
    1 1/2 cups granulated sugar
      1 8-ounce package PHILADELPHIA
       BRAND® Cream Cheese,
       softened
    2 eggs
    2 tablespoons lemon juice
    1 1/2 teaspoons grated lemon peel
    4 1/2 cups flour
    1 1/2 teaspoons baking powder
      KRAFT® Apricot Preserves
      Powdered sugar

• Combine margarine, granulated sugar and cream cheese, mixing until well blended. Blend in eggs, juice and peel. Add combined flour and baking powder; mix well.

• Chill several hours.

• Preheat oven to 350°F.

• Shape level measuring tablespoonfuls of dough into balls. Place on ungreased cookie sheet; flatten slightly. Indent centers; fill with preserves.

• Bake at 350°F, 15 minutes. Cool; sprinkle with powdered sugar.

Makes about 7 dozen cookies

Orange & Chocolate Ribbon Cookies

1 cup butter or margarine, softened
$^1/_2$ cup sugar
3 egg yolks
2 teaspoons grated orange peel
1 teaspoon orange extract
2$^1/_4$ cups all-purpose flour, divided
3 tablespoons unsweetened cocoa
1 teaspoon vanilla
1 teaspoon chocolate extract

Cream butter, sugar and egg yolks in large bowl until light and fluffy. Remove half of the mixture; place in another bowl. Add orange peel, orange extract and 1$^1/_4$ cups of the flour to one half of mixture; mix until blended and smooth. Shape into a ball. Add cocoa, vanilla and chocolate extract to second half of mixture; beat until smooth. Stir in remaining 1 cup flour; mix until blended and smooth. Shape into a ball. Cover doughs; refrigerate 10 minutes.

Empty a 12×2×2-inch food wrap box, such as foil or plastic wrap; set aside. Roll out each dough separately on lightly floured surface to a 12×4-inch rectangle. Pat edges of dough to straighten; use rolling pin to level off thickness. Place one of the doughs on top of the other. Using a sharp knife, make a lengthwise cut through center of doughs. Lift half of the dough onto the other to make a long, 4-layer strip of dough. With hands, press dough strips together. Wrap in plastic wrap; fit into food wrap box, pressing down at the top. Close box; refrigerate at least 1 hour or up to 3 days. (For longer storage, freeze up to 6 weeks.)

Preheat oven to 350°F. Lightly grease cookie sheets or line with parchment paper. Cut dough crosswise into $^1/_4$-inch-thick slices; place 2 inches apart on prepared cookie sheets. Bake 10 to 12 minutes or until very lightly browned. Remove to wire racks to cool.
Makes about 5 dozen cookies

Chocolate Mint Sandwiches

2 squares (1 ounce each) unsweetened chocolate
$^1/_2$ cup butter or margarine, softened
1 cup packed light brown sugar
1 teaspoon vanilla
1 egg
$^1/_8$ teaspoon baking soda
2 cups all-purpose flour
Creamy Mint Filling (page 140)

Melt chocolate in top of double boiler over hot, not boiling, water. Remove from heat; cool. Cream butter and brown sugar in large bowl. Beat in vanilla, egg, melted chocolate and baking soda until light and fluffy. Stir in flour to make stiff dough. Divide dough into four parts. Shape each part into a roll about 1$^1/_2$ inches in diameter. Wrap in plastic wrap; refrigerate at least 1 hour or up to 2 weeks. (For longer storage, freeze up to 6 weeks.)

Preheat oven to 375°F. Cut rolls into $^1/_8$-inch-thick slices; place 2 inches apart on ungreased cookie sheets. Bake 6 to 7 minutes or until firm. Remove to wire racks to cool. Prepare Creamy Mint Filling. Spread filling on bottoms of half the cookies. Top with remaining cookies, bottom sides down.
Makes about 3 dozen sandwich cookies
continued on page 140

Orange & Chocolate Ribbon Cookies, Chocolate Mint Sandwiches, Cinnamon Chocolate Cutouts (page 140)

Creamy Mint Filling

**2 tablespoons butter or margarine,
  softened**
1¹/₂ cups powdered sugar
**3 to 4 tablespoons light cream or
  half-and-half**
¹/₄ teaspoon peppermint extract
Few drops green food coloring

Cream butter with powdered sugar and
cream in a small bowl until smooth and
blended. Stir in peppermint extract and
food coloring; blend well.

Cinnamon Chocolate Cutouts

**2 squares (1 ounce each)
  unsweetened chocolate**
¹/₂ cup butter or margarine, softened
1 cup granulated sugar
1 egg
1 teaspoon vanilla
3 cups all-purpose flour
2 teaspoons ground cinnamon
¹/₂ teaspoon baking soda
¹/₄ teaspoon salt
¹/₂ cup sour cream
Decorator Icing (recipe follows)

Melt chocolate in top of double boiler
over hot, not boiling, water. Remove
from heat; cool. Cream butter, melted
chocolate, granulated sugar, egg and
vanilla in large bowl until light.
Combine flour, cinnamon, baking soda
and salt in small bowl. Stir into
creamed mixture with sour cream until
smooth. Cover; refrigerate at least
30 minutes.

Preheat oven to 400°F. Lightly grease
cookie sheets or line with parchment
paper. Roll out dough, ¹/₄ at a time, to
¹/₄-inch thickness on lightly floured
surface. Cut out with cookie cutters.
Place 2 inches apart on prepared cookie
sheets. Bake 10 minutes or until lightly
browned, but not dark. Remove to wire
racks to cool. Prepare Decorator Icing.
Spoon into pastry bag fitted with small
tip or small heavy-duty plastic bag. (If
using plastic bag, close securely. With
scissors, snip off small corner from one
side of bag.) Decorate cookies with
icing.   *Makes about 6 dozen cookies*

Decorator Icing

1 egg white*
3¹/₂ cups powdered sugar
1 teaspoon almond or lemon extract
2 to 3 tablespoons water

Beat egg white in large bowl until
frothy. Gradually beat in powdered
sugar until blended. Add almond
extract and enough water to moisten.
Beat until smooth and glossy.

*Use clean, uncracked egg.

Chocolate Thumbprints

Cookies

- ½ cup BUTTER FLAVOR CRISCO®
- ½ cup granulated sugar
- 1 tablespoon milk
- ½ teaspoon vanilla
- 1 egg yolk
- 1 square (1 ounce) unsweetened baking chocolate, melted and cooled
- 1 cup all-purpose flour
- ¼ teaspoon salt
- ⅓ cup mini semi-sweet chocolate chips

Peanut Butter Cream Filling

- 2 tablespoons BUTTER FLAVOR CRISCO®
- ⅓ cup JIF® Creamy Peanut Butter
- 1 cup confectioners sugar
- 2 tablespoons milk
- ½ teaspoon vanilla

1. Preheat oven to 350°F. Grease cookie sheet with Butter Flavor Crisco®.

2. For cookies, combine ½ cup Butter Flavor Crisco®, granulated sugar, 1 tablespoon milk, vanilla and egg yolk in large bowl. Beat at medium speed of electric mixer until well blended. Add melted chocolate. Mix well.

3. Combine flour and salt. Add gradually to chocolate mixture at low speed. Mix until blended. Add chocolate chips. Shape dough into 1-inch balls. Place 2 inches apart on greased cookie sheet. Press thumb gently in center of each cookie.

4. Bake at 350°F for 8 minutes. Press centers again with small measuring spoon. Remove to cooling rack. Cool completely.

5. For peanut butter cream filling, combine 2 tablespoons Butter Flavor Crisco® and peanut butter in medium bowl. Stir with spoon until blended. Add confectioners sugar. Stir well. Add 2 tablespoons milk and vanilla. Stir until smooth. Fill centers of cookies.

Makes about 2½ dozen cookies

Chocolate Thumbprints

Biscochitos

3 cups all-purpose flour
2 teaspoons anise seed
$^1/_2$ teaspoon baking powder
$^1/_2$ teaspoon salt
1 cup shortening or butter
$^3/_4$ cup sugar, divided
1 egg
$^1/_4$ cup orange juice
2 teaspoons ground cinnamon

Preheat oven to 350°F. Combine flour, anise seed, baking powder and salt in medium bowl; set aside. Beat shortening in large bowl of electric mixer on medium speed until creamy. Add $^1/_2$ cup sugar; beat until fluffy. Blend in egg. Gradually add flour mixture alternately with orange juice, mixing well after each addition.

Divide dough in half; roll out one portion at a time on lightly floured surface to $^1/_4$-inch thickness; cover remaining dough to prevent drying. Cut out cookies with fancy cookie cutters 2 to $2^1/_2$ inches in diameter. While cutting cookies, add scraps to remaining dough. If dough becomes too soft to handle, refrigerate briefly. Place cookies 1 inch apart on ungreased cookie sheet.

To prepare cinnamon topping, combine remaining $^1/_4$ cup sugar and cinnamon; lightly sprinkle over cookies. Bake 8 to 10 minutes or until edges are lightly browned. Cool on racks, then store in airtight container.

Makes 4 to 5 dozen cookies

Double Chocolate Chunk Cookies

4 squares BAKER'S® Semi-Sweet Chocolate
$^1/_2$ cup (1 stick) margarine or butter, slightly softened
$^1/_2$ cup granulated sugar
$^1/_4$ cup firmly packed brown sugar
1 egg
1 teaspoon vanilla
1 cup all-purpose flour
$^1/_2$ teaspoon CALUMET® Baking Powder
$^1/_4$ teaspoon salt
$^3/_4$ cup chopped walnuts (optional)
4 squares BAKER'S® Semi-Sweet Chocolate

Melt 1 square chocolate; set aside. Cut 3 squares chocolate into large ($^1/_2$-inch) chunks; set aside.

Beat margarine, sugars, egg and vanilla until light and fluffy. Stir in melted chocolate. Mix in flour, baking powder and salt. Stir in chocolate chunks and walnuts. Refrigerate 30 minutes.

Preheat oven to 375°F. Drop dough by heaping tablespoonfuls, about 2 inches apart, onto greased cookie sheets. Bake for 8 minutes or until lightly browned. Cool 5 minutes on cookie sheets. Remove and finish cooling on wire racks.

Melt 4 squares chocolate. Dip half each cookie into melted chocolate. Let stand on waxed paper until chocolate is firm.

Makes about 2 dozen cookies

Prep Time: 30 minutes
Chill Time: 30 minutes
Bake Time: 8 minutes

Lemon Pecan Crescents

**1 package DUNCAN HINES®
Golden Sugar Cookie Mix
2 egg whites
³/₄ cup toasted pecans, chopped
¹/₄ cup all-purpose flour
1 tablespoon grated lemon peel
Confectioners sugar**

1. Preheat oven to 375°F.

2. Combine cookie mix, buttery flavor packet from Mix, egg whites, pecans, flour and lemon peel in large bowl. Stir until thoroughly blended. Form level ¹/₂ measuring tablespoonfuls dough into crescent shapes. Place 2 inches apart on ungreased cookie sheets. Bake at 375°F for 7 to 8 minutes or until set but not browned. Cool 2 minutes on cookie sheets. Remove to cooling racks. Roll warm cookies in confectioners sugar. Cool completely. Roll cookies again in confectioners sugar. Store between layers of waxed paper in airtight container.   *Makes about 5 dozen cookies*

Lemon Pecan Crescents

Roasted Honey Nut Sandwich Cookies

**1¹/₂ cups quick oats
¹/₂ cup flour
¹/₂ teaspoon baking powder
¹/₂ teaspoon baking soda
¹/₈ teaspoon salt
¹/₂ cup Roasted Honey Nut SKIPPY®
Creamy Peanut Butter
¹/₂ cup MAZOLA® Margarine,
softened
¹/₂ cup sugar
¹/₂ cup packed brown sugar
1 egg
¹/₂ teaspoon vanilla
Cookie Filling (recipe follows)**

Preheat oven to 350°F. In medium bowl, combine oats, flour, baking powder, baking soda and salt. In large bowl with mixer at medium speed, beat peanut butter, margarine and sugars until well blended. Beat in egg and vanilla. Stir in oat mixture until well mixed. Shape dough by heaping teaspoonfuls into balls; place 2 inches apart on ungreased cookie sheets. Flatten each ball to 2-inch round. Bake in 350°F oven 8 minutes or until golden brown. Cool 3 minutes on cookie sheet. Remove to rack; cool completely. Spread bottoms of half the cookies with heaping teaspoonfuls of Cookie Filling; top with remaining cookies.

Makes about 2¹/₂ dozen sandwich cookies.

Cookie Filling: In small bowl, combine 1 cup Roasted Honey Nut Skippy® Peanut Butter and ¹/₂ cup confectioners' sugar; stir until smooth.

Double Chocolate Cherry Cookies

1¼ cups margarine or butter, softened
1¾ cups sugar
2 eggs
1 tablespoon vanilla extract
3½ cups unsifted flour
¾ cup HERSHEY'S Cocoa
½ teaspoon baking powder
½ teaspoon baking soda
¼ teaspoon salt
2 (6-ounce) jars maraschino cherries, well drained and halved (about 60 cherries)
1 cup (6 ounces) HERSHEY'S Semi-Sweet Chocolate Chips
1 (14-ounce) can EAGLE® Brand Sweetened Condensed Milk (NOT evaporated milk)

Preheat oven to 350°F. In large mixer bowl, beat margarine and sugar until fluffy; add eggs and vanilla. Mix well. Combine dry ingredients; stir into margarine mixture (dough will be stiff). Shape into 1-inch balls. Place 1 inch apart on ungreased cookie sheets. Press cherry half into center of each cookie. Bake 8 to 10 minutes. Cool.

In heavy saucepan, over medium heat, melt chips with sweetened condensed milk; continue cooking about 3 minutes or until mixture thickens. Frost each cookie, covering cherry. Store loosely covered at room temperature.

Makes about 10 dozen cookies

Double Chocolate Pecan Cookies:
Prepare cookies as directed, omitting cherries; flatten. Bake as directed and frost tops. Garnish each cookie with pecan half.

Double Chocolate Cherry Cookies

Oats 'n' Pumpkin Pinwheels

1½ cups sugar, divided
½ cup (1 stick) margarine, softened
2 egg whites
1½ cups all-purpose flour
1 cup QUAKER® Oats (quick or old fashioned, uncooked)
¼ teaspoon baking soda
1 cup canned pumpkin
½ teaspoon pumpkin pie spice
¼ cup sesame seeds

Beat 1 cup sugar and margarine until fluffy; mix in egg whites. Stir in combined flour, oats and baking soda. On waxed paper, press into 16×12-inch rectangle. Spread combined pumpkin, remaining ½ cup sugar and spice over dough to ½ inch from edge. From narrow end, roll up dough. Sprinkle sesame seeds over roll, pressing gently. Wrap in waxed paper; freeze overnight or until firm.

Preheat oven to 400°F. Spray cookie sheet with no-stick cooking spray. Cut frozen dough into ¼-inch slices; place 1 inch apart on prepared cookie sheet.

Bake 9 to 11 minutes or until golden brown. Remove to wire rack; cool completely.

Makes about 4 dozen cookies

Butter-Flavored Brickle Drizzles

Cookies

    1 cup BUTTER FLAVOR CRISCO®
    1 cup granulated sugar
    1 cup firmly packed brown sugar
    1 can (14 ounces) sweetened
        condensed milk (not evaporated
        milk)
    1 teaspoon vanilla
1^3/$_4$ cups all-purpose flour
    1 teaspoon salt
    ^{1}/$_2$ teaspoon baking soda
    3 cups quick oats, uncooked
    1 cup almond brickle chips

Drizzle

    1 cup milk chocolate chips

1. Preheat oven to 350°F. Grease cookie sheet with Butter Flavor Crisco®.

2. For cookies, combine Butter Flavor Crisco®, granulated sugar and brown sugar in large bowl. Stir with spoon until well blended and creamy. Stir in condensed milk and vanilla. Mix well.

3. Combine flour, salt and baking soda. Stir into creamed mixture. Stir in oats.

4. Shape dough into 1-inch balls. Press tops into brickle chips. Place cookies, brickle side up, 2 inches apart on prepared cookie sheet.

5. Bake at 350°F for 9 to 10 minutes or until set but not browned. Remove to cooling rack. Cool completely.

6. For drizzle, place chocolate chips in heavy resealable plastic bag. Seal. Microwave at 50% (MEDIUM). Knead bag after 1 minute. Repeat until smooth (or melt by placing in bowl of hot water). Cut tiny tip off corner of bag. Squeeze out and drizzle over cookies.

Makes about 6 dozen cookies

Chocolate Sandwich Cookies

Cookies

    2 cups all-purpose flour
    ^{1}/$_3$ cup unsweetened cocoa powder
    1 teaspoon baking soda
    ^{1}/$_4$ teaspoon salt
    6 tablespoons butter, softened
    1 cup sugar
    1 egg
    1 cup milk

Filling

    ^{1}/$_2$ cup milk
    2 tablespoons all-purpose flour
    ^{1}/$_2$ cup butter, softened
    ^{1}/$_2$ cup sugar
    1 teaspoon vanilla

Preheat oven to 425°F. For cookies, in medium bowl, stir together 2 cups flour, cocoa, baking soda and salt. In large mixer bowl, cream 6 tablespoons butter and 1 cup sugar until fluffy. Beat in egg. Add flour mixture and 1 cup milk alternately to butter mixture, beating after each addition. Drop dough by rounded teaspoonfuls onto greased cookie sheets. Bake about 7 minutes or until set. Remove to wire racks to cool.

For filling, in a small saucepan over low heat, stir together ^{1}/$_2$ cup milk and 2 tablespoons flour. Cook and stir until thick and bubbly; cook and stir 1 to 2 minutes more. Cool slightly. In small mixer bowl, cream ^{1}/$_2$ cup butter and ^{1}/$_2$ cup sugar until fluffy. Add cooled flour mixture and vanilla. Beat until smooth. Spread filling on flat side of half the cooled cookies; top with remaining cookies.

Makes about 2^1/$_2$ dozen sandwich cookies

Favorite recipe from Wisconsin Milk Marketing Board © 1993

Butter-Flavored Brickle Drizzles

Oatmeal Toffee Lizzies

1 cup BUTTER FLAVOR CRISCO®
1 cup granulated sugar
1 cup firmly packed brown sugar
2 eggs, beaten
1 tablespoon milk
1 teaspoon vanilla
2 cups all-purpose flour
1 teaspoon baking soda
1 teaspoon salt
2 cups quick oats, uncooked
2 cups semi-sweet chocolate chips
$3/4$ cup almond brickle chips
$1/2$ cup finely chopped pecans

1. Preheat oven to 350°F. Grease cookie sheet with Butter Flavor Crisco®.

2. Combine Butter Flavor Crisco®, granulated sugar and brown sugar in large bowl. Beat until well blended. Add eggs, milk and vanilla. Mix well.

3. Combine flour, baking soda and salt. Add to creamed mixture. Mix well. Stir in oats, chocolate chips, brickle chips and nuts until well blended. Shape dough into $1^1/4$- to $1^1/2$-inch balls with lightly floured hands. Place 2 inches apart on greased cookie sheet. Flatten slightly.

4. Bake at 350°F for 12 to 15 minutes or until cookies begin to brown around edges. Remove to flat surface to cool.

Makes about 4$^1/2$ dozen cookies

Chocolate Pinwheel Cookies

$3/4$ cup MAZOLA® Margarine
1 cup sugar
2 eggs
1 teaspoon vanilla
$2^1/2$ cups flour
1 teaspoon baking powder
1 teaspoon cinnamon
1 teaspoon salt
2 ounces unsweetened chocolate, melted and cooled

In medium bowl, beat margarine and sugar until light and fluffy. Add eggs, 1 at a time, and vanilla; beat until smooth. In small bowl, combine flour, baking powder, cinnamon and salt; add to margarine mixture. Beat until smooth. Remove half of dough; reserve. Blend chocolate into remaining half of dough. Cover; chill chocolate dough 20 minutes.

With floured rolling pin, on lightly floured surface, roll reserved dough into a 12×9-inch rectangle. Roll chilled chocolate dough into 12×9-inch rectangle. Place chocolate rectangle on top of plain rectangle. With rolling pin, roll dough to $1/4$-inch thickness. Roll up tightly, beginning with the 12-inch side. Chill.

Preheat oven to 400°F. Cut dough crosswise into $1/4$-inch-thick slices. Place slices 1 inch apart on ungreased cookie sheets. Bake 8 to 10 minutes or until lightly browned. Cool on cookie sheets 2 minutes. Remove; cool completely on wire rack. *Makes about 4 dozen cookies*

Raspberry Freckles

Cookies

    1 cup sugar
    ¹/₂ cup BUTTER FLAVOR CRISCO®
    1 egg
    1 tablespoon raspberry-flavored
        liqueur
  2²/₃ cups all-purpose flour
    1 teaspoon baking powder
    ¹/₂ teaspoon baking soda
    ¹/₂ teaspoon salt
    ¹/₂ cup dairy sour cream
    1 cup cubed (¹/₈- to ¹/₄-inch) white
        confectionery coating
    ³/₄ cup mini semi-sweet chocolate
        chips
    ¹/₂ cup (2¹/₄-ounce bag) crushed,
        sliced almonds

Topping

    ¹/₄ cup seedless red raspberry jam
    1 teaspoon raspberry-flavored
        liqueur
    ¹/₃ cup chopped white confectionery
        coating
    2 teaspoons BUTTER FLAVOR
        CRISCO®

Raspberry Freckles

1. Preheat oven to 375°F. Grease cookie sheet with Butter Flavor Crisco®.

2. For Cookies, combine sugar and ¹/₂ cup Butter Flavor Crisco® in large bowl. Stir with spoon until well blended. Stir in egg and 1 tablespoon liqueur.

3. Combine flour, baking powder, baking soda and salt. Add alternately with sour cream to creamed mixture. Stir in cubed confectionery coating, chocolate chips and nuts.

4. Roll dough to ¹/₄-inch thickness on floured surface. Cut with 3-inch scalloped round cutter. Place 2 inches apart on greased cookie sheet.

5. Bake at 375°F for 7 minutes or just until beginning to brown. Cool 2 minutes on cookie sheet before removing to paper towels. Cool completely.

6. For Topping, combine raspberry jam and 1 teaspoon liqueur in microwave-safe measuring cup or bowl. Microwave at 50% (MEDIUM) until jam melts (or melt on rangetop in small saucepan on very low heat). Drop mixture in 10 to 12 dots to resemble freckles on top of each cookie.

7. Combine chopped confectionery coating and 2 teaspoons Butter Flavor Crisco® in heavy resealable plastic bag. Seal. Microwave at 50% (MEDIUM). Knead bag after 1 minute. Repeat until smooth (or melt by placing in bowl of hot water). Cut tiny tip off corner of bag. Squeeze out and drizzle over cookies. *Makes about 3 dozen cookies*

"Radical" Peanut Butter Pizza Cookie

Cocoa-Pecan Kiss Cookies

1 cup butter or margarine, softened
$^2/_3$ cup sugar
1 teaspoon vanilla
1$^2/_3$ cups unsifted all-purpose flour
$^1/_4$ cup HERSHEY'S Cocoa
1 cup finely chopped pecans
54 HERSHEY'S KISSES® Chocolates
(9-ounce package), unwrapped
Confectioners' sugar

Preheat oven to 350°F. Cream butter, sugar and vanilla in large mixer bowl until light and fluffy. Combine flour and cocoa; blend into creamed mixture. Add pecans; beat on low speed until well blended. Chill dough 1 hour or until firm enough to handle.

Shape scant tablespoon of dough around each unwrapped KISS®, covering completely; shape into balls. Place on ungreased cookie sheet. Bake 10 to 12 minutes or until almost set. Cool slightly. Remove from cookie sheet; cool completely on wire rack. Roll in confectioners' sugar.

Makes about 4$^1/_2$ dozen cookies

"Radical" Peanut Butter Pizza Cookies

Cookies

1 cup BUTTER FLAVOR CRISCO®
1$^1/_4$ cups granulated sugar, divided
1 cup firmly packed dark brown sugar
1 cup JIF® Creamy Peanut Butter
2 eggs
1 teaspoon baking soda
1 teaspoon vanilla
$^1/_2$ teaspoon salt
2 cups all-purpose flour
2 cups quick oats, uncooked

Pizza Sauce

2 cups milk chocolate chips
$^1/_4$ cup BUTTER FLAVOR CRISCO®

Pizza Topping

Any of the following:
Mmmmm—candy coated chocolate pieces
Beary good—gummy bears
Jumbo jewels—small pieces of gumdrops
Bubble gum-like—round sprinkles and balls
German chocolate—chopped pecans and flake coconut
Cherries jubilee—candied cherries and slivered almonds
Rocky road—miniature marshmallows and mini semisweet chocolate chips
Harvest mix—candy corn and chopped peanuts
Ants and logs—cashews and raisins

Drizzle

1 cup chopped white confectionery coating

1. Preheat oven to 350°F.

2. For Cookies, combine 1 cup Butter Flavor Crisco®, 1 cup granulated sugar and brown sugar in large bowl. Beat at low speed of electric mixer until well blended. Add peanut butter, eggs, baking soda, vanilla and salt. Mix about 2 minutes or until well blended. Stir in flour and oats with spoon.

3. Place remaining 1/4 cup granulated sugar in small bowl.

4. Measure 1/4 cup dough. Shape into ball. Repeat with remaining dough. Roll each ball in sugar. Place 4 inches apart on ungreased cookie sheet. Flatten into 4-inch circles.

5. Bake at 350°F for 8 to 10 minutes. Use back of spoon to flatten center and up to edge of each hot cookie to resemble pizza crust. Cool 5 to 8 minutes on cookie sheet before removing to flat surface.

6. For pizza sauce, combine chocolate chips and 1/4 cup Butter Flavor Crisco® in large microwave-safe measuring cup or bowl. Microwave at 50% (MEDIUM) for 2 to 3 minutes or until chips are shiny and soft (or melt on rangetop in small saucepan on very low heat). Stir until smooth. Spoon 2 teaspoons melted chocolate into center of each cookie. Spread to inside edge. Sprinkle desired topping over chocolate.

7. For drizzle, place confectionery coating in heavy resealable plastic bag. Seal. Microwave at 50% (MEDIUM). Knead bag after 1 minute. Repeat until smooth (or melt by placing in bowl of hot water). Cut tiny tip off corner of bag. Squeeze out and drizzle over cookies.   *Makes about 2 dozen cookies*

Cinnamon Stars

  2 tablespoons sugar
3/4 teaspoon ground cinnamon
3/4 cup butter or margarine, softened
  2 egg yolks
  1 teaspoon vanilla extract
  1 package DUNCAN HINES® Moist Deluxe French Vanilla Cake Mix

1. Preheat oven to 375°F.

2. Combine sugar and cinnamon in small bowl. Set aside.

3. Combine butter, egg yolks and vanilla extract in large bowl. Gradually blend in Duncan Hines® Moist Deluxe French Vanilla Cake Mix. Roll to 1/8-inch thickness on lightly floured surface. Cut with 2 1/2-inch star cookie cutter. Place 2 inches apart on ungreased cookie sheets. Sprinkle cookies with cinnamon-sugar mixture. Bake at 375°F for 6 to 8 minutes or until edges are light golden brown. Cool 1 minute on cookie sheets. Remove to cooling racks. Cool completely. Store in airtight container.

Makes 3 to 3 1/2 dozen cookies

Cinnamon Stars

Festive Butter Cookies

Cookies

1½ cups butter, softened
¾ cup granulated sugar
3 egg yolks
3 cups all-purpose flour
1 teaspoon baking powder
2 tablespoons orange juice
1 teaspoon vanilla

Frosting (optional)

4 cups powdered sugar
½ cup butter, softened
3 to 4 tablespoons milk
2 teaspoons vanilla
Food coloring (optional)
Colored sugars, flaked coconut
and cinnamon candies for
decoration

For cookies, in large bowl, cream butter and granulated sugar. Add egg yolks; beat until light and fluffy. Add flour, baking powder, orange juice and vanilla; beat until well mixed. Cover; refrigerate until firm, 2 to 3 hours.

Preheat oven to 350°F. Roll out dough, half at a time, ¼ inch thick on well-floured surface. Cut out with holiday cookie cutters. Place 1 inch apart on ungreased cookie sheets. Bake 6 to 10 minutes or until edges are golden brown. Remove to wire racks to cool completely.

For frosting, in medium bowl, combine all frosting ingredients except food coloring and decorations; beat until fluffy. If desired, divide frosting into small bowls and tint with food coloring. Frost cookies and decorate with colored sugars, coconut and candies, if desired.

Makes about 4 dozen cookies

Date Menenas

2¾ cups all-purpose flour
½ teaspoon DAVIS® Baking Powder
¾ cup sugar
⅔ cup FLEISCHMANN'S®
Margarine, softened
1 teaspoon vanilla extract
¼ cup EGG BEATERS® 99% Egg
Product
8 ounces pitted dates, finely
chopped
½ cup water
1 tablespoon lemon juice

In medium bowl, combine flour and baking powder. Reserve 2 tablespoons sugar for date filling. In large bowl of electric mixer, on medium speed, beat margarine and remaining sugar until creamy. On low speed, add vanilla and egg product alternately with flour mixture. Beat until well combined. Form into flattened disk and wrap in plastic wrap. Refrigerate 1 hour.

To make date filling, place dates, water, reserved sugar and lemon juice in medium saucepan. Bring to a simmer; reduce heat and simmer, covered, 10 minutes. Remove from heat and let cool to room temperature.

Preheat oven to 400°F. Cut dough in half. On floured waxed paper, roll dough to 12×10-inch rectangle. Spread half the filling (½ cup) on dough. Beginning with 12-inch side, roll up as a jelly-roll. With thread, cut ⅜-inch cookies from log. Place on greased cookie sheet. Repeat with remaining dough and filling.

Bake 10 minutes or until bottoms are lightly browned. Remove to wire rack to cool. Store in airtight container.

Makes about 5 dozen cookies

Festive Butter Cookies

Frosted Peanut Butter Peanut Brittle Cookies

Peanut Brittle

1½ cups granulated sugar
1½ cups shelled unroasted Spanish
    peanuts
¾ cup light corn syrup
½ teaspoon salt
1 tablespoon BUTTER FLAVOR
    CRISCO®
1½ teaspoons vanilla
1½ teaspoons baking soda

Cookies

½ cup BUTTER FLAVOR CRISCO®
½ cup granulated sugar
½ cup firmly packed brown sugar
½ cup JIF® Creamy Peanut Butter
1 tablespoon milk
1 egg
1⅓ cups all-purpose flour
¾ teaspoon baking soda
½ teaspoon baking powder
¼ teaspoon salt

Frosting

1¼ cups peanut butter chips
    Reserved 1 cup crushed peanut
    brittle

*Frosted Peanut Butter
Peanut Brittle Cookies*

1. For peanut brittle, grease 15½×12-inch cookie sheet with Butter Flavor Crisco®.

2. Combine 1½ cups granulated sugar, nuts, corn syrup and salt in 3-quart saucepan. Cook and stir on medium-low heat until mixture registers 240°F on candy thermometer.

3. Stir in 1 tablespoon Butter Flavor Crisco® and vanilla. Cook and stir until mixture registers 300°F on candy thermometer. Watch closely so mixture does not burn.

4. Remove from heat. Stir in 1½ teaspoons baking soda. Pour onto prepared cookie sheet. Spread to ¼-inch thickness. Cool. Break into pieces. Crush into medium-fine pieces to measure 1 cup. Set aside.

5. Preheat oven to 375°F.

6. For cookies, combine ½ cup Butter Flavor Crisco®, ½ cup granulated sugar, brown sugar, peanut butter and milk in large bowl. Beat at medium speed of electric mixer until well blended. Beat in egg.

7. Combine flour, ¾ teaspoon baking soda, baking powder and salt. Add gradually at low speed. Mix until well blended.

8. Shape dough into 1¼-inch balls. Place 3½ inches apart on ungreased cookie sheet. Flatten each into 3-inch circle.

9. Bake at 375°F for 8 to 9 minutes or until light brown. Cool 2 minutes on cookie sheet before removing to flat surface. Cool completely.

10. For frosting, place peanut butter chips in microwave-safe measuring cup or bowl. Microwave at 50% (MEDIUM). Stir after 1 minute. Repeat until smooth (or melt in saucepan on very low heat). Spread frosting on half of each cookie.

11. Sprinkle reserved peanut brittle over frosting. Refrigerate to set quickly or let stand at room temperature.

Makes about 2 dozen cookies

Cocoa Almond
Cut-out Cookies

³/₄ cup margarine or butter, softened
1 (14-ounce) can EAGLE® Brand
    Sweetened Condensed Milk
    (NOT evaporated milk)
2 eggs
1 teaspoon vanilla extract
¹/₂ teaspoon almond extract
2³/₄ cups unsifted flour
²/₃ cup HERSHEY₅S Cocoa
2 teaspoons baking powder
¹/₂ teaspoon baking soda
¹/₂ cup finely chopped almonds
    Chocolate Glaze

Cocoa Almond Cut-out Cookies

In large mixer bowl, beat margarine, sweetened condensed milk, eggs and extracts until well blended. Combine dry ingredients; add to margarine mixture, beating until well blended. Stir in almonds. Divide dough into 4 equal portions. Wrap each in plastic wrap; flatten. Chill until firm enough to roll, about 2 hours.

Preheat oven to 350°F. Working with 1 portion at a time (keep remaining dough in refrigerator), on floured surface, roll to about ¹/₈-inch thickness. Cut into desired shapes. Place on lightly greased cookie sheets. Bake 6 to 8 minutes or until set. Remove from cookie sheets. Cool completely. Drizzle with Chocolate Glaze. Store tightly covered at room temperature.
Makes about 6 dozen 3-inch cookies

Chocolate Glaze: Melt 1 cup (6 ounces) HERSHEY₅S Semi-Sweet Chocolate Chips with 2 tablespoons shortening. Makes about ²/₃ cup.

Chocolate-Filled Bonbons

¹/₂ cup BUTTER FLAVOR CRISCO®
¹/₂ cup granulated sugar
¹/₄ cup firmly packed brown sugar
1 teaspoon vanilla
1 egg
1²/₃ cups all-purpose flour
¹/₂ teaspoon baking soda
¹/₄ teaspoon salt
6 chocolate kisses, unwrapped
36 nut halves

1. Preheat oven to 400°F.

2. Combine Butter Flavor Crisco®, granulated sugar, brown sugar, vanilla and egg in large bowl. Beat at medium speed of electric mixer.

3. Combine flour, baking soda and salt. Stir into creamed mixture with spoon.

4. Press two level measuring teaspoonfuls of dough around each kiss, covering kiss completely. Top each with nut half. Place 2 inches apart on ungreased cookie sheet.

5. Bake at 400°F for 6 to 7 minutes. Cookies will not brown. Do not overbake. Press nuts gently into hot cookies. Cool on cookie sheet 1 minute before removing to cooling rack.
Makes about 3 dozen cookies

Chocolate Chip Sandwich Cookies

Chocolate Chip Sandwich Cookies

Cookies

    1 package DUNCAN HINES®
        Chocolate Chip Cookie Mix
    1 egg
    2 teaspoons water

Cream Filling

    1 cup marshmallow creme
    $1/2$ cup butter or margarine, softened
    $1^2/3$ cups confectioners sugar
    1 teaspoon vanilla extract

1. Preheat oven to 375°F.

2. For cookies, combine cookie mix, buttery flavor packet from Mix, egg and water in large bowl. Stir until thoroughly blended. Drop by rounded teaspoonfuls 2 inches apart onto ungreased cookie sheets. Bake at 375°F for 8 to 10 minutes or until light golden brown. Cool 1 minute on cookie sheets. Remove to cooling racks.

3. For cream filling, combine marshmallow creme and butter in small bowl. Add confectioners sugar and vanilla extract, beating until smooth.

4. To assemble, spread bottoms of half the cookies with 1 tablespoon cream filling; top with remaining cookies. Press together to make sandwich cookies. Refrigerate to quickly set filling, if desired.

Makes about 18 sandwich cookies

Toasted Anise Biscuits

    $2/3$ cup EGG BEATERS® 99% Egg
        Product
    $3/4$ cup sugar
    $1/4$ cup FLEISCHMANN'S®
        Margarine, melted
    2 cups all-purpose flour
    2 teaspoons baking powder
    2 teaspoons anise extract*
    1 cup confectioner's sugar
    3 to 4 teaspoons water
    $1/2$ cup sliced almonds, toasted
        (optional)

Preheat oven to 350°F. Blend egg product and sugar; stir in margarine, flour, baking powder and anise extract until blended.

Divide batter in half. On greased cookie sheet, spread each half into a 14×4-inch rectangle. Bake 20 minutes or until golden brown. Immediately cut loaves on a diagonal into 1-inch-thick biscuits. Turn biscuits on their sides on same cookie sheet; broil 2 to 3 minutes on each side until light golden brown. Cool on wire rack.

Mix confectioner's sugar and enough water to make frosting consistency. Spread on biscuit tops; sprinkle with almonds if desired.

*Toasted Almond Biscuits: 2 teaspoons almond extract may be substituted for anise extract.

Caramel Pecan Cookies

Cookies

- 1/2 cup BUTTER FLAVOR CRISCO®, melted
- 1 package DUNCAN HINES® Moist Deluxe Yellow Cake Mix
- 1 cup JIF® Extra Crunchy Peanut Butter
- 2 eggs
- 2 tablespoons orange juice or water

Caramel and Chocolate Topping

- 28 caramels, unwrapped
- 2 tablespoons milk
- 2 cups pecan halves
- 1 package (6 ounces) semi-sweet chocolate chips

1. Preheat oven to 350°F. For cookies, combine Butter Flavor Crisco®, cake mix, peanut butter, eggs and juice in large bowl. Beat at medium speed of electric mixer until well blended.

2. Drop rounded tablespoonfuls of dough, 3 inches apart, onto ungreased cookie sheet.

3. Bake 10 to 12 minutes or until set. Cool 1 minute on cookie sheet. Remove to wire rack to cool completely.

4. For topping, combine caramels and milk in microwave-safe bowl. Cover with waxed paper. Microwave at 50% (MEDIUM). Stir after 1 minute. Repeat until smooth (or melt on range top in small saucepan on very low heat). Drop rounded teaspoonfuls on top of each cookie. Place 3 pecan halves around edge of caramel to resemble turtles.

5. Place chocolate chips in microwave-safe cup. Microwave at 50% (MEDIUM). Stir after 1 minute. Repeat until smooth (or melt on range top in small saucepan on very low heat). Spread rounded teaspoonfuls over top of caramel. Do not cover pecans. Cool completely.   *Makes about 4 dozen cookies*

Confetti Chocolate Chip Cookies

- 1 1/4 cups firmly packed brown sugar
- 3/4 cup BUTTER FLAVOR CRISCO®
- 2 tablespoons milk
- 1 tablespoon vanilla
- 1 egg
- 1 1/2 cups all-purpose flour
- 1 teaspoon salt
- 3/4 teaspoon baking soda
- 1 cup walnut pieces
- 1/2 cup semi-sweet chocolate chunks
- 1/2 cup large vanilla chunks
- 1/2 cup milk chocolate chips

1. Preheat oven to 375°F.

2. Combine brown sugar, Butter Flavor Crisco®, milk and vanilla in large mixer bowl. Beat at medium speed of electric mixer until well blended. Beat in egg.

3. Combine flour, salt and baking soda. Add gradually to creamed mixture at low speed. Mix until blended.

4. Stir in nuts, chocolate chunks, vanilla chunks and chocolate chips with spoon. Drop by rounded tablespoonfuls 3 inches apart onto ungreased cookie sheet.

5. Bake at 375°F for 8 to 10 minutes. Cookies will look light and moist. *Do not overbake*. Cool 2 minutes on cookie sheet before removing to cooling rack.
Makes about 2 dozen cookies

ESPECIALLY
ELEGANT

Double-Dipped Chocolate Peanut Butter Cookies

1/2 cup butter or margarine, softened
1/2 cup granulated sugar
1/2 cup packed light brown sugar
1/2 cup chunky or creamy peanut butter
1 large egg
1 teaspoon vanilla
1 1/4 cups all-purpose flour
1/2 teaspoon baking powder
1/2 teaspoon baking soda
1/2 teaspoon salt
1 1/2 cups semisweet chocolate chips
3 teaspoons shortening, divided
1 1/2 cups milk chocolate chips

Preheat oven to 350°F. Beat butter, granulated sugar and brown sugar in large bowl until light and fluffy. Beat in peanut butter, egg and vanilla. Gradually stir in combined flour, baking powder, baking soda and salt; mix well. Roll heaping tablespoonfuls dough into 1 1/2-inch balls. Place balls 2 inches apart on cookie sheets. (If dough is too soft to roll into balls, refrigerate 30 minutes.)

Dip fork into sugar; press criss-cross indentation on each ball, flattening to 1/2-inch thickness. Bake 12 minutes or until set. Let cookies stand on cookie sheets 2 minutes. Remove cookies to wire cooling rack; cool completely.

Melt semisweet chocolate chips and 1 1/2 teaspoons shortening in top of double boiler over hot, not boiling water. Dip one third of each cookie into semisweet chocolate; place on waxed paper. Let stand until chocolate is set, about 30 minutes.

Melt milk chocolate chips with remaining 1 1/2 teaspoons shortening in top of double boiler over hot, not boiling water. Dip opposite one third of each cookie into milk chocolate; place on waxed paper. Let stand until chocolate is set, about 30 minutes.

Makes about 2 dozen 3-inch cookies

Double-Dipped Chocolate Peanut Butter Cookies

Cherry Surprises

1 package DUNCAN HINES®
  Golden Sugar Cookie Mix
36 to 42 candied cherries
1/2 cup semi-sweet chocolate chips
1 teaspoon CRISCO® Shortening

1. Preheat oven to 375°F. Grease cookie sheets.

2. Prepare cookie mix following package directions for original recipe. Shape thin layer of dough around each candied cherry. Place 2 inches apart on prepared cookie sheets. Bake at 375°F for 8 minutes or until set but not browned. Cool 1 minute on cookie sheets. Remove to cooling racks. Cool completely.

3. Combine chocolate chips and shortening in small resealable plastic bag. Place bag in bowl of hot water for several minutes. Dry with paper towel. Knead until blended and chocolate is smooth. Snip pinpoint hole in corner of bag. Drizzle chocolate over cookies. Allow drizzle to set before storing between layers of waxed paper in airtight container.

Makes 3 to 3 1/2 dozen cookies

Cherry Surprises

Chocolate-Dipped Cinnamon Thins

1 cup unsalted butter, softened
1 cup powdered sugar
1 large egg
1 teaspoon vanilla
1/4 teaspoon salt
1 1/4 cups all-purpose flour
1 1/2 teaspoons ground cinnamon
1 (4-ounce) bittersweet chocolate candy bar, broken

Beat butter in large bowl until light and fluffy. Add sugar; beat well. Add egg, vanilla and salt; beat well. Gradually add combined flour and cinnamon. Beat until well blended. Place dough on sheet of waxed paper. Using waxed paper to hold dough, roll back and forth to form a log about 12 inches long and 2 1/2 inches wide. Securely wrap waxed paper around log. Refrigerate at least 2 hours or until firm. (Log may be frozen up to 3 months; wrap airtight in plastic wrap before freezing. Thaw in refrigerator before baking).

Preheat oven to 350°F. Cut dough with sharp knife into 1/4-inch thick slices. Place 2 inches apart on cookie sheets. Bake 10 minutes or until set. Let cookies stand on cookie sheets 2 minutes. Remove cookies to wire racks; cool completely.

Melt chocolate in 1 cup glass measuring cup set in bowl of very hot water, stirring twice, about 10 minutes. Dip each cookie into chocolate, coating 1 inch deep and letting excess chocolate drip back into cup. Transfer to wire racks or waxed paper; let stand at cool room temperature about 40 minutes until chocolate has set.

Makes about 2 dozen cookies

Caramel Lace Chocolate Chip Cookies

Caramel Lace Chocolate Chip Cookies

¹/₄ cup **BUTTER FLAVOR CRISCO®**
¹/₂ **cup light corn syrup**
  1 **tablespoon brown sugar**
¹/₂ **teaspoon vanilla**
1¹/₂ **teaspoons grated orange peel**
   (optional)
¹/₂ **cup all-purpose flour**
¹/₄ **teaspoon salt**
¹/₃ **cup semi-sweet chocolate chips**
¹/₃ **cup coarsely chopped pecans**

1. Preheat oven to 375°F. Grease cookie sheet with Butter Flavor Crisco®.

2. Combine Butter Flavor Crisco®, corn syrup, brown sugar, vanilla and orange peel in large bowl. Beat at medium speed of electric mixer until well blended.

3. Combine flour and salt. Mix into creamed mixture at low speed until blended. Stir in chocolate chips and nuts. Drop teaspoonfuls of dough 4 inches apart onto cookie sheet.

4. Bake 5 minutes or until edges are golden brown. (Chips and nuts will remain in center while dough spreads out.) *Do not overbake.* Cool 2 minutes on cookie sheet. Lift each cookie edge with spatula. Grasp cookie edge gently and lightly pinch or flute the edge, bringing it up to chips and nuts in center. Work around each cookie until completely fluted. Remove to cooling rack.

Makes about 3 dozen cookies

Hidden Treasures

Hidden Treasures

²/₃ **cup BUTTER FLAVOR CRISCO®**
³/₄ **cup sugar**
1 **egg**
1 **tablespoon milk**
1 **teaspoon vanilla**
1³/₄ **cups all-purpose flour**
1 **teaspoon baking powder**
¹/₂ **teaspoon salt**
¹/₂ **teaspoon baking soda**
48 **maraschino cherries, well drained on paper towels**

White Dipping Chocolate

1 **cup white melting chocolate, cut into small pieces**
2 **tablespoons BUTTER FLAVOR CRISCO®**

Dark Dipping Chocolate

1 **cup semi-sweet chocolate chips**
2 **tablespoons BUTTER FLAVOR CRISCO®**

Finely chopped pecans
Slivered white chocolate

1. Preheat oven to 350°F. Cream Butter Flavor Crisco®, sugar, egg, milk and vanilla in large bowl at medium speed of electric mixer until well blended.

2. Combine flour, baking powder, salt and baking soda. Beat into creamed mixture at low speed. Divide into 48 equal pieces.

3. Press dough into very thin layer around well drained cherries. Place 2 inches apart on ungreased cookie sheet.

4. Bake 10 minutes. Cool 1 minute on cookie sheet. Remove to wire rack to cool completely.

5. For dipping chocolate, place chocolate of choice and Butter Flavor Crisco® in glass measuring cup. Microwave at 50% (MEDIUM). Stir after 1 minute. Repeat until smooth (or melt on range top in small saucepan on very low heat).

6. Drop 1 cookie at a time into chocolate. Use fork to turn. Cover completely with chocolate.* Lift cookie out of chocolate with fork. Allow excess to drip off. Place on waxed paper-lined cookie sheet.

7. Sprinkle chopped pecans on top of white chocolate cookies before chocolate sets. Sprinkle white chocolate on dark chocolate cookies before chocolate sets. Chill in refrigerator to set chocolate.

Makes 4 dozen cookies

*If chocolate becomes too firm, reheat in microwave or on range top.

Two-Toned Spritz Cookies

1 **square (1 ounce) unsweetened chocolate, coarsely chopped**
1 **cup butter or margarine, softened**
1 **cup sugar**
1 **large egg**
1 **teaspoon vanilla**
2¹/₄ **cups all-purpose flour**
¹/₄ **teaspoon salt**

Two-Toned Spritz Cookies

Melt chocolate in small, heavy saucepan over low heat, stirring constantly; set aside. Beat butter and sugar in large bowl until light and fluffy. Beat in egg and vanilla. Gradually add combined flour and salt. Reserve 2 cups dough. Beat chocolate into dough in bowl until smooth. Cover both doughs and refrigerate until easy to handle, about 20 minutes.

Preheat oven to 400°F. Roll out vanilla dough between two sheets of waxed paper to ¹/₂-inch thickness. Cut into 5×4-inch rectangles. Place chocolate dough on sheet of waxed paper. Using waxed paper to hold dough, roll back and forth to form a log about 1 inch in diameter. Cut into 5-inch-long logs. Place chocolate log in center of vanilla rectangle. Wrap vanilla dough around log and fit into cookie press fitted with star disc. Press dough onto cookie sheets 1¹/₂ inches apart. Bake about 10 minutes or until just set. Remove cookies with spatula to wire racks; cool completely.

Makes about 4 dozen cookies

Raspberry Almond Sandwich Cookies

1 package DUNCAN HINES®
  Golden Sugar Cookie Mix
1 egg
1 tablespoon water
¹/₂ teaspoon almond extract
³/₄ cup sliced natural almonds,
  broken
  Seedless red raspberry jam

1. Preheat oven to 375°F.

2. Combine cookie mix, buttery flavor packet from Mix, egg, water and almond extract in large bowl. Stir until thoroughly blended. Drop half of dough by level measuring teaspoonfuls 2 inches apart onto ungreased cookie sheets. (It is a small amount of dough but will spread during baking to 1¹/₂ to 1³/₄ inches.)

3. Place almonds on waxed paper. Drop other half of dough by level measuring teaspoonfuls onto nuts. Place almond side up 2 inches apart on cookie sheets.

4. Bake both plain and almond cookies at 375°F for 6 minutes or until set but not browned. Cool 1 minute on cookie sheets. Remove to cooling racks. Cool completely.

5. Spread bottoms of plain cookies with jam; top with almond cookies. Press together to make sandwiches. Store in airtight container.

Makes 4¹/₂ to 5 dozen cookies

Raspberry Almond Sandwich Cookies

Elegant Lace Cookie Cups

1/2 cup light corn syrup
1/2 cup butter or margarine
2 tablespoons whipping cream
1 cup all-purpose flour
1/4 cup firmly packed brown sugar
1/4 cup granulated sugar
1/2 cup slivered almonds, finely
     chopped
   Semisweet chocolate chips, melted
   Ice cream

Preheat oven to 300°F. In 2-quart saucepan over medium heat, bring corn syrup to a full boil, 2 to 3 minutes. Add butter; reduce heat to low. Continue cooking, stirring occasionally, until butter melts, 2 to 3 minutes. Remove from heat. Stir in whipping cream, flour, brown sugar, granulated sugar and almonds. Drop tablespoonfuls of dough 4 inches apart onto greased cookie sheets. Bake 11 to 13 minutes or until cookies bubble and are golden brown. *Cool 30 seconds on cookie sheets.* Working quickly, remove and shape cookies over inverted small custard cups to form cups. Cool completely; remove from custard cups.

For *each* cup, spread 1 tablespoon melted chocolate on outside bottom and 1 inch up outside edge of each cooled cookie cup. Refrigerate, chocolate side up, until hardened, about 30 minutes. Just before serving, fill each cup with large scoop of ice cream. If desired, drizzle with additional melted chocolate.

Makes about 2 dozen cookie cups

Tip: Make desired number of cups. With remaining dough, bake as directed above except shape into cones or leave flat. Serve as cookies.

Mini Pecan Tarts

Tart Shells

1 1/2 sticks cold butter or margarine, cut
     into pieces
  2 cups flour
  1 teaspoon granulated sugar
    Pinch of salt
1/3 cup ice water

Filling

  1 cup powdered sugar
1/2 cup butter or margarine
1/3 cup dark corn syrup
  1 cup chopped pecans
36 pecan halves

Preheat oven to 375°F. For tart shells, in large bowl combine margarine, flour, granulated sugar and salt. Using pastry blender or two knives, cut margarine into dry ingredients until mixture resembles crumbly corn meal. Add water, 1 tablespoon at a time, kneading mixture until dough forms. Wrap dough in plastic wrap, flatten and refrigerate at least 30 minutes.

Roll out dough on lightly floured surface to 1/8-inch thickness. Cut out 3-inch circles using cookie cutter; press into greased mini-muffin cups and bake about 8 minutes or until very lightly browned. *Reduce oven temperature to 350°F.*

For filling, in 2-quart saucepan combine powdered sugar, 1/2 cup butter and corn syrup. Cook over medium heat, stirring occasionally, until mixture comes to a full boil, 4 to 5 minutes. Remove from heat; stir in chopped pecans. Spoon into baked shells. Top *each* with a pecan half. Bake 5 minutes. Cool completely; remove from pans.

Makes 3 dozen tarts

Elegant Lace Cookie Cups, Mini Pecan Tarts

Yummy Chocolate Chip Flower Cookies

1 package DUNCAN HINES®
    Chocolate Chip Cookie Mix
1 egg
2 teaspoons water
24 flat ice cream sticks
1 container (16 ounces) DUNCAN
    HINES® Creamy Homestyle
    Vanilla Frosting
    Yellow and red food colorings
    Assorted decors

1. Preheat oven to 375°F.

2. Combine cookie mix, buttery flavor packet from Mix, egg and water in large bowl. Stir until thoroughly blended. Shape dough into 24 (1-inch) balls. Place 3 inches apart on ungreased cookie sheets. Push ice cream stick into center of each ball. Flatten dough slightly. Bake at 375°F for 7 to 8 minutes or until light golden brown. Cool 1 minute on cookie sheets. Remove to cooling racks. Cool completely.

3. Spoon half the vanilla frosting into small bowl. Add 3 to 4 drops yellow food coloring. Stir until blended. Add 3 to 4 drops red food coloring to frosting in container. Stir until blended. Place each tinted frosting in small resealable plastic bag; seal. Snip pinpoint hole in bottom corner of each bag. Decorate one cookie with frostings. Sprinkle with assorted decors. Repeat with remaining cookies. *Makes 24 cookies*

Yummy Chocolate Chip Flower Cookies

Chocolate Sugar Spritz

2 squares (1 ounce each)
    unsweetened chocolate, coarsely
    chopped
1 cup butter or margarine, softened
3/4 cup granulated sugar
1 large egg
1 teaspoon almond extract
2 1/4 cups all-purpose flour
1/4 teaspoon salt
1/2 cup powdered sugar
1 teaspoon ground cinnamon

Preheat oven to 400°F. Melt chocolate in small, heavy saucepan over low heat, stirring constantly; set aside. Beat butter and granulated sugar in large bowl until light and fluffy. Beat in egg and almond extract. Beat in chocolate. Gradually add combined flour and salt. (Dough will be stiff.) Fit cookie press with desired plate. Fill press with dough; press 1 inch apart on cookie sheets. Bake 7 minutes or until just set.

Combine powdered sugar and cinnamon in small bowl. Sprinkle over hot cookies while still on cookie sheet. Remove cookies to wire rack; cool completely. *Makes 4 to 5 dozen cookies*

Jeremy's Famous Turtles

Cookies

    3 egg whites
    1 egg yolk
 1¼ cups BUTTER FLAVOR CRISCO®
    ¾ cup firmly packed brown sugar
    ½ cup granulated sugar
    1 teaspoon vanilla
 1¾ cups all-purpose flour
    1 teaspoon baking soda
    ¾ teaspoon salt
    ½ cup butterscotch chips
    ½ cup semi-sweet chocolate chips
    ½ cup chopped dates
    ½ cup chopped pecans
    ½ cup diced dried fruit bits
    ⅓ cup cinnamon applesauce
    ¼ cup toasted wheat germ
    ¼ cup ground shelled sunflower
       seeds
    2 tablespoons honey
    3 cups oats (quick or old fashioned),
       uncooked
    8 ounces pecan halves (2 cups)

Coating

    1 to 2 egg whites, lightly beaten
    ½ cup granulated sugar

Jeremy's Famous Turtles

1. For cookies, place 3 egg whites in medium bowl. Beat at medium speed of electric mixer until frothy. Beat in egg yolk until well blended.

2. Combine Butter Flavor Crisco®, brown sugar and granulated sugar in large bowl. Beat at medium speed until well blended. Add egg mixture and vanilla. Beat until well blended.

3. Combine flour, baking soda and salt. Add gradually to creamed mixture at low speed. Stir in, 1 at a time, butterscotch chips, chocolate chips, dates, chopped nuts, fruit bits, applesauce, wheat germ, sunflower seeds, honey and oats. Cover. Refrigerate dough 1 hour.

4. Heat oven to 350°F. Grease cookie sheet with Butter Flavor Crisco®.

5. Shape dough into 1½-inch balls. Cut pecan halves into 4 lengthwise pieces for legs. Save broken pieces for heads and tails.

6. For coating, dip top of cookie ball in beaten egg white, then dip in sugar. Place cookies, sugar side up, 2½ inches apart on prepared cookie sheet. Insert lengthwise nut pieces for legs. Flatten slightly. Place nut sliver for tail and rounded nut piece for head.

7. Bake at 350°F for 9 to 11 minutes or until lightly browned. Reposition nuts, if necessary. Cool 30 seconds on cookie sheet before removing to paper towels.

Makes about 7½ dozen cookies

Black and White Cut-Outs

1 cup butter or margarine, softened
3/4 cup granulated sugar
3/4 cup packed light brown sugar
2 large eggs
1 teaspoon vanilla
2 3/4 cups *plus* 2 tablespoons all-purpose
    flour, divided
1 teaspoon baking soda
3/4 teaspoon salt
1/4 cup unsweetened cocoa
1 (4-ounce) white baking bar,
    broken into 1/2-inch pieces
1 (4-ounce package) semisweet
    chocolate chips
    Assorted decorative candies
    (optional)

Beat butter, granulated sugar and brown sugar in large bowl until light and fluffy. Beat in eggs, 1 at a time. Beat in vanilla. Gradually add combined 2 3/4 cups flour, baking soda and salt. Beat until well combined. Remove half of dough from bowl; reserve. To make chocolate dough, beat cocoa into remaining dough with spoon until well blended. To make butter cookie dough, beat remaining 2 tablespoons flour into reserved dough. Flatten each piece of dough into a disc; wrap in plastic wrap and refrigerate about 1 1/2 hours or until firm. (Dough may be refrigerated up to 3 days before baking).

Preheat oven to 375°F. Working with one type of dough at a time, place dough on lightly floured surface. Roll out dough to 1/4-inch thickness. Cut dough into desired shapes with cookie cutters. Place cut-outs 1 inch apart on cookie sheets. Bake 9 to 11 minutes or until set. Let cookies stand on cookie sheets 2 minutes. Remove cookies to wire rack; cool completely.

For white chocolate drizzle, place baking bar pieces in small resealable plastic bag; seal bag. Heat in microwave oven at MEDIUM (50% power) 2 minutes. Turn bag over; heat at MEDIUM (50% power) 2 to 3 minutes or until melted. Knead bag until baking bar is smooth. Cut off very tiny corner of bag; pipe or drizzle melted chocolate onto chocolate cookies. Decorate as desired with assorted candies. Let stand until white chocolate is set, about 30 minutes.

For chocolate drizzle, place chocolate chips in small resealable plastic bag; seal bag. Heat in microwave oven at HIGH (100% power) 1 minute. Turn bag over; heat at HIGH (100% power) 1 to 2 minutes or until chocolate is melted. Knead bag until chocolate is smooth. Cut off tiny corner of bag; pipe or drizzle chocolate onto butter cookies. Decorate as desired with assorted candies. Let stand until chocolate is set, about 40 minutes.

Makes 3 to 4 dozen cookies

Black and White Sandwiches: Cut cookies out with cookie cutter. Spread thin layer of prepared frosting on bottom side of chocolate cookie. Place bottom side of butter cookie over frosting. Drizzle either side of cookie with melted chocolate or white chocolate.

Black and White Cut-Outs

Austrian Tea Cookies

Austrian Tea Cookies

1¹/₂ cups sugar, divided
¹/₂ cup butter, softened
¹/₂ cup shortening
1 egg, beaten
¹/₂ teaspoon vanilla extract
2 cups all-purpose flour
2 cups HONEY ALMOND
   DELIGHT® Brand Cereal,
   crushed to 1 cup
¹/₂ teaspoon baking powder
¹/₄ teaspoon ground cinnamon
14 ounces almond paste
2 egg whites
5 tablespoons raspberry or apricot
   jam, warmed

In large bowl, beat 1 cup sugar, butter and shortening. Add egg and vanilla; mix well. Stir in flour, cereal, baking powder and cinnamon until well blended. Refrigerate 1 to 2 hours or until firm.

Preheat oven to 350°F. Roll dough out on lightly floured surface to ¹/₄-inch thickness; cut into 2-inch circles with floured cookie cutter. Place on ungreased cookie sheet: set aside.

In small bowl, beat almond paste, egg whites and remaining ¹/₂ cup sugar until smooth. With pastry tube fitted with medium-sized star tip, pipe almond paste mixture ¹/₂ inch thick on top of each cookie along outside edge. Place ¹/₄ teaspoon jam in center of each cookie, spreading out to paste.

Bake 8 to 10 minutes or until lightly browned. Let stand 1 minute before removing from cookie sheet. Cool on wire rack.

Makes about 3¹/₂ dozen cookies

Peanut Butter & Jelly Cookies

**1 package DUNCAN HINES®
Peanut Butter Cookie Mix
³/4 cup quick-cooking oats (not
instant or old-fashioned)
1 egg
¹/2 cup grape jelly
¹/2 cup confectioners sugar
2 teaspoons water**

1. Preheat oven to 375°F.

2. Combine cookie mix, peanut butter packet from Mix, oats and egg in large bowl. Stir until thoroughly blended. Divide dough into 4 equal portions. Shape each portion into 12-inch-long log on waxed paper. Place logs on ungreased cookie sheets. Press back of spoon down center of each log to form indentation. Bake at 375°F for 9 to 11 minutes or until light golden brown. Press back of spoon down center of each log again. Cool 2 minutes on cookie sheets. Remove to cooling racks. Cool completely. Spoon 2 tablespoons jelly along indentation of each log.

3. Combine confectioners sugar and water in small bowl. Stir until smooth. Drizzle over each log. Allow glaze to set. Cut each log diagonally into 12 slices with large, sharp knife. Store between layers of waxed paper in airtight container.

Makes about 48 cookies

Peanut Butter & Jelly Cookies

No-Bake Cherry Crisps

No-Bake Cherry Crisps

**¹/4 cup butter or margarine, softened
1 cup powdered sugar
1 cup peanut butter
¹/4 cup *plus* 2 tablespoons mini
semisweet chocolate chips
¹/4 cup chopped pecans
1¹/3 cups crisp rice cereal
¹/2 cup maraschino cherries, drained,
dried and chopped
1 to 2 cups flaked coconut (for
rolling)**

In large mixing bowl, cream butter, sugar and peanut butter. Stir in chips, pecans, cereal and cherries. Mix well. Shape teaspoonfuls of dough into 1-inch balls. Roll in coconut. Place on cookie sheet and chill in refrigerator 1 hour. Store in refrigerator.

Makes about 3 dozen treats

Watermelon Slices

3. For red cookie dough, combine remaining dough with red food coloring. Stir until evenly tinted. On waxed paper, shape dough into 12-inch-long roll with one side flattened. Cover; refrigerate with flat side down until firm.

4. Preheat oven to 375°F.

5. To assemble, remove green dough rectangle from refrigerator. Remove top layer of waxed paper. Trim edges along both 12-inch sides. Remove red dough log from refrigerator. Place red dough log, flattened side up, along center of green dough. Mold green dough up to edge of flattened side of red dough. Remove bottom layer of waxed paper. Trim excess green dough, if necessary.

6. Cut chilled roll, flat side down, into ¼-inch-thick slices with sharp knife. Place slices 2 inches apart on ungreased cookie sheets. Sprinkle chocolate sprinkles on red dough for seeds. Bake for 7 minutes or until set. Cool 1 minute on cookie sheets. Remove to cooling racks. Cool completely. Store between layers of waxed paper in airtight container.   *Makes 3 to 4 dozen cookies*

Watermelon Slices

1 package DUNCAN HINES®
   Golden Sugar Cookie Mix
1 egg
5 drops green food coloring
12 drops red food coloring
   Chocolate sprinkles

1. Combine cookie mix, buttery flavor packet from Mix and egg in large bowl. Stir until thoroughly blended.

2. For green cookie dough, combine ⅓ cup dough with green food coloring in small bowl. Stir until evenly tinted. Place between 2 layers of waxed paper. Roll dough into 12×4-inch rectangle. Refrigerate for 15 minutes.

Chocolate-Dipped Brandy Snaps

½ cup butter
½ cup sugar
⅓ cup dark corn syrup
½ teaspoon cinnamon
¼ teaspoon ginger
   1 cup all-purpose flour
   2 teaspoons brandy
   1 cup (6-ounce package) NESTLÉ®
      Toll House® Semi-Sweet
      Chocolate Morsels
   1 tablespoon vegetable shortening
⅓ cup finely chopped nuts

Chocolate-Dipped Brandy Snaps

Preheat oven to 300°F. In heavy saucepan, combine butter, sugar, corn syrup, cinnamon and ginger; cook over medium heat, stirring constantly, until melted and smooth. Remove from heat; stir in flour and brandy. Drop by rounded teaspoonfuls onto ungreased cookie sheets about 3 inches apart. (Do *not* bake more than 6 cookies at one time.)

Bake at 300°F for 10 to 12 minutes. Remove from oven; let stand a few seconds. Remove cookies from cookie sheets and immediately roll around wooden spoon handle; cool completely. Combine over hot (not boiling) water, Nestlé® Toll House® Semi-Sweet Chocolate Morsels and vegetable shortening; stir until morsels are melted and mixture is smooth. Dip Brandy Snap halfway in melted chocolate. Sprinkle with nuts; set on waxed paper-lined cookie sheets. Chill until set. Store in airtight container in refrigerator.

Makes about 3 dozen 2¹/₂-inch snaps

Chocolate Chip Cordials

Cookies

    1 package DUNCAN HINES®
        Chocolate Chip Cookie Mix
    1 egg
    2 teaspoons water
    1 cup chopped pecans
    ¹/₄ cup chopped red candied cherries
    ¹/₄ cup flaked coconut
        Pecan or cherry halves for garnish

Chocolate Glaze

    1 square (1 ounce) semi-sweet
        chocolate
  1¹/₂ tablespoons butter or margarine

1. Preheat oven to 375°F. Place 1³/₄-inch paper liners in 28 mini muffin cups.

2. For cookies, combine cookie mix, buttery flavor packet from Mix, egg and water in large bowl. Stir until thoroughly blended. Stir in chopped pecans, chopped cherries and coconut. Fill cups with cookie dough. Top with pecan or cherry halves. Bake at 375°F for 13 to 15 minutes or until light golden brown. Cool completely.

3. For chocolate glaze, melt chocolate and butter in small bowl over hot water. Stir until smooth. Drizzle over cordials. Refrigerate until chocolate is firm. Store in airtight container.

Makes 28 cordials

Chocolate Chip Cordials

Chocolate-Dipped Almond Horns

1½ cups powdered sugar
1 cup butter or margarine, softened
2 egg yolks
1½ teaspoons vanilla
2 cups all-purpose flour
½ cup ground almonds
1 teaspoon cream of tartar
1 teaspoon baking soda
1 cup semisweet chocolate chips, melted
Powdered sugar

Preheat oven to 325°F. In large mixer bowl, combine powdered sugar and butter. Beat at medium speed, scraping bowl often, until creamy, 1 to 2 minutes. Add egg yolks and vanilla; continue beating until well mixed, 1 to 2 minutes. Reduce speed to low. Add flour, almonds, cream of tartar and baking soda. Continue beating, scraping bowl often, until well mixed, 1 to 2 minutes. Shape into 1-inch balls. Roll balls into 2-inch ropes; shape into crescents. Place 2 inches apart on cookie sheets. Flatten slightly with glass bottom covered in waxed paper. Bake 8 to 10 minutes or until set. (Cookies will not brown.) Cool completely. Dip half of each cookie into chocolate; sprinkle remaining half with powdered sugar. Refrigerate until set.

Makes about 3 dozen cookies

Mint Chocolate Pinwheels

⅔ cup butter or margarine, softened
1 cup sugar
1 large egg
1 teaspoon vanilla
1¼ cups all-purpose flour
1 teaspoon baking powder
½ teaspoon salt
1 cup uncooked quick-cooking oats
1 cup mint chocolate chips

Beat butter and sugar in large bowl until light and fluffy. Add egg and vanilla; beat well. Gradually add combined flour, baking powder and salt. Beat until well blended. Stir in oats.

Place mint chocolate chips in 1 cup glass measuring cup. Heat in microwave oven at HIGH (100% power) about 2 minutes or until melted, stirring after 1½ minutes of cooking.

Divide cookie dough in half. Add melted chocolate to one half; mix well. Roll out each half of dough between two sheets of waxed paper into 15×10-inch rectangle. Remove waxed paper from top of each rectangle. Place chocolate dough over plain dough; remove waxed paper from bottom of chocolate dough. Using bottom sheet of waxed paper as a guide and starting at long side, tightly roll up dough jelly-roll fashion, removing waxed paper while rolling. Wrap roll in plastic wrap; refrigerate at least 2 hours or overnight.

Preheat oven to 350°F. Unwrap log. With large, sharp knife, cut dough into ¼-inch slices. Place 3 inches apart on greased cookie sheets. Bake 10 to 12 minutes or until set. Remove cookies to wire racks; cool completely.

Makes about 3 dozen cookies

Chocolate-Dipped Almond Horns

Left to right: Double-Dipped Hazelnut Crisps, Pecan Florentines

Double-Dipped Hazelnut Crisps

³/₄ cup semisweet chocolate chips
1¹/₄ cups all-purpose flour
³/₄ cup powdered sugar
²/₃ cup whole hazelnuts, toasted,
    hulled and pulverized*
¹/₄ teaspoon instant espresso powder
    Dash salt
¹/₂ cup butter or margarine, softened
2 teaspoons vanilla
4 squares (1 ounce each) bittersweet
    or semisweet chocolate
4 ounces white chocolate
2 teaspoons shortening, divided

Preheat oven to 350°F. Lightly grease cookie sheets or line with parchment paper. Melt chocolate chips in top of double boiler over hot, not boiling, water. Remove from heat; cool. Blend flour, sugar, hazelnuts, espresso powder and salt in large bowl. Blend in butter, melted chocolate and vanilla until dough is stiff but smooth. (If dough is too soft to handle, cover and refrigerate until firm.)

Roll out dough, ¹/₄ at a time, to ¹/₈-inch thickness on lightly floured surface. Cut out with 2-inch scalloped round cutters. Place 2 inches apart on prepared cookie sheets. Bake 8 minutes or until not quite firm. (Cookies should not brown. They will puff up during baking and then fall again.) Remove to wire racks to cool.

Place bittersweet and white chocolates into separate small bowls. Add 1 teaspoon shortening to each bowl. Place bowls over hot water; stir until chocolate is melted and smooth. Dip cookies, 1 at a time, halfway into bittersweet chocolate. Place on waxed paper; refrigerate until chocolate is set. Dip other halves of cookies into white chocolate; refrigerate until set. Store cookies in airtight container in cool place. (If cookies are frozen, chocolate may discolor.)

Makes about 4 dozen cookies

*To pulverize hazelnuts, place in food processor or blender. Process until thoroughly ground with a dry, not pasty, texture.

Pecan Florentines

$3/4$ cup pecan halves, pulverized*
$1/2$ cup all-purpose flour
$1/3$ cup packed brown sugar
$1/4$ cup light corn syrup
$1/4$ cup butter or margarine
2 tablespoons milk
$1/3$ cup semisweet chocolate chips

Preheat oven to 350°F. Line cookie sheets with foil; lightly grease foil. Combine pecans and flour in small bowl. Combine sugar, syrup, butter and milk in medium saucepan. Stir over medium heat until mixture comes to a boil. Remove from heat; stir in flour mixture.

Drop batter by teaspoonfuls about 3 inches apart onto prepared cookie sheets. Bake 10 to 12 minutes or until lacy and golden brown (cookies are soft when hot, but become crispy as they cool). Cool completely on foil.

Place chocolate chips in small resealable heavy-duty plastic bag; close securely. Set bag in bowl of hot water until chips are melted, being careful not to let any water into bag. Remove bag from water. Knead bag lightly to check that chips are completely melted. Pat bag dry. With scissors, snip off a small corner from one side of bag. Squeeze melted chocolate over cookies to decorate. Let stand until chocolate is set. Peel cookies off foil.   *Makes about 3 dozen cookies*

*To pulverize pecans, place in food processor or blender. Process until thoroughly ground with a dry, not pasty, texture.

Easter Egg Cookies

1 package DUNCAN HINES®
    Golden Sugar Cookie Mix
1 egg
    Assorted colored decors
    Corn syrup
    Food coloring
    Nonpareils (optional)

1. Preheat oven to 375°F.

2. Combine cookie mix, buttery flavor packet from Mix and egg in large bowl. Stir with wooden spoon until thoroughly blended.

3. Place 1 level *measuring* teaspoonful dough on ungreased cookie sheet about 2 inches apart for each cookie. Flatten dough into egg shape (an oval with one narrow end and one wide end). Decorate half the cookies with assorted decors. Press lightly into cookie dough. Bake at 375°F for 6 to 7 minutes or until cookies are light golden brown around the edges. Cool 1 minute on cookie sheets. Remove to cooling racks. Cool completely.

4. To decorate plain cookies, combine 1 tablespoon corn syrup and 1 or 2 drops food coloring in small bowl for each color. Stir to blend. Paint designs with tinted corn syrup using clean artist paint brushes. Sprinkle painted areas with nonpareils, if desired. Store between layers of waxed paper in airtight container.

Makes about 4 dozen cookies

Easter Egg Cookies

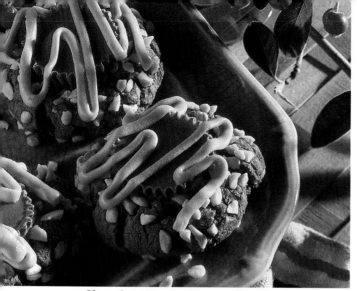
Chocolate Peanut Butter Cup Cookies

Chocolate Peanut Butter Cup Cookies

Cookies

    1 cup semi-sweet chocolate chips
    2 squares (1 ounce each)
        unsweetened baking chocolate
    1 cup sugar
    $^1/_2$ cup BUTTER FLAVOR CRISCO®
    2 eggs
    1 teaspoon salt
    1 teaspoon vanilla
  $1^1/_2$ cups *plus* 2 tablespoons all-
      purpose flour
    $^1/_2$ teaspoon baking soda
    $^3/_4$ cup finely chopped peanuts
    36 miniature peanut butter cups,
        unwrapped

Drizzle

    1 cup peanut butter chips

1. Heat oven to 350°F.

2. For cookies, combine chocolate chips and chocolate squares in microwave-safe measuring cup or bowl. Microwave at 50% (MEDIUM). Stir after 2 minutes. Repeat until smooth (or melt on rangetop in small saucepan on very low heat). Cool slightly.

3. Combine sugar and Butter Flavor Crisco® in large bowl. Beat at medium speed of electric mixer until blended and crumbly. Beat in eggs, 1 at a time, then salt and vanilla. Reduce speed to low. Add chocolate slowly. Mix until well blended. Stir in flour and baking soda with spoon until well blended. Shape dough into $1^1/_4$-inch balls. Roll in nuts. Place 2 inches apart on ungreased cookie sheet.

4. Bake at 350°F for 8 to 10 minutes or until set. Press peanut butter cup into center of each cookie immediately. Press cookie against cup. Cool 2 minutes on cookie sheet before removing to cooling rack. Cool completely.

5. For drizzle, place peanut butter chips in heavy resealable sandwich bag. Seal. Microwave at 50% (MEDIUM). Knead bag after 1 minute. Repeat until smooth (or melt by placing bag in hot water). Snip pinpoint hole in corner of bag. Squeeze out and drizzle over cookies.

Makes about 3 dozen cookies

Almond Hearts

    1 package DUNCAN HINES®
        Golden Sugar Cookie Mix
    $^3/_4$ cup ground almonds
    2 egg yolks
    1 tablespoon water
    14 ounces (6 cubes) vanilla flavored
        candy coating
        Pink candy coating, for garnish

1. Preheat oven to 375°F.

2. Combine cookie mix, buttery flavor packet from Mix, ground almonds, egg yolks and water in large bowl. Stir until thoroughly blended.

3. Divide dough in half. Roll half the dough between 2 sheets of waxed paper into 11-inch circle. Slide onto flat surface. Refrigerate about 15 minutes. Repeat with remaining dough. Loosen top sheet of waxed paper from dough. Turn over and remove second sheet of waxed paper. Cut dough with 2½-inch heart cookie cutter. Place cut-outs 2 inches apart on ungreased cookie sheets. (Roll leftover cookie dough to ⅛-inch thickness between sheets of waxed paper. Chill before cutting.) Repeat with remaining dough circle. Bake at 375°F for 6 to 8 minutes or until light golden brown. Cool 1 minute on cookie sheets. Remove to cooling racks. Cool completely.

4. Place vanilla candy coating in 1-quart saucepan on low heat; stir until melted and smooth. Dip half of one heart cookie into candy coating. Allow excess to drip back into pan. Place cookie on waxed paper. Repeat with remaining cookies. Place pink candy coating in small saucepan on low heat. Stir until melted and smooth. Pour into pastry bag fitted with small writing tip. Decorate tops of cookies as desired. Allow candy coating to set before storing between layers of waxed paper in airtight container.

Makes 4 to 5 dozen cookies

Almond Hearts

Surprise Cookies

2 squares (1 ounce each) semisweet
   baking chocolate, coarsely
   chopped
½ cup butter or margarine, softened
½ cup sugar
1 large egg
1 teaspoon vanilla
1¼ cups all-purpose flour
½ teaspoon baking powder
¼ teaspoon salt
   Fillings as desired: maraschino
      cherries (well drained) or
      candied cherries; chocolate mint
      candies, broken in half; white
      baking bar, cut into chunks;
      thick milk chocolate candy bar,
      cut into chunks; semi-sweet
      chocolate chunks; raspberry jam
      or apricot preserves

Preheat oven to 350°F. Grease mini-muffin cups; set aside. Melt chocolate in small, heavy saucepan over low heat, stirring constantly; set aside. Beat butter and sugar in large bowl until light and fluffy. Beat in egg and vanilla. Gradually beat in chocolate. Gradually add combined flour, baking powder and salt. Drop dough by level teaspoonfuls into prepared muffin cups. Smooth dough down and form small indentation with back of teaspoon. Fill as desired with assorted filling ingredients. Top with heaping teaspoonful of dough, smoothing top lightly with back of spoon.

Bake 15 to 17 minutes or until center of cookie is set. Remove pan to wire rack; cool completely before removing cookies from pan. *Makes about 1 dozen cookies*

HOMEMADE HOLIDAY

Spicy Gingerbread Cookies

Cookies

- ¹/₂ **cup firmly packed brown sugar**
- ³/₄ **cup (1¹/₄ sticks) butter or margarine, softened**
- ²/₃ **cup light molasses**
- 1 **egg**
- 1¹/₂ **teaspoons grated lemon peel**
- 2¹/₂ **cups all-purpose flour**
- 1¹/₄ **teaspoons ground cinnamon**
- 1 **teaspoon vanilla**
- 1 **teaspoon ground allspice**
- ¹/₂ **teaspoon ground ginger**
- ¹/₂ **teaspoon baking soda**
- ¹/₂ **teaspoon salt**
- ¹/₄ **teaspoon baking powder**

Frosting

- 4 **cups powdered sugar**
- ¹/₂ **cup butter, softened**
- 4 **tablespoons milk**
- 2 **teaspoons vanilla**
-   **Food coloring**

For cookies, in large mixer bowl combine brown sugar, ³/₄ cup butter, molasses, egg and lemon peel. Beat at medium speed, scraping bowl often, until smooth and creamy, 1 to 2 minutes. Add all remaining cookie ingredients. Reduce speed to low. Continue beating, scraping bowl often, until well mixed, 1 to 2 minutes. Cover; refrigerate at least 2 hours.

Preheat oven to 350°F. On well floured surface, roll out dough, half at a time (keeping remaining dough refrigerated), to ¹/₄-inch thickness. Cut with 3- to 4-inch cookie cutters. Place 1 inch apart on greased cookie sheets. Bake 6 to 8 minutes or until no indentation remains when touched. Remove immediately. Cool completely.

For frosting, in small mixer bowl combine powdered sugar, ¹/₂ cup butter, milk and vanilla. Beat at low speed, scraping bowl often, until fluffy, 1 to 2 minutes. If desired, color frosting with food coloring. Decorate cookies with frosting.   *Makes about 4 dozen cookies*

Spicy Gingerbread Cookies, Cocoa Cream Cheese Cookies (page 182)

Cocoa Cream Cheese Cookies

1¼ cups sugar
1 cup butter, softened
2 (3-ounce) packages cream cheese, softened
1 (1-ounce) square unsweetened chocolate, melted
2 teaspoons vanilla
¾ teaspoon instant espresso dissolved in 1 tablespoon water
2 cups all-purpose flour
¼ cup unsweetened cocoa
  Semisweet chocolate chips, melted (optional)
  Vanilla-flavored candy coating, melted (optional)
  Finely chopped almonds, pecans or walnuts (optional)
  Candy coated milk chocolate pieces (optional)
  Flaked coconut (optional)
  Fruit preserves (optional)
  Colored sugars and multi-colored decorator candies for toppings (optional)

Preheat oven to 350°F. In large mixer bowl, combine sugar, butter, cream cheese, chocolate, vanilla and diluted espresso. Beat at medium speed, scraping bowl often, until mixture is light and fluffy, 2 to 3 minutes. Continue beating, gradually adding flour and cocoa, until well mixed, 2 to 3 minutes. With lightly floured hands, shape rounded teaspoonfuls of dough into 1-inch balls. Place 1 inch apart on ungreased cookie sheets. Shape as desired. Bake 7 to 9 minutes or until set. Cool completely. Decorate cookies with suggested coatings and toppings, as desired. *Makes 4 to 5 dozen cookies*

Sugar Cookie Wreaths

1 package DUNCAN HINES® Golden Sugar Cookie Mix
1 egg
  Green food coloring
  Candied or maraschino cherry pieces

1. Preheat oven to 375°F.

2. Combine cookie mix, buttery flavor packet from Mix and egg in large bowl. Stir until thoroughly blended.

3. Tint dough with green food coloring. Stir until desired color. Form into balls the size of miniature marshmallows. For each wreath, arrange 9 or 10 balls with sides touching into a ring. Place wreaths 2 inches apart on ungreased cookie sheets. Flatten slightly with fingers. Place small piece of candied cherry on each ball.

4. Bake at 375°F for 5 to 7 minutes or until set but not browned. Cool 1 minute on cookie sheets. Remove to cooling racks. Cool completely. Store in airtight container.
Makes about 2 dozen cookies

Note: If using maraschino cherries, drain well after chopping into pieces.

Sugar Cookie Wreaths

Happy Pumpkin Faces

Happy Pumpkin Faces

2 cups packed brown sugar
1/2 cup butter or margarine, softened
1/2 cup shortening
2 eggs
2 cups all-purpose flour
1 teaspoon baking soda
1/4 teaspoon salt
1/2 teaspoon ground cinnamon
2 cups uncooked quick oats
1 cup "M&M's"® Plain Chocolate
    Candies
1 can (16 ounces) frosting, tinted
    with food coloring if desired
    "M&M's"® Brand HOLIDAYS®
    Chocolate Candies in Harvest
    Colors to decorate

Preheat oven to 350°F. In large bowl, beat sugar, butter and shortening until light and fluffy. Add eggs, 1 at a time, beating well after each addition. Stir in flour, baking soda, salt and cinnamon; fold in oats and "M&M's"® Plain Chocolate Candies.

On cookie sheets, place heaping tablespoonfuls of dough about 3 inches apart. Shape dough into ovals. Add a bit of dough for stems. Bake 12 to 14 minutes or until golden. Remove cookies to wire racks to cool. Spread with frosting; decorate with "M&M's"®.

Makes about 3 1/2 dozen cookies

Chocolate Gingerbread Cookies

Chocolate Gingerbread Cookies

Cookies

    2¼ **cups all-purpose flour**
    ¾ **cup NESTLÉ® Cocoa**
    1 **teaspoon baking soda**
    1 **teaspoon ginger**
    ½ **teaspoon baking powder**
    ½ **teaspoon cinnamon**
    ½ **teaspoon cloves**
    ¼ **teaspoon salt**
    ½ **cup (1 stick) butter or margarine,**
      softened
    1 **cup granulated sugar**
    1 **egg**
    ½ **cup molasses**

Glaze

    1 **cup confectioners' sugar**
    2 **to 3 tablespoons milk**
    1 **foil-wrapped bar (2 ounces)**
      NESTLÉ® Semi-Sweet Chocolate
      Baking Bar, broken

Cookies: In small bowl, combine flour, Nestlé® Cocoa, baking soda, ginger, baking powder, cinnamon, cloves and salt; set aside.

In large mixer bowl, beat butter and granulated sugar until creamy. Blend in egg and molasses. Gradually beat in flour mixture. Divide dough into four equal pieces; wrap in plastic wrap. Refrigerate at least 2 hours until firm.

Preheat oven to 350°F. Lightly grease two large cookie sheets. On floured board, roll dough, 1 piece at a time, to ⅛-inch thickness. Cut with 4½-inch cookie cutters. With metal spatula, transfer cutouts to prepared cookie sheets. Repeat with remaining dough.

Bake 8 to 10 minutes until set. Let stand 2 minutes. Remove from cookie sheets; cool completely.

Glaze: In small bowl, combine confectioners' sugar and 2 tablespoons milk; stir until smooth. (Add additional 1 tablespoon milk if necessary for desired consistency.) Set aside.

In small saucepan over low heat, melt Nestlé® Semi-Sweet Chocolate Baking Bar. Pipe cookies with Glaze or decorate with melted chocolate baking bar.

Makes about 2 dozen cookies

Linzer Hearts

    1 **package DUNCAN HINES®**
      Golden Sugar Cookie Mix
    ½ **cup all-purpose flour**
    ½ **cup finely ground almonds**
    1 **egg**
    1 **tablespoon water**
    3 **tablespoons confectioners sugar**
    ½ **cup *plus* 1 tablespoon seedless red**
      raspberry jam, warmed

Linzer Hearts

1. Preheat oven to 375°F.

2. Combine cookie mix, buttery flavor packet from Mix, flour, almonds, egg and water in large bowl. Stir until blended. Roll dough to 1/8-inch thickness on lightly floured board. Cut out 3-inch hearts with floured cookie cutter. Cut out centers of half the hearts with smaller heart cookie cutter. Reroll dough as needed. Place 2 inches apart on ungreased cookie sheets. Bake whole hearts at 375°F for 8 to 9 minutes and cut-out hearts for 6 to 7 minutes or until edges are lightly browned. Cool 1 minute on cookie sheets. Remove to cooling racks. Cool completely.

3. To assemble, dust cut-out hearts with sifted confectioners sugar. Spread warm jam over whole hearts almost to edges; top with cut-out hearts. Press together to make sandwiches. Fill center with 1/4 teaspoon jam. Store between layers of waxed paper in airtight container.

Makes about 22 (3-inch) sandwich cookies

Spooky Ghost Cookies

1 recipe Butter Cookie dough (see page 212)
Fluffy White Frosting (recipe follows)
1/2 cup semisweet chocolate chips (about 60 chips)

1. Preheat oven to 350°F. Roll dough on floured surface to 1/4-inch thickness. Using photo as guide, cut out 2 1/2-inch ghost-shaped pattern from clean cardboard; place on dough. Trace pattern with sharp knife to cut out ghosts.

2. Bake on ungreased cookie sheets 10 to 12 minutes until edges begin to brown. Remove to wire racks to cool.

3. Spread Fluffy White Frosting over cookies. Position 2 chocolate chips on each cookie for eyes.

Makes about 2 1/2 dozen cookies

Fluffy White Frosting

1 container (16 ounces) vanilla frosting
3/4 cup marshmallow creme

Combine all ingredients; mix well.

Makes about 2 cups

Spooky Ghost Cookies

Versatile Cut-Out Cookies

3½ cups unsifted flour
  1 tablespoon baking powder
 ½ teaspoon salt
  1 (14-ounce) can EAGLE® Brand
    Sweetened Condensed Milk
    (NOT evaporated milk)
 ¾ cup margarine or butter, softened
  2 eggs
  1 tablespoon vanilla extract *or*
    2 teaspoons almond or lemon
    extract

Combine flour, baking powder and salt. In large mixer bowl, beat sweetened condensed milk, margarine, eggs and vanilla until well blended. Add dry ingredients; mix well. Cover; chill 2 hours.

Preheat oven to 350°F. On floured surface, knead dough to form a smooth ball. Divide into thirds. On well-floured surface, roll out each portion to ⅛-inch thickness. Cut with floured cookie cutter. Reroll as necessary to use all dough. Place 1 inch apart on greased

Versatile Cut-Out Cookies

cookie sheets. Bake 7 to 9 minutes or until lightly browned around edges (do not overbake). Cool. Frost and decorate as desired. Store loosely covered at room temperature.

Makes about 6 1/2 dozen cookies

Chocolate Cookies: Decrease flour to 3 cups. Add 1/2 cup HERSHEY®S Cocoa to dry ingredients. Chill and roll dough as directed. Makes about 6 1/2 dozen cookies.

Chocolate Snow Balls: Prepare dough as directed for Chocolate Cookies, increasing eggs to 3; add 1 cup finely chopped nuts. Chill. Shape into 1-inch balls. Roll in confectioners' sugar. Bake 8 to 10 minutes. Cool. Roll again in confectioners' sugar. Makes about 7 1/2 dozen cookies.

Sandwich Cookies: Prepare, chill and roll dough as directed. Use 2 1/2-inch floured cookie cutter. Bake as directed. Sandwich 2 cookies together with ready-to-spread frosting. Sprinkle tops with confectioners' sugar if desired. Makes about 3 dozen cookies.

Cookie Pecan Critters: Prepare and chill dough as directed. For each critter, arrange 3 pecan halves together on ungreased cookie sheets. Shape 1 teaspoonful dough into 1-inch ball. Press firmly onto center of arranged pecans. Repeat until all dough is used. Bake 12 to 14 minutes. Spread tops with Chocolate Frosting (recipe follows). Makes about 6 1/2 dozen cookies.

Chocolate Frosting: In small saucepan, melt 1/4 cup margarine or butter with 1/4 cup water. Stir in 1/2 cup Hershey®s Cocoa. Remove saucepan from heat; beat in 2 cups confectioners' sugar and 1 teaspoon vanilla until smooth. Stir in additional water for a thinner consistency if desired. Makes about 1 cup.

Mincemeat Peek-a-Boo Cookies: Prepare, chill and roll dough as directed. Use 3-inch floured round cookie cutter. Using sharp knife, cut "X" in centers of half the rounds. Place 1 teaspoon mincemeat in centers of remaining rounds. Top with cut rounds. Bake 8 to 10 minutes. Cool. Sprinkle with confectioners' sugar if desired. Makes about 4 dozen cookies.

Stained Glass Cookies: Prepare, chill and roll dough as directed. Use 3-inch floured cookie cutter to cut into desired shapes. Cut out holes for "stained glass" in each cookie with small cutters or knife. Place on aluminum foil-lined cookie sheets. Fill holes with crushed hard candies. (If planning to hang cookies, make hole in each cookie in dough near edge with straw.) Bake 6 to 8 minutes or until candy has melted. Cool 10 minutes; remove from foil. Makes about 8 dozen cookies.

Cinnamon Pinwheel Cookies: Decrease baking powder to 2 teaspoons. Prepare and chill dough as directed. Divide into quarters. Roll each quarter of dough into a 16×8-inch rectangle. Brush with melted margarine or butter. Top each with 2 tablespoons sugar combined with 1/2 teaspoon ground cinnamon. Roll up tightly, beginning with 8-inch side. Wrap tightly; freeze until firm, about 20 minutes. Unwrap; cut into 1/4-inch slices. Place on ungreased cookie sheets. Bake 12 to 14 minutes or until lightly browned. Makes about 6 1/2 dozen cookies.

Peanut Butter Reindeer

Cookies

   1 package DUNCAN HINES®
      Peanut Butter Cookie Mix
   1 egg
   2 teaspoons all-purpose flour

Assorted Decorations

   Semi-sweet mini chocolate chips
   Vanilla milk chips
   Candy-coated semi-sweet chocolate
      chips
   Colored sprinkles

1. For cookies, combine cookie mix, peanut butter packet from Mix and egg in large bowl. Stir until thoroughly blended. Form dough into ball. Place flour in jumbo (15×13-inch) resealable plastic bag. Place ball of dough in bag. Shake to coat with flour. Place dough in center of bag (do not seal). Roll dough with rolling pin out to edges of bag. Slide bag onto cookie sheet. Chill in refrigerator at least 1 hour.

2. Preheat oven to 375°F.

3. Use scissors to cut bag down center and across ends. Turn plastic back to uncover dough. Dip reindeer cookie cutter in flour. Cut dough with reindeer cookie cutter. Dip cookie cutter in flour after each cut. Transfer cutout cookies using floured pancake turner to ungreased cookie sheets. Reroll dough by folding cut plastic bag back over dough scraps. Decorate as desired making eyes, mouth, nose and tail with assorted decorations. Bake at 375°F for 5 to 7 minutes or until set but not browned. Cool 2 minutes on cookie sheets. Remove to cooling racks. Cool completely. Store between layers of waxed paper in airtight container.

Makes about 2 dozen cookies

Norwegian Molasses Cookies

   2¼ cups all-purpose flour
   2 teaspoons baking soda
   1 cup firmly packed light brown
      sugar
   ¾ cup FLEISCHMANN'S®
      Margarine, softened
   ¼ cup EGG BEATERS® 99% Egg
      Product
   ¼ cup BRER RABBIT® Light or Dark
      Molasses
   ¼ cup granulated sugar
      Water
      Confectioner's Sugar Glaze
      (recipe follows)
      Colored sprinkles, optional

In small bowl, combine flour and baking soda; set aside.

In medium bowl, with electric mixer on medium speed, cream brown sugar and margarine. Add egg product and molasses, beating until smooth. Stir in flour mixture. Cover; chill dough 1 hour.

Preheat oven to 350°F. Shape dough into 48 (1¼-inch) balls; roll in granulated sugar. Place on greased and floured cookie sheets about 2 inches apart. Lightly sprinkle dough with water. Bake at 350°F for 18 to 20 minutes or until done. Remove from sheets; cool on wire racks. Decorate with Confectioner's Sugar Glaze and colored sprinkles, if desired.   *Makes 4 dozen cookies*

Confectioner's Sugar Glaze: Combine 1 cup confectioner's sugar and 5 to 6 teaspoons skim milk.

Prep Time: 20 minutes
Total Time: 2 hours

Peanut Butter Reindeer

Peppermint Refrigerator Slices

Peppermint Refrigerator Slices

**3 packages DUNCAN HINES®
    Golden Sugar Cookie Mix,
    divided
3 eggs, divided
3 to 4 drops red food coloring
³/₄ teaspoon peppermint extract,
    divided
3 to 4 drops green food coloring**

1. For pink cookie dough, combine
1 buttery flavor packet from Mix, 1 egg,
red food coloring and ¹/₄ teaspoon
peppermint extract in large bowl. Stir
until evenly tinted. Add 1 cookie mix
and stir until thoroughly blended. Set
aside.

2. For green cookie dough, combine
1 buttery flavor packet from Mix, 1 egg,
green food coloring and ¹/₄ teaspoon
peppermint extract in large bowl. Stir
until evenly tinted. Add 1 cookie mix
and stir until thoroughly blended. Set
aside.

3. For plain cookie dough, combine
remaining cookie mix, buttery flavor
packet from Mix, egg and ¹/₄ teaspoon
peppermint extract in large bowl. Stir
until thoroughly blended.

4. To assemble, divide each batch of
cookie dough into 4 equal portions.
Shape each portion into 12-inch-long
roll on waxed paper. Lay 1 pink roll
beside 1 green roll; press together
slightly. Place 1 plain roll on top. Press
rolls together to form 1 tri-colored roll;
wrap in waxed paper or plastic wrap.
Repeat with remaining rolls to form 3
more tri-colored rolls; wrap separately
in waxed paper or plastic wrap.
Refrigerate rolls for several hours or
overnight.

5. Preheat oven to 375°F.

6. Cut chilled rolls into ¹/₄-inch-thick
slices. Place 2 inches apart on
ungreased cookie sheets. Bake at 375°F
for 7 to 8 minutes or until set but not
browned. Cool 1 minute on cookie
sheets. Remove to cooling racks. Cool
completely. Store in airtight containers.

Makes about 15 dozen small cookies

Yule Tree Namesakes

**1 recipe Butter Cookie dough (see
    page 212)
1 recipe Cookie Glaze (see page 208)
    Green food color
    Powdered sugar
    Assorted candies
3 packages (12 ounces each)
    semisweet chocolate chips,
    melted
1 cup flaked coconut, tinted green***

1. Preheat oven to 350°F. Roll dough on
floured surface to ¹/₈-inch thickness. Cut
out cookies using 3- to 4-inch tree-shaped
cookie cutter. Place 2 inches apart on
ungreased cookie sheets.

2. Bake 12 to 14 minutes until edges
begin to brown. Remove to wire racks;
cool completely.

Yule Tree Namesakes

3. Reserve ¹/₃ cup Cookie Glaze; color remaining glaze green with food color. Place cookies on wire rack over waxed paper-lined cookie sheet. Spoon green glaze over cookies.

4. Add 1 to 2 tablespoons powdered sugar to reserved Cookie Glaze. Spoon into pastry bag fitted with small writing tip. Pipe names onto trees as shown in photo. Decorate with assorted candies as shown. Let stand until glaze is set.

5. Spoon melted chocolate into 1³/₄-inch baking cups, filling evenly. Let stand until chocolate is very thick and partially set. Place trees upright in chocolate.

6. Sprinkle tinted coconut over chocolate.   *Makes 24 place cards*

*Tinting coconut: Dilute a few drops of food color with ¹/₂ teaspoon water in a large plastic bag. Add 1 to 1¹/₃ cups flaked coconut. Close bag and shake well until the coconut is evenly coated. If a deeper color is desired, add more diluted food color and shake again.

Jammy Fantasia

Crust

  1¹/₂ **cups all-purpose flour**
  1¹/₂ **cups quick oats (not instant)**
  ¹/₂ **cup firmly packed brown sugar**
  ¹/₂ **teaspoon baking soda**
  ³/₄ **cup BUTTER FLAVOR CRISCO®**
  2 **tablespoons water**
  1 **cup apricot or raspberry preserves**

Drizzle

  ³/₄ **cup confectioners sugar**
  1 **tablespoon** *plus* ¹/₂ **teaspoon milk**
  ¹/₄ **teaspoon vanilla**

1. Preheat oven to 375°F.

2. For crust, combine flour, oats, brown sugar and baking soda. Cut in Butter Flavor Crisco® until coarse crumbs form. Reserve 1³/₄ cups of mixture. Set aside.

3. Drizzle water over remaining crumbs. Toss to mix. Press firmly into ungreased 13×9-inch baking pan. Spread preserves over crust. Sprinkle with reserved crumbs. Pat gently.

4. Bake at 375°F for 25 to 30 minutes. Cool in pan.

5. For drizzle, combine confectioners sugar, milk and vanilla. Stir well. Drizzle over tops of cookies. Cut into triangles or 2×1¹/₂-inch bars.

Makes about 36 bars

Prep Time: 25 minutes
Bake Time: 25 to 30 minutes

Jammy Fantasia

Cherry Chewbilees

Crust

1 cup walnut pieces, divided
1¼ cups all-purpose flour
½ cup firmly packed brown sugar
½ cup BUTTER FLAVOR CRISCO®
½ cup flake coconut

Filling

2 (8-ounce) packages cream cheese, softened
⅔ cup granulated sugar
2 eggs
2 teaspoons vanilla
1 (21-ounce) can cherry pie filling

1. Preheat oven to 350°F. Grease 13×9-inch pan with Butter Flavor Crisco®. Set aside.

2. Chop ½ cup nuts coarsely for topping. Set aside. Chop remaining ½ cup nuts finely.

3. For crust, combine flour and brown sugar. Cut in Butter Flavor Crisco® until fine crumbs form. Add ½ cup finely chopped nuts and coconut. Mix well. Remove ½ cup. Set aside. Press remaining crumbs in bottom of prepared pan.

4. Bake at 350°F for 12 to 15 minutes until edges are lightly browned.

5. For filling, beat cream cheese, granulated sugar, eggs and vanilla in small bowl at medium speed of electric mixer until smooth. Spread over hot baked crust. Return to oven. Bake 15 minutes longer or until set. Spread cherry pie filling over cheese layer. Combine reserved coarsely chopped nuts and reserved crumbs. Sprinkle evenly over cherry pie filling. Return to oven. Bake 15 minutes longer. Chill. Refrigerate several hours. Cut into 2×1½-inch bars.   *Makes about 36 bars*

Cherry Chewbilee

Holiday Almond Wreaths

¾ cup FLEISCHMANN'S® Margarine, softened
½ cup sugar
¼ cup EGG BEATERS® Cholesterol-Free 99% Egg Product
1 teaspoon almond extract
2 cups all-purpose flour
½ cup ground PLANTERS® Almonds
Green and red glacé cherries, optional

Preheat oven to 400°F. In medium bowl, using electric mixer at medium speed, cream margarine and sugar. Add egg product and almond extract. Stir in flour and ground almonds. Using pastry bag with ½-inch star tip, pipe dough into 1-inch wreaths 2 inches apart on ungreased cookie sheets. Decorate wreaths with green and red glacé cherries if desired. Bake for 10 to 12 minutes or until golden brown. Cool on wire racks.

Makes about 3 dozen cookies

Brownie Cookies-on-a-Stick

About twelve 10- to 12-inch
  wooden skewers
2 cups all-purpose flour
½ cup NESTLÉ® Cocoa
¾ teaspoon baking powder
¾ cup (1½ sticks) butter or
  margarine, softened
1 cup granulated sugar
½ cup firmly packed brown sugar
1 egg
2 teaspoons vanilla extract
1 cup (½ of 12-ounce package)
  NESTLÉ® Toll House® Semi-
  Sweet Chocolate Mini Morsels
2 foil-wrapped bars (4 ounces)
  NESTLÉ® Premier White®
  Baking Bars, melted

In small bowl, combine flour, Nestlé®
Cocoa and baking powder; set aside. In
large mixer bowl, beat butter, granulated
sugar and brown sugar until creamy.
Beat in egg and vanilla extract. Gradually
beat in flour mixture, working last bit in
with wooden spoon. Stir in Nestlé® Toll
House® Semi-Sweet Chocolate Mini
Morsels. Divide dough in half; shape
into balls. Flatten; wrap with plastic
wrap. Refrigerate about 1½ hours until
firm.

Preheat oven to 350°F. Between two
sheets of waxed paper, roll dough to
¼-inch thickness. Peel off waxed paper.
Using 3- to 4-inch cookie cutters, cut
two matching shapes to make each
finished cookie. Place cutouts on cookie
sheets; refrigerate 10 minutes. Using
metal spatula, transfer one cookie of
each shape to greased cookie sheets.
Place one skewer on each cookie, to
within ¼-inch of top. Using metal
spatula, place matching cookie over
skewer; press gently over skewer.

Brownie Cookies-on-a-Stick

Bake 11 to 13 minutes until set. Let
stand 5 minutes. Remove from cookie
sheets; cool completely. Decorate with
melted Nestlé® Premier White® Baking
Bars.   *Makes about 1 dozen cookies*

"Buttery" Drop Cookies

½ cup BUTTER FLAVOR CRISCO®
¾ cup sugar
1 tablespoon milk
1 egg
½ teaspoon vanilla
1¼ cups all-purpose flour
¼ teaspoon salt
¼ teaspoon baking powder
¼ cup BUTTER FLAVOR CRISCO®, melted

1. Preheat oven to 375°F. Grease cookie sheets with Butter Flavor Crisco®. Set aside.

2. Cream ½ cup Butter Flavor Crisco®, sugar and milk in medium bowl at medium speed of electric mixer until well blended. Beat in egg and vanilla.

3. Combine flour, salt and baking powder. Mix into creamed mixture. Drop by level measuring tablespoonfuls 2 inches apart onto prepared cookie sheets.

4. Bake at 375°F for 7 to 9 minutes. Brush surface of warm cookies with melted Butter Flavor Crisco® for more buttery taste. Remove to cooling rack.   *Makes about 3 dozen cookies*

Prep Time: 20 minutes
Bake Time: 7 to 9 minutes

Creamy Vanilla Frosting*: Combine ½ cup BUTTER FLAVOR CRISCO®, 1 pound (4 cups) confectioners sugar, ⅓ cup milk and 1 teaspoon vanilla in small bowl at low speed of electric mixer for 15 seconds. Scrape bowl. Beat at high speed for 2 minutes, or until smooth and creamy.

* 1 or 2 drops food color can be used to tint part of frosting, if desired.

Frosted "Buttery" Drop: Bake and cool "Buttery" Drop Cookies. Frost cooled cookies as wreaths or ornaments for the holiday season.

Chocolate Dipped: Bake and cool "Buttery" Drop Cookies. Melt 1 cup semi-sweet chocolate chips with 1 teaspoon BUTTER FLAVOR CRISCO® on very low heat or 50% (MEDIUM) in microwave. Stir well. Spoon into glass measuring cup. Dip half of cooled cookie in chocolate. Place on waxed paper until chocolate is firm.

Chocolate Nut: Dip in melted chocolate as above. Sprinkle with finely chopped nuts before chocolate hardens.

Raspberry Coconut: Bake "Buttery" Drop Cookies. Spread ½ to 1 teaspoon raspberry jam on each hot cookie. Sprinkle with flake coconut.

Chocolate Frosting: Melt ⅓ cup BUTTER FLAVOR CRISCO® in 2-quart saucepan. Remove from heat. Add ¾ cup cocoa and ¼ teaspoon salt. Blend at low speed of hand-held electric mixer. Add ½ cup milk and 2 teaspoons vanilla. Mix at low speed. Blend in 1 pound (4 cups) confectioners sugar, 1 cup at a time. Mix until smooth and creamy. Add more sugar to thicken or milk to thin for good spreading consistency.

"Buttery" Drop Cookies

Original Toll House® Chocolate Chip Cookies

2¼ cups all-purpose flour
1 teaspoon baking soda
1 teaspoon salt
1 cup (2 sticks) butter, softened
¾ cup granulated sugar
¾ cup firmly packed brown sugar
2 eggs
1 teaspoon vanilla extract
2 cups (12-ounce package) NESTLÉ®
    Toll House® Semi-Sweet
    Chocolate Morsels
1 cup nuts, chopped

Preheat oven to 375°F. In small bowl, combine flour, baking soda and salt; set aside.

In large mixer bowl, beat butter, granulated sugar and brown sugar until creamy. Add eggs, 1 at a time, beating well after each addition. Blend in vanilla extract. Gradually beat in flour mixture. Stir in Nestlé® Toll House® Semi-Sweet Chocolate Morsels and nuts. Drop by rounded measuring tablespoonfuls onto ungreased cookie sheets.

Bake 9 to 11 minutes until edges are golden brown. Let stand 2 minutes. Remove from cookie sheets; cool.

Makes about 5 dozen cookies

Toll House® Pan Cookies: Preheat oven to 375°F. Prepare dough as directed; spread in greased 15½×10½×1-inch baking pan. Bake 20 to 25 minutes until golden brown. Cool completely. Cut into 2-inch squares. Makes about 3 dozen squares.

Refrigerator Toll House® Cookies: Prepare dough as directed. Divide dough in half; wrap halves separately in waxed paper. Refrigerate 1 hour or until firm. On waxed paper, shape each dough half into 15-inch log; wrap with waxed paper. Refrigerate 30 minutes.*

Preheat oven to 375°F. Cut each log into thirty ½-inch slices. Place on ungreased cookie sheets. Bake 8 to 10 minutes until edges are golden brown. Makes about 5 dozen cookies.

* Dough may be stored up to 1 week in refrigerator or up to 8 weeks in freezer if foil or freezer-wrapped.

Original Toll House® Chocolate Chip Cookies

Santa's Thumbprints

1 cup (2 sticks) margarine, softened
1/2 cup firmly packed brown sugar
1 whole egg *or* egg white
1 teaspoon vanilla
1 1/2 cups QUAKER® Oats (quick or old
    fashioned, uncooked)
1 1/2 cups all-purpose flour
1 cup finely chopped nuts
1/3 cup jelly or preserves

Preheat oven to 350°F. Beat margarine
and sugar until fluffy. Blend in egg and
vanilla. Add combined oats and flour;
mix well. Shape to form l-inch balls; roll
in chopped nuts. Place 2 inches apart
on ungreased cookie sheet. Press center
of each ball with thumb. Fill each
thumbprint with about 1/4 teaspoon
jelly. Bake 12 to 15 minutes or until light
golden brown. Cool completely on wire
rack. Store loosely covered.

Makes about 3 dozen cookies

Glazed Sugar Cookies

Glazed Sugar Cookies

Cookies

1 package DUNCAN HINES®
    Golden Sugar Cookie Mix
1 egg

Glaze

1 cup sifted confectioners sugar
1 to 2 tablespoons water or milk
1/2 teaspoon vanilla extract
    Food coloring (optional)
    Red and green sugar crystals,
      nonpareils or cinnamon candies

1. Preheat oven to 375°F.

2. For cookies, combine cookie mix,
buttery flavor packet from Mix and egg
in large bowl. Stir until thoroughly
blended. Roll dough to 1/8-inch
thickness on lightly floured surface. Cut
dough into desired shapes using floured
cookie cutters. Place cookies 2 inches
apart on ungreased cookie sheets. Bake
at 375°F for 5 to 6 minutes or until
edges are light golden brown. Cool 1
minute on cookie sheets. Remove to
cooling racks. Cool completely.

3. For glaze, combine confectioners
sugar, water and vanilla extract in small
bowl. Beat until smooth. Tint glaze with
food coloring, if desired. Brush glaze on
each cookie with clean pastry brush.
Sprinkle cookies with sugar crystals,
nonpareils or cinnamon candies before
glaze sets. Allow glaze to set before
storing between layers of waxed paper
in airtight container.

Makes 2 1/2 to 3 dozen cookies

Peanut Butter Cut-Out Cookies

1/2 cup butter or margarine
1 cup REESE'S® Peanut Butter Chips
2/3 cup packed light brown sugar
1 egg
3/4 teaspoon vanilla extract
1 1/3 cups all-purpose flour
3/4 teaspoon baking soda
1/2 cup finely chopped pecans
Chocolate Chip Glaze

In medium saucepan, place butter and peanut butter chips; cook over low heat, stirring constantly until melted. Pour into large mixer bowl; add brown sugar, egg and vanilla, beating until well blended. Stir in flour, baking soda and pecans, blending well. Refrigerate 15 to 20 minutes or until firm enough to roll.

Preheat oven to 350°F. Roll a small portion of dough at a time on lightly floured board or between 2 pieces of waxed paper to 1/4-inch thickness. (Keep remaining dough in refrigerator.) With cookie cutters, cut into desired shapes; place on ungreased cookie sheet. Bake 7 to 8 minutes or until almost set (do not overbake). Cool 1 minute; remove from cookie sheet to wire rack. Cool completely. Drizzle Chocolate Chip Glaze onto each cookie; allow to set.

Makes about 3 dozen cookies

Chocolate Chip Glaze: In top of double boiler over hot, not boiling, water melt 1 cup HERSHEY'S Semi-Sweet Chocolate Chips with 1 tablespoon shortening; stir until smooth. Remove from heat; cool slightly, stirring occasionally.

Chocolate Cherry Brownies

1 jar (16 ounces) maraschino cherries
2/3 cup (1 stick *plus* 3 tablespoons) margarine
1 cup (6-ounce package) semi-sweet chocolate pieces, divided
1 cup sugar
1 teaspoon vanilla
2 eggs
1 1/4 cups all-purpose flour
3/4 cup QUAKER® Oats (quick or old fashioned, uncooked)
1 teaspoon baking powder
1/4 teaspoon salt (optional)
1/2 cup chopped nuts (optional)
2 teaspoons vegetable shortening

Preheat oven to 350°F. Lightly grease 13×9-inch baking pan. Drain cherries; reserve 12 and chop remainder. In large saucepan over low heat, melt margarine and 1/2 cup chocolate pieces, stirring until smooth. Remove from heat; cool slightly. Add sugar and vanilla. Beat in eggs, 1 at a time. Add combined flour, oats, baking powder and salt. Stir in chopped cherries and nuts. Spread into prepared pan.

Bake about 25 minutes or until brownie pulls away from sides of pan. Cool completely in pan on wire rack.

Cut reserved cherries in half; place evenly on top of brownies. In small saucepan over low heat, melt remaining 1/2 cup chocolate pieces and vegetable shortening, stirring constantly until smooth.* Drizzle over brownies; cut into about 2 1/2-inch squares. Store tightly covered.

Makes about 2 dozen bars

*Microwave Directions: Place chocolate pieces and shortening in microwavable bowl. Microwave at HIGH (100% power) 1 to 1 1/2 minutes, stirring after 1 minute.

Peanut Butter Cut-Out Cookies

Peanut Butter Sugar Cookies

3 foil-wrapped bars (6-ounce package) NESTLÉ® Premier White® Baking Bars, divided
2¹/₂ cups all-purpose flour
³/₄ teaspoon salt
³/₄ cup (1¹/₂ sticks) butter or margarine, softened
³/₄ cup peanut butter
1 cup sugar
1 egg
1 teaspoon vanilla extract
    Assorted NESTLÉ® Toll House® Morsels

In small saucepan over low heat, melt 1 foil-wrapped bar (2 ounces) Premier White® Baking Bar; set aside. In small bowl, combine flour and salt; set aside.

In large mixer bowl, beat butter, peanut butter and sugar until creamy. Blend in egg and vanilla extract. Beat in melted Premier White® Baking Bar. Gradually beat in flour mixture. Divide dough in half. Shape each half into ball. Wrap with plastic wrap. Refrigerate 3 to 4 hours until firm enough to roll.

Preheat oven to 350°F. Between two sheets of waxed paper, roll each ball to ¹/₈-inch thickness. Peel off top sheets of waxed paper; cut with 2¹/₂- to 3-inch cookie cutters. Slide waxed paper onto ungreased cookie sheets; refrigerate 10 minutes. Transfer cutouts to ungreased cookie sheets. Decorate with assorted Nestlé® Toll House® Morsels.

Bake 10 to 12 minutes until set. Let stand 2 minutes. Remove from cookie sheets; cool completely.

In small saucepan over low heat, melt remaining 2 foil-wrapped bars (4 ounces) Nestlé® Premier White® Baking Bars. Drizzle over cookies.

Makes about 5 dozen cookies

Peanut Butter Sugar Cookies

Snowballs

¹/₂ cup DOMINO® Confectioners 10-X Sugar
¹/₄ teaspoon salt
1 cup butter or margarine, softened
1 teaspoon vanilla extract
2¹/₄ cups all-purpose flour
¹/₂ cup chopped pecans
    Additional DOMINO® Confectioners 10-X Sugar

In large bowl, combine ¹/₂ cup sugar, salt and butter; mix well. Add vanilla. Gradually stir in flour. Work nuts into dough. Cover and chill until firm.

Preheat oven to 400°F. Form dough into 1-inch balls. Place 1 inch apart on ungreased cookie sheets. Bake 8 to 10 minutes or until set, but not brown. Roll in additional sugar immediately. Cool on wire racks. Roll in sugar again. Store in airtight container.

Makes about 5 dozen cookies

Holiday Citrus Logs

1 (12-ounce) package vanilla wafers, crushed (about 3 cups)
1 (8-ounce) package candied cherries, coarsely chopped
1 (8-ounce) package chopped dates (1³/₄ cups)
1 cup chopped pecans or almonds
¹/₄ cup REALEMON® Lemon Juice from Concentrate
2 tablespoons orange-flavored liqueur
1 tablespoon light corn syrup
Additional light corn syrup, heated
Additional finely chopped pecans or sliced almonds, toasted

In large bowl, combine all ingredients except additional corn syrup and finely chopped nuts. Shape into two 10-inch logs. Brush with additional corn syrup; roll in finely chopped nuts. Wrap tightly; refrigerate 3 to 4 days to blend flavors. To serve, cut into ¹/₄-inch slices.
Makes 2 (10-inch) logs

Chocolate Cherry Drops

Fudge Filling
1 cup (6-ounce package) semi-sweet chocolate chips
¹/₂ cup sweetened condensed milk
2 tablespoons maraschino cherry juice

Cookies
1 package DUNCAN HINES® Chocolate Chip Cookie Mix
1 egg
¹/₃ cup chopped maraschino cherries, well drained
42 maraschino cherry halves, well drained, for garnish

Chocolate Cherry Drops

1. Preheat oven to 350°F.

2. For fudge filling, combine chocolate chips, sweetened condensed milk and maraschino cherry juice in small saucepan. Cook on low heat until chocolate chips are melted, stirring until smooth. Set aside.

3. For cookies, combine cookie mix, buttery flavor packet from Mix and egg in large bowl. Stir until thoroughly blended. Stir in chopped maraschino cherries. Drop by rounded teaspoonfuls 2 inches apart onto ungreased cookie sheets. Bake at 350°F for 5 minutes. Remove from oven. Drop 1 rounded teaspoonful fudge filling on top of each partially baked cookie. Top each with maraschino cherry half. Bake 4 to 5 minutes longer or until edges are light golden brown. Cool 2 minutes on cookie sheets. Remove to cooling racks. Cool completely. Store between layers of waxed paper in airtight container.
Makes about 3¹/₂ dozen cookies

Chocolate-Frosted Lebkuchen

4 eggs
1 cup sugar
1½ cups all-purpose flour
1 cup (6 ounces) pulverized
    almonds*
⅓ cup candied lemon peel, finely
    chopped
⅓ cup candied orange peel, finely
    chopped
1½ teaspoons ground cinnamon
1 teaspoon grated lemon peel
½ teaspoon ground cardamom
½ teaspoon ground nutmeg
¼ teaspoon ground cloves
    Bittersweet Glaze (recipe follows)

In large bowl of electric mixer, combine eggs and sugar. Beat at high speed for 10 minutes. In separate bowl, combine flour, almonds, candied lemon and orange peels, cinnamon, lemon peel, cardamom, nutmeg and cloves. Blend in egg mixture, stirring until evenly mixed. Cover; refrigerate 12 hours.

Preheat oven to 350°F. Grease cookie sheets and dust with flour or line with parchment paper. Drop dough by rounded teaspoonfuls 2 inches apart onto prepared cookie sheets.

Bake 8 to 10 minutes or until just barely browned. Do not overbake. Remove to wire racks. While cookies bake, prepare Bittersweet Glaze. Spread over tops of warm cookies using pastry brush. Cool until glaze is set. Store in airtight container. *Makes about 5 dozen cookies*

* To pulverize almonds, place in food processor or blender. Process until thoroughly ground with a dry, not pasty, texture.

Bittersweet Glaze: Melt 3 chopped squares (1 ounce each) bittersweet or semisweet chocolate and 1 tablespoon butter or margarine in small bowl over hot water. Stir until smooth.

Honey-Ginger Bourbon Balls

1 cup gingersnap cookie crumbs
1¼ cups powdered sugar, divided
1 cup finely chopped pecans or
    walnuts
1 square (1 ounce) unsweetened
    chocolate, chopped
1½ tablespoons honey
¼ cup bourbon

Combine crumbs, 1 cup sugar and nuts in large bowl. Combine chocolate and honey in small bowl over hot water; stir until chocolate is melted. Blend in bourbon. Stir bourbon mixture into crumb mixture until well blended. Shape into 1-inch balls. Sprinkle remaining powdered sugar over balls. Refrigerate until firm.
Makes about 4 dozen balls

Note: These improve with aging; store in airtight container in refrigerator. They will keep several weeks, but are best after 2 to 3 days.

Chocolate-Frosted Lebkuchen,
Honey-Ginger Bourbon Balls

Spritz Christmas Trees

Spritz Christmas Trees

$^1/_3$ cup ($3^1/_2$ ounces) almond paste
1 egg
1 package DUNCAN HINES®
    Golden Sugar Cookie Mix
8 drops green food coloring
1 container (16 ounces) DUNCAN
    HINES® Creamy Homestyle
    Vanilla Frosting
    Cinnamon candies, for garnish

1. Preheat oven to 375°F.

2. Combine almond paste and egg in large bowl. Beat at low speed with electric mixer until blended. Add buttery flavor packet from Mix and green food coloring. Beat until smooth and evenly tinted. Add cookie mix. Beat at low speed until thoroughly blended.

3. Fit cookie press with Christmas tree plate; fill with dough. Force dough through press 2 inches apart onto ungreased cookie sheets. Bake at 375°F for 6 to 7 minutes or until set but not browned. Cool 1 minute on cookie sheets. Remove to cooling racks. Cool completely.

4. To decorate, fill resealable plastic bag half full with Vanilla frosting. Do not seal bag. Cut pinpoint hole in bottom corner of bag. Pipe small dot of frosting on tip of 1 cookie tree and top with cinnamon candy. Repeat with remaining cookies. Pipe remaining frosting to form garland on cookie trees. Allow frosting to set before storing between layers of waxed paper in airtight container.

Makes about 5 dozen cookies

Mini Morsel Meringue Wreaths

2 egg whites
$^1/_4$ teaspoon cream of tartar
$^1/_3$ cup sugar
$^1/_2$ cup ($^1/_4$ of 12-ounce package)
    NESTLÉ® Toll House® Semi-
    Sweet Chocolate Mini Morsels
1 (3-ounce) package candied
    cherries, quartered

Preheat oven to 275°F. In small mixer bowl, beat egg whites and cream of tartar until soft peaks form. Gradually add sugar; beat until stiff peaks form. Fold in Nestlé® Toll House® Semi-Sweet Chocolate Mini Morsels. Spoon into pastry bag fitted with plain #7 pastry tip. Pipe 2-inch circles onto parchment paper-lined cookie sheets. Top each wreath with two candied cherry pieces. Bake 20 minutes. Turn oven off; let stand in oven 30 minutes with door ajar. Cool; peel off paper. Store in airtight container.

Makes about $2^1/_2$ dozen cookies

Chocolate Peanut Butter Squares

1½ cups chocolate-covered graham
   crackers, broken into crumbs
   (about 17 crackers)
3 tablespoons PARKAY® Margarine,
   melted
1 (8-ounce) package
   PHILADELPHIA BRAND®
   Cream Cheese, softened
½ cup chunk style peanut butter
1 cup powdered sugar
¼ cup BAKER'S® Semi-Sweet Real
   Chocolate Chips
1 teaspoon shortening

Preheat oven to 350°F.

Stir together crumbs and margarine in
small bowl. Press onto bottom of 9-inch
square baking pan. Bake 10 minutes.
Cool.

Beat cream cheese, peanut butter and
sugar in small mixing bowl at medium
speed with electric mixer until well
blended. Spread over crust.

Melt chocolate chips with shortening in
small saucepan over low heat, stirring
until smooth. Drizzle over cream cheese
mixture. Chill 6 hours or overnight. Cut
into squares.   *Makes about 1 dozen bars*

Lemon Blossom Cookies

2 cups margarine or butter, softened
1½ cups confectioners' sugar
¼ cup REALEMON® Lemon Juice
   from Concentrate
4 cups unsifted flour
   Finely chopped nuts, optional
   Assorted BAMA® Fruit Preserves
   and Jams or pecan halves

In large mixer bowl, beat margarine and
sugar until fluffy. Add ReaLemon®
brand; beat well. Gradually add flour;
mix well. Chill 2 hours. Preheat oven to
350°F. Shape dough into 1-inch balls;
roll in nuts if desired. Place 1 inch apart
on greased cookie sheets. Press thumb
in center of each ball; fill with preserves
or pecans. Bake 14 to 16 minutes or
until lightly browned.
    Makes about 6 dozen cookies

Chocolate Peanut Butter Squares

Hanukkah Cookies

Hanukkah Cookies

Cookies

> ³/₄ cup butter or margarine, softened
> 2 egg yolks
> 2 tablespoons grated orange peel
> 1 package DUNCAN HINES® Moist
>   Deluxe White Cake Mix

Frosting

> 1 container (16 ounces) DUNCAN
>   HINES® Creamy Homestyle
>   Vanilla Frosting
> 3 to 4 drops blue food coloring
> 3 to 4 drops yellow food coloring

1. For cookies, combine butter, egg yolks and orange peel in large bowl. Beat at low speed with electric mixer until blended. Add Duncan Hines® Moist Deluxe White Cake Mix gradually, beating until thoroughly blended. Form dough into ball. Cover with plastic wrap and refrigerate for 1 to 2 hours or until chilled but not firm.

2. Preheat oven to 375°F.

3. Roll dough to ¹/₈-inch thickness on lightly floured surface. Cut with Hanukkah cookie cutters. Place 2 inches apart on ungreased cookie sheets. Bake at 375°F for 6 to 7 minutes or until edges are light golden brown. Cool 1 minute on cookie sheets. Remove to cooling racks. Cool completely.

4. For frosting, tint ¹/₂ cup Vanilla frosting with blue food coloring. Warm frosting in microwave oven at HIGH (100% power) for 5 to 10 seconds, if desired. Place writing tip in pastry bag. Fill with tinted frosting. Pipe outline pattern on cookies. Tint ¹/₂ cup frosting with yellow food coloring and leave ¹/₂ cup frosting untinted; decorate as desired. Allow frosting to set before storing between layers of waxed paper in airtight container.

Makes 3¹/₂ to 4 dozen cookies

Angel Pillows

> ¹/₂ cup BUTTER FLAVOR CRISCO®
> 1 (3-ounce) package cream cheese,
>   softened
> 1 tablespoon milk
> ¹/₄ cup firmly packed brown sugar
> ¹/₂ cup apricot preserves
> 1¹/₄ cups all-purpose flour
> 1¹/₂ teaspoons baking powder
> 1¹/₂ teaspoons cinnamon
> ¹/₄ teaspoon salt
> ¹/₂ cup coarsely chopped pecans or
>   flake coconut

Frosting

> 1 cup confectioners' sugar
> ¹/₄ cup apricot preserves
> 1 tablespoon BUTTER FLAVOR
>   CRISCO®
> Flake coconut or finely chopped
>   pecans (optional)

1. Preheat oven to 350°F. Grease cookie sheets with Butter Flavor Crisco®. Set aside.

2. Cream ¹/₂ cup Butter Flavor Crisco®, cream cheese and milk at medium speed of electric mixer until well blended. Beat in brown sugar. Beat in ¹/₂ cup preserves. Combine flour, baking powder, cinnamon and salt. Mix into creamed mixture. Stir in ¹/₂ cup nuts.

3. Drop 2 level measuring tablespoons of dough into a mound to form each cookie. Place 2 inches apart on cookie sheets.

4. Bake at 350°F for 14 minutes. Cool on cookie sheets one minute. Remove to cooling racks. Cool completely before frosting.

5. Fcr frosting, combine confectioners' sugar, ¹/₄ cup preserves and 1 tablespoon Butter Flavor Crisco® in small mixing bowl. Beat with electric mixer until well blended. Frost cooled cookies. Sprinkle coconut over frosting, if desired.

Makes about 1¹/₂ dozen cookies

Tip: Try peach or pineapple preserves instead of apricot.

Prep Time: 25 minutes
Bake Time: 14 minutes

Angel Pillow

Kringle's Cutout

Kringle's Cutouts

²/₃ cup **BUTTER FLAVOR CRISCO®**
³/₄ **cup sugar**
  1 tablespoon *plus* 1 teaspoon milk
  1 teaspoon vanilla
  1 egg
  2 cups all-purpose flour
1¹/₂ **teaspoons baking powder**
¹/₄ **teaspoon salt**

1. Cream Butter Flavor Crisco®, sugar, milk and vanilla in large bowl at medium speed of electric mixer until well blended. Beat in egg. Combine flour, baking powder and salt. Mix into creamed mixture. Cover; refrigerate several hours or overnight.

2. Preheat oven to 375°F.

3. Roll dough, half at a time, to ¹/₈-inch thickness on floured surface. Cut into desired shapes. Place cookies 2 inches apart on ungreased cookie sheet. Sprinkle with colored sugar and decors, or leave plain to frost when cool.

4. Bake at 375°F for 7 to 9 minutes. Cool slightly. Remove to cooling rack.

Makes about 3 dozen cookies

Hint: Floured pastry cloth and rolling pin cover make rolling out dough easier.

Kittens and Mittens

1 recipe Butter Cookie Dough (see page 212)
1 recipe Cookie Glaze (recipe follows)
Assorted food colors
Assorted candies

1. Preheat oven to 325°F. Grease cookie sheets.

2. Roll dough on floured surface to ⅛-inch thickness. Using diagrams as guides, cut out kitten and mitten cookies. Place cookies on prepared cookie sheets. With plastic straw, make holes in tops of cookies, about ½ inch from top edges.

3. Bake 8 to 10 minutes until edges begin to brown. Remove to wire racks; cool completely. If necessary, push straw through warm cookies to remake holes.

4. Place cookies on racks on waxed paper-lined cookie sheets. Spoon Cookie Glaze into several small bowls. Color as desired with food colors. Spoon glaze over cookies. Place some of remaining glaze in plastic bag. Cut tiny tip from corner of bag. Use to pipe decorations as shown in photo. Decorate with candies as shown. Let stand until glaze has set.

5. Thread yarn or ribbon through holes to make garland.

Makes about 2 dozen cookies

Cookie Glaze

4 cups powdered sugar
4 to 6 tablespoons milk
Assorted food colors

Combine powdered sugar and enough milk to make a medium-thick pourable glaze.   *Makes about 4 cups glaze*

Kittens and Mittens

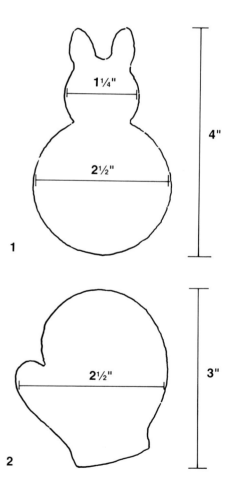

Triple Chocolate Pretzels

2 squares (1 ounce each)
  unsweetened chocolate
$^1/_2$ cup butter or margarine, softened
$^1/_2$ cup granulated sugar
 1 egg
 2 cups cake flour
 1 teaspoon vanilla
$^1/_4$ teaspoon salt
  Mocha Glaze (recipe follows)
 2 ounces white chocolate, chopped

Melt unsweetened chocolate in top of double boiler over hot, not boiling, water. Remove from heat; cool. Cream butter and granulated sugar in large bowl until light. Add egg and melted chocolate; beat until fluffy. Stir in cake flour, vanilla and salt until well blended. Cover; refrigerate until firm, about 1 hour.

Preheat oven to 400°F. Lightly grease cookie sheets or line with parchment paper. Divide dough into 4 equal parts. Divide each part into 12 pieces. To form pretzels, knead each piece briefly to soften dough. Roll into a rope about 6 inches long. Form each rope on prepared cookie sheet into a pretzel shape. Repeat with each piece of dough, spacing cookies 2 inches apart. Bake 7 to 9 minutes or until firm. Remove to wire racks to cool.

Prepare Mocha Glaze. Dip pretzels, 1 at a time, into glaze to coat completely. Place on waxed paper. Let stand until glaze is set. Melt white chocolate in small bowl over hot water. Squeeze melted chocolate through pastry bag or drizzle over pretzels to decorate. Let stand until chocolate is completely set.
Makes 4 dozen cookies

Triple Chocolate Pretzels

Mocha Glaze

1 cup (6 ounces) semisweet chocolate
  chips
1 teaspoon light corn syrup
1 teaspoon shortening
1 cup powdered sugar
3 to 5 tablespoons hot coffee or
  water

Combine chocolate chips, corn syrup and shortening in small heavy saucepan. Stir over low heat until chocolate is melted. Stir in powdered sugar and enough coffee to make a smooth glaze.

Almond Cream Cookies

¾ cup (1½ sticks) margarine,
  softened
¾ cup granulated sugar
½ cup *plus* 2 tablespoons soft-style
  cream cheese
1 egg
1 teaspoon almond extract
1¼ cups all-purpose flour
¾ cup QUAKER® Corn Meal
½ teaspoon baking powder
½ cup coarsely chopped almonds
1 cup powdered sugar
1 tablespoon milk or water
  Red or green candied cherries
  (optional)

Preheat oven to 350°F. Beat margarine,
granulated sugar and ½ cup cream
cheese at medium speed of electric
mixer until fluffy. Add egg and almond
extract; mix until well blended.
Gradually add combined flour, corn
meal and baking powder; mix well. Stir
in almonds. Drop by rounded
teaspoonfuls onto ungreased cookie
sheet. Bake 12 to 14 minutes or until
edges are golden brown. Cool on cookie
sheet for 2 minutes; remove to wire
rack. Cool completely.

Almond Cream Cookies

Mix remaining 2 tablespoons cream
cheese and powdered sugar until
blended. Add milk; mix until smooth.
Spread over cookies. Garnish with
halved red or green candied cherries, if
desired. Store tightly covered.
Makes about 4 dozen cookies

Cherry Thumbprint Cookies

¾ cup sugar
½ cup HELLMANN'S® or BEST
  FOODS® Real Mayonnaise
½ cup MAZOLA® Margarine
2 eggs, separated
1 teaspoon vanilla
2 cups all-purpose flour
¼ teaspoon ground nutmeg
1½ cups finely chopped walnuts or
  almonds
  Red and green candied cherries

In large bowl, beat sugar, mayonnaise,
margarine, egg yolks and vanilla. Beat
in flour and nutmeg until well blended.
Cover; refrigerate until firm, at least 3
hours.

Preheat oven to 350°F. Shape dough
into ¾-inch balls. In small bowl, beat
egg whites with fork until foamy. Dip
each ball into egg whites; roll in nuts.
Place 1½ inches apart on greased cookie
sheets. Press thumb into centers of
balls. Place 1 whole cherry in each
center. Bake 15 to 17 minutes or until
bottoms are browned. Let cookies cool
slightly before removing from cookie
sheets to wire racks.
Makes about 5 dozen cookies

Mini Chocolate Clouds

4 egg whites
1 cup sugar
1/4 cup NESTLÉ® Cocoa
2 cups (12-ounce package) NESTLÉ®
    Toll House® Semi-Sweet
    Chocolate Mini Morsels
    Additional NESTLÉ® Cocoa,
    optional

Preheat oven to 325°F. Grease 4 large cookie sheets. In small mixer bowl, beat egg whites until soft peaks form. Gradually add sugar, beating until stiff peaks form.

Transfer egg mixture to large bowl. Sift 1/4 cup Nestlé® Cocoa over top; fold in. Fold in Nestlé® Toll House® Semi-Sweet Chocolate Mini Morsels. Drop slightly rounded measuring teaspoonfuls onto cookie sheets.

Bake 20 to 23 minutes until dry and firm. Let stand 1 minute. Remove from cookie sheets; cool on wire racks. If desired, sprinkle with additional cocoa. Store in airtight containers at room temperature.

Makes about 7 dozen cookies

Mini Chocolate Clouds,
Butterscotch Fruit Drops

Butterscotch Fruit Drops

2 cups all-purpose flour
1 teaspoon baking soda
1/2 teaspoon salt
1/2 cup (1 stick) butter or margarine,
    softened
3/4 cup firmly packed brown sugar
1 egg
2 tablespoons milk
1 teaspoon grated lemon rind,
    optional
2 cups (12-ounce package) NESTLÉ®
    Toll House® Butterscotch
    Flavored Morsels
1 cup diced mixed dried fruit bits or
    raisins

Preheat oven to 350°F. In small bowl, combine flour, baking soda and salt; set aside.

In large mixer bowl, beat butter and brown sugar until creamy. Blend in egg, milk and lemon rind. Gradually beat in flour mixture. Stir in Nestlé® Toll House® Butterscotch Flavored Morsels and fruit. Drop by rounded measuring teaspoonfuls onto ungreased cookie sheets.

Bake 9 to 11 minutes until golden brown. Let stand 2 minutes. Remove from cookie sheets; cool on wire racks.

Makes about 6 dozen cookies

Butter Cookies

$^3/_4$ **cup butter or margarine, softened**
$^1/_4$ **cup granulated sugar**
$^1/_4$ **cup packed light brown sugar**
   1 egg yolk
$1^3/_4$ **cups all-purpose flour**
$^3/_4$ **teaspoon baking powder**
$^1/_8$ **teaspoon salt**

1. Combine butter, granulated sugar, brown sugar and egg yolk in medium bowl. Add flour, baking powder and salt; mix well. Cover; refrigerate until firm, about 4 hours or overnight.

2. Preheat oven to 350°F.

3. Roll dough on floured surface to $^1/_4$-inch thickness. Cut into desired shapes with cookie cutters. Place on ungreased cookie sheets.

4. Bake 8 to 10 minutes or until edges begin to brown. Remove to wire racks; cool completely.

Makes about 2 dozen cookies

Autumn Mobile

1 recipe Butter Cookie dough
3 egg yolks, divided
3 teaspoons water, divided
   Yellow, red and green food colors

1. Preheat oven to 350°F. Roll dough on floured surface to $^1/_4$-inch thickness. Using diagrams as guides, cut out 1 large and 3 small pumpkins, and 2 leaves. Cut out remaining dough as desired.

2. Place large pumpkin on ungreased cookie sheet and remaining cookies on another ungreased cookie sheet. Using straw, make hole in top of each small pumpkin, about $^1/_2$ inch from top. Make holes in sides of each leaf. Make 3 evenly spaced holes along bottom edge of large pumpkin, about $^1/_2$ inch from edge.

Autumn Mobile

3. Place 1 egg yolk in each of 3 separate bowls. Add 1 teaspoon water to each; beat lightly. Color egg wash in 1 bowl orange,* another yellow and the last green. Using a small brush, decorate cookies as shown in photo.

4. Bake smaller cookies 10 to 12 minutes until lightly browned around edges. Bake large cookie about 14 minutes. Remove to wire racks; cool completely.

5. Using ribbon, tie cookies together as shown. For ease in balancing mobile, tie large pumpkin cookie to cabinet handle while tying on other cookies.

Makes 1 mobile and about 1 dozen cookies

* Use about 1 drop red food color to every 3 drops yellow to make orange color.

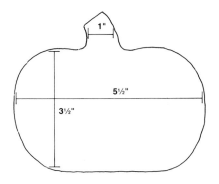

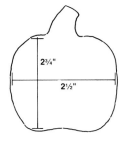

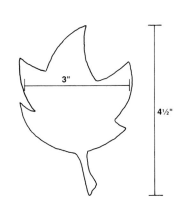

Choco Peanut Butter Dreams

1½ cups firmly packed brown sugar
1 cup creamy or chunk-style peanut butter
¾ cup (1½ sticks) margarine, softened
⅓ cup water
1 egg
1 teaspoon vanilla
3 cups QUAKER® Oats (quick or old fashioned, uncooked)
1½ cups all-purpose flour
½ teaspoon baking soda
1½ cups semi-sweet chocolate pieces
4 teaspoons vegetable shortening
⅓ cup chopped peanuts (optional)

Preheat oven to 350°F. Beat brown sugar, peanut butter and margarine until fluffy. Blend in water, egg and vanilla. Add combined oats, flour and baking soda; mix well. Shape into 1-inch balls. Place on ungreased cookie sheet. Using bottom of glass dipped in sugar, press into ¼-inch thick circles. Bake 8 to 10 minutes or until edges are golden brown. Remove to wire rack; cool completely.

In saucepan over low heat, melt chocolate pieces and shortening, stirring until smooth.* Top each cookie with ½ teaspoon melted chocolate; sprinkle with chopped peanuts. Chill until set. Store tightly covered.

Makes about 6 dozen cookies

Microwave Directions: Place chocolate pieces and shortening in microwavable bowl. Microwave at HIGH (100% power) 1 to 2 minutes, stirring after 1 minute and then every 30 seconds until smooth.

Acknowledgments

The publishers would like to thank the companies and organizations listed below for the use of their recipes in this book.

Best Foods, a Division of CPC International Inc.
Borden Kitchens, Borden, Inc.
Checkerboard Kitchens, Ralston Purina Company
Dole Food Company, Inc.
Hershey Chocolate U.S.A.
Kahlúa Liqueur
Kellogg Company
Kraft General Foods, Inc.
Leaf, Inc.
M&M/Mars
Nabisco Foods Group
National Cherry Foundation
Nestlé Food Company
The Procter & Gamble Company
The Quaker Oats Company
Wisconsin Milk Marketing Board
Willy Wonka Brands

Photo Credits

The publishers would like to thank the companies and organizations listed below for the use of their photographs in this book.

Best Foods, a Division of CPC International Inc.
Borden Kitchens, Borden, Inc.
Checkerboard Kitchens, Ralston Purina Company
Dole Food Company, Inc.
Hershey Chocolate U.S.A.
Kahlúa Liqueur
Kraft General Foods, Inc.
Leaf, Inc.
M&M/Mars
National Cherry Foundation
Nestlé Food Company
The Quaker Oats Company
Wisconsin Milk Marketing Board
Willy Wonka Brands

INDEX

A

All American Heath® Brownies, 32
Almond Cream Cookies, 210
Almond Delightful Cookies, 82
Almond Frosting, 134
Almond Fudge Topped Shortbread, 64
Almond Hearts, 178
Almond Milk Chocolate Chippers, 87
Almonds
  Almond Cream Cookies, 210
  Almond Frosting, 134
  Almond Fudge Topped Shortbread, 64
  Almond Hearts, 178
  Almond Milk Chocolate Chippers, 87
  Almond Shortbread Cookies, 134
  Almond Toffee Squares, 45
  Almond Toffee Triangles, 46
  Anise Cookie Cordials, 81
  Austrian Tea Cookies, 170
  Chocolate Almond Cookie Bites, 120
  Chocolate-Dipped Almond Horns, 174
  Chocolate-Frosted Lebkuchen, 203
  Cocoa Almond Cut-out Cookies, 155
  Double Chocolate Banana Cookies, 90
  Fudge-wiches, 61
  Fudgy Almond Bars, 54
  Holiday Almond Wreaths, 192
  Linzer Hearts, 184
  Norwegian Almond Bars, 58
  Pineapple Almond Shortbread Bars, 72
  Raspberry Almond Sandwich Cookies, 163
  Snow Covered Almond Crescents, 131
Almond Shortbread Cookies, 134
Almond Toffee Squares, 45
Almond Toffee Triangles, 46
Angel Pillows, 206
Anise Cookie Cordials, 81

Apple Crumb Squares, 75
Apples
  Apple Crumb Squares, 75
  Caramel Apple Oatmeal Squares, 71
  Chocolate Apple Crisp, 67
  Four-Layer Oatmeal Bars, 65
Apricots
  Chewy Oatmeal-Apricot-Date Bars, 48
  Fruit and Nut Chippers, 81
  Jammy Fantasia, 191
  "Philly" Apricot Cookies, 137
Austrian Tea Cookies, 170
Autumn Mobile, 212

B

Baked Truffle Treasures, 110
Baker's® Chocolate Chip Cookies, 88
Banana Chocolate Chip Softies, 103
Banana Gingerbread Bars, 76
Bananas
  Banana Chocolate Chip Softies, 103
  Banana Gingerbread Bars, 76
  Banana Split Bars, 70
  Double Chocolate Banana Cookies, 90
Banana Split Bars, 70
Bar Cookie Crust, 46
Bar Cookies (see also **Brownies)**
  Almond Fudge Topped Shortbread, 64
  Almond Toffee Squares, 45
  Almond Toffee Triangles, 46
  Apple Crumb Squares, 75
  Banana Gingerbread Bars, 76
  Banana Split Bars, 70
  Blueberry Cheesecake Bars, 76
  Butter Pecan Squares, 63
  Candy Bar Cookies, 68
  Caramel Apple Oatmeal Squares, 71
  Caramel Marshmallow Bars, 73
  Cheese Crunchers, 61
  Cherry Butterscotch Squares, 60

Bar Cookies (continued)
  Cherry Chewbilees, 192
  Chewy Oatmeal-Apricot-Date Bars, 48
  Chippy Cheeseys, 42
  Choco Cheesecake Squares, 68
  Chocolate 'n' Oat Bars, 56
  Chocolate Apple Crisp, 67
  Chocolate Caramel-Pecan Bars, 51
  Chocolate Cheesecake Bars, 66
  Chocolate Chip Shortbread, 90
  Chocolate-Drizzled Peanut Bars, 46
  Chocolate Filled Walnut-Oatmeal Bars, 53
  Chocolate Fruit Bars, 60
  Chocolate Mint Cheesecake Bars, 49
  Chocolate Peanut Butter Squares, 205
  Chocolate Pecan Pie Squares, 58
  Chocolate Raspberry Coconut Squares, 42
  Chocolate Streusel Bars, 72
  Cranberry Jewel Bars, 67
  English Toffee Bars, 56
  Four-Layer Oatmeal Bars, 65
  Fudge-wiches, 61
  Fudgy Almond Bars, 54
  Fudgy Walnut Cookie Wedges, 43
  Gorp Bars, 70
  Jammy Fantasia, 191
  Kahlúa® Pumpkin Squares with Praline Topping, 40
  Lemon Nut Bars, 56
  Lemon Raspberry Cheesecake Bars, 54
  Magic Cookie Bars, 55
  Marble Squares, 51
  Marshmallow Krispie Bars, 56
  No-Fuss Bar Cookies, 113
  Norwegian Almond Bars, 58
  Orange Chess Bars, 45
  Orange Shortbread Squares, 63
  Peachy Oatmeal Bars, 75
  Peanut Butter Bars, 59
  Peanut Butter Chips and Jelly Bars, 64
  Pecan Date Bars, 63
  Pecan Pie Bars, 44

Bar Cookies *(continued)*
Pineapple Almond Shortbread Bars, 72
Pumpkin Cheesecake Bars, 44
Pumpkin Jingle Bars, 55
Raspberry Coconut Layer Bars, 40
Special Treat No-Bake Squares, 118
Strawberry Streusel Bars, 75
Streusel Caramel Bars, 52
Streusel Peanut Butter Bars, 71
Triple Layer Chocolate Bars, 53
Tropical Sun Bars, 77
Walnut Shortbread Bars, 49
Walnut Toffee Bars, 73
Best Brownies, 17
Biscochitos, 142
Bittersweet Glaze, 203
Black & White Cheesecake Brownies, 37
Black and White Cut-Outs, 169
Black Russian Brownies, 27
Blueberry Cheesecake Bars, 76
Brian's Buffalo Cookies, 80
Brickle
All American Heath® Brownies, 32
Butter-Flavored Brickle Drizzles, 147
Oatmeal Toffee Lizzies, 148
Peanut Butter Brickle Cookies, 115
Pecan Pie Bars, 44
Brownie Candy Cups, 15
Brownie Cheesecake Bars, 26
Brownie Cookies-on-a-Stick, 193
Brownie Kiss Cups, 31
Brownies
All American Heath® Brownies, 32
Best Brownies, 17
Black & White Cheesecake Brownies, 37
Black Russian Brownies, 27
Brownie Candy Cups, 15
Brownie Cheesecake Bars, 26
Brownie Kiss Cups, 31
Brownie Sundaes for Kids, 28
Buckeye Cookie Bars, 19
Butterscotch Brownies, 35
Candy Dandy Brownies, 36
Cappuccino Brownies, 30
Chocolate Cherry Brownies, 198
Chocolate Chunk Blonde Brownies, 14
Chocolate Macaroon Squares, 30
Chocolatey Rocky Road Brownies, 28
Coconut Crowned Cappuccino Brownies, 17
Coconut-Pecan Brownies, 26
Decadent Blonde Brownies, 22
Double "Topped" Brownies, 19
Extra Moist & Chunky Brownies, 22

Brownies *(continued)*
Fancy Walnut Brownies, 27
Frosted Maraschino Brownies, 21
Fudgy Bittersweet Brownie Pie, 13
Fudgy Cheesecake Swirl Brownies, 38
Fudgy Mocha Brownies with a Crust, 20
German Sweet Chocolate Cream Cheese Brownies, 15
Irish Brownies, 24
Kahlúa® Mudslide Brownies, 14
Minted Chocolate Chip Brownies, 10
Minty Fudge Brownies, 37
Mississippi Mud Brownies, 22
Oatmeal Brownies, 20
Outrageous Brownies, 18
Peanut Butter Brownie Cups, 39
Peanut Butter Paisley Brownies, 12
Peanutty Picnic Brownies, 10
Praline Brownies, 21
Rich 'n' Creamy Brownie Bars, 12
Rich Chocolate Caramel Brownies, 35
Rocky Road Brownies, 36
Scrumptious Minted Brownies, 25
Sour Cream Walnut Brownies, 31
Sweets-for-the-Sweet Brownies, 18
Tex-Mex Brownies, 39
Ultimate Designer Brownies, 33
Vanilla Chip Orange Brownies, 38
White Chocolate Brownies, 32
White Chocolate Chunk Brownies, 25
Brownie Sandwich Cookies, 137
Brownie Sundaes for Kids, 28
Buckeye Cookie Bars, 19
Butter Cookies, 212
Butter-Flavored Brickle Drizzles, 147
Butter-Pecan Squares, 63
Butterscotch
Butterscotch Brownies, 35
Butterscotch Fruit Drops, 211
Butterscotch Granola Cookies, 106
Butterscotch Lemon Cookies, 86
Butterscotch Walnut Crisps, 85
Cheese Crunchers, 61
Cherry Butterscotch Squares, 60
Chocolate Scotcheroos, 99
Jeremy's Famous Turtles, 167
Oatmeal Scotchies™, 86
Pudding Drop Cookies, 103
Butterscotch Brownies, 35
Butterscotch Fruit Drops, 211
Butterscotch Granola Cookies, 106
Butterscotch Lemon Cookies, 86
Butterscotch Walnut Crisps, 85
"Buttery" Drop Cookies, 195

C

Candies
Gorp Bars, 70
Happy Pumpkin Faces, 183
Nerds® Sprinkle Cookies, 111
Sweets-for-the-Sweet Brownies, 18
Walnut Toffee Bars, 73
Candy Bar Cookies, 68
Candy Dandy Brownies, 36
Cappuccino Brownies, 30
Caramel
Candy Bar Cookies, 68
Caramel Apple Oatmeal Squares, 71
Caramel Lace Chocolate Chip Cookies, 161
Caramel Marshmallow Bars, 73
Caramel Pecan Cookies, 157
Chocolate Caramel-Pecan Bars, 51
Rich Chocolate Caramel Brownies, 35
Streusel Caramel Bars, 52
Caramel Apple Oatmeal Squares, 71
Caramel Lace Chocolate Chip Cookies, 161
Caramel Marshmallow Bars, 73
Caramel Pecan Cookies, 157
Cereals
Almond Delightful Cookies, 82
Austrian Tea Cookies, 170
Chocolate Chip Cookies, 106
Circus Cookies, 125
Corn Flake Macaroons, 130
Gorp Bars, 70
Jumbo Corn Flake Cookies, 104
Marshmallow Krispie Bars, 56
No-Bake Cherry Crisps, 171
Cheery Chocolate Teddy Bear Cookies, 114
Cheese Crunchers, 61
Cherries
Almond Cream Cookies, 210
Cherry Butterscotch Squares, 60
Cherry Chewbilees, 192
Cherry Surprises, 160
Cherry Thumbprint Cookies, 210
Chocolate Cherry Brownies, 198
Chocolate Cherry Drops, 201
Chocolate Chip Cordials, 173
Chocolate Fruit Bars, 60
Double Chocolate Cherry Cookies, 145
Frosted Maraschino Brownies, 21
Hidden Treasures, 162
Holiday Citrus Logs, 201
Mini Morsel Meringue Wreaths, 204
No-Bake Cherry Crisps, 171
Sugar Cookie Wreaths, 182
Cherry Butterscotch Squares, 60

Cherry Chewbilees, 192
Cherry Surprises, 160
Cherry Thumbprint Cookies, 210
Chewy Choco-Peanut Pudgies, 134
Chewy Oatmeal-Apricot-Date Bars, 48
Child's Choice, 101
Chippy Cheeseys, 42
Choco Cheesecake Squares, 68
Choco Peanut Butter Dreams, 213
Choco-Scutterbotch, 104
Chocolate (*see also* **Brownies, Chocolate Chips, Cocoa, White Chocolate**)
    Almond Fudge Topped Shortbread, 64
    Baked Truffle Treasures, 110
    Bittersweet Glaze, 203
    Black and White Cut-Outs, 169
    Brownie Cookies-on-a-Stick, 193
    Brownie Sandwich Cookies, 137
    Cheery Chocolate Teddy Bear Cookies, 114
    Chocolate Almond Cookie Bites, 120
    Chocolate Apple Crisp, 67
    Chocolate Butter-Pecan Crescents, 113
    Chocolate Caramel-Pecan Bars, 51
    Chocolate Cheesecake Bars, 66
    Chocolate Cherry Brownies, 198
    Chocolate Chip Chocolate Cookies, 95
    Chocolate-Dipped Almond Horns, 174
    Chocolate-Dipped Brandy Snaps, 172
    Chocolate-Dipped Cinnamon Thins, 160
    Chocolate-Drizzled Peanut Bars, 46
    Chocolate-Filled Bonbons, 155
    Chocolate Filled Walnut-Oatmeal Bars, 53
    Chocolate Filling, 53
    Chocolate-Frosted Lebkuchen, 203
    Chocolate Frosting, 195
    Chocolate Gingerbread Cookies, 184
    Chocolate Glaze: 46, 49, 155
    Chocolate Mint Cheesecake Bars, 49
    Chocolate Mint Cookies, 132
    Chocolate Mint Meltaways, 133
    Chocolate Mint Sandwiches, 139
    Chocolate Mint Snow-Top Cookies, 110
    Chocolate Peanut Butter Cup Cookies, 178
    Chocolate Peanut Butter Squares, 205
    Chocolate Pecan Pie Squares, 58
    Chocolate Pinwheel Cookies, 148
    Chocolate Sandwich Cookies, 147
    Chocolate Streusel Bars, 72
    Chocolate Sugar Spritz, 166
    Chocolate Thumbprints, 141
    Cinnamon-Chocolate Cutouts, 140

Chocolate (*continued*)
    Cocoa-Pecan Kiss Cookies, 150
    Creamy Brownie Frosting, 17
    Double Chocolate Chip Cookies, 100
    Double Chocolate Chunk Cookies, 142
    Double Chocolate Cookies, 94
    Double Chocolate Dream Cookies, 88
    Double Chocolate Mint Chip Cookies, 105
    Double-Dipped Chocolate-Peanut Butter Cookies, 158
    Double-Dipped Hazelnut Crisps, 176
    Dreamy Chocolate Chip Cookies, 83
    English Toffee Bars, 66
    Fudge-wiches, 61
    Fudgy Almond Bars, 54
    Fudgy Raisin Pixies, 123
    Fudgy Walnut Cookie Wedges, 43
    Happy Pumpkin Faces, 183
    Hidden Treasures, 162
    Kahlúa® Glaze, 14
    Marble Squares, 51
    Marshmallow Krispie Bars, 56
    Marshmallow Sandwich Cookies, 121
    Mint Chocolate Pinwheels, 174
    No-Bake Peanutty Cookies, 127
    Old-Fashioned Ice Cream Sandwiches, 117
    Orange & Chocolate Ribbon Cookies, 139
    Peanut Butter and Chocolate Cookie Sandwich Cookies, 128
    Peanut Butter Bars, 59
    Peanut Butter Stars, 131
    Pinwheels and Checkerboards, 130
    Quick Chocolate Softies, 108
    Surprise Cookies, 179
    Triple Chocolate Pretzels, 209
    Two-Toned Spritz Cookies, 162
Chocolate Almond Cookie Bites, 120
Chocolate 'n' Oat Bars, 56
Chocolate Apple Crisp, 67
Chocolate Butter-Pecan Crescents, 113
Chocolate Caramel-Pecan Bars, 51
Chocolate Cheesecake Bars, 66
Chocolate Cherry Brownies, 198
Chocolate Cherry Drops, 201
Chocolate Chip Chocolate Cookies, 95
Chocolate Chip Cookies, 106
Chocolate Chip Cordials, 173
Chocolate Chip Crispers, 83
Chocolate Chip Glaze, 198
Chocolate Chip Macaroons, 127
Chocolate Chip Oatmeal Raisin Cookies, 106
Chocolate Chip Pretzel Cookies, 92
Chocolate Chip Sandwich Cookies, 156
Chocolate Chip Shortbread, 90

Chocolate Chips
    Almond Delightful Cookies, 82
    Almond Milk Chocolate Chippers, 87
    Anise Cookie Cordials, 81
    Baker's® Chocolate Chip Cookies, 88
    Banana Chocolate Chip Softies, 103
    Brian's Buffalo Cookies, 80
    Butter-Flavored Brickle Drizzles, 147
    Butter-Pecan Squares, 63
    Butterscotch Brownies, 35
    Candy Bar Cookies, 68
    Caramel Lace Chocolate Chip Cookies, 161
    Caramel Pecan Cookies, 157
    Cherry Surprises, 160
    Child's Choice, 101
    Chippy Cheeseys, 42
    Choco Cheesecake Squares, 68
    Choco Peanut Butter Dreams, 213
    Choco-Scutterbotch, 104
    Chocolate 'n' Oat Bars, 56
    Chocolate Caramel-Pecan Bars, 51
    Chocolate Cherry Drops, 201
    Chocolate Chip Chocolate Cookies, 95
    Chocolate Chip Cookies, 106
    Chocolate Chip Cordials, 173
    Chocolate Chip Crispers, 83
    Chocolate Chip Glaze, 198
    Chocolate Chip Macaroons, 127
    Chocolate Chip Oatmeal Raisin Cookies, 106
    Chocolate Chip Pretzel Cookies, 92
    Chocolate Chip Sandwich Cookies, 156
    Chocolate Chip Shortbread, 90
    Chocolate Chunk Blonde Brownies, 14
    Chocolate-Dipped Sandwich Macaroons, 82
    Chocolate Mint Sugar Cookie Drops, 105
    Chocolate Oatmeal Chippers, 98
    Chocolate Orange Granola Cookies, 94
    Chocolate Peanut Butter Cup Cookies, 178
    Chocolate-Pecan Angels, 115
    Chocolate Raspberry Coconut Squares, 42
    Chocolate Scotcheroos, 99
    Chunky Chocolate Cookies, 116
    Coconut Chocolate Chip Cookies, 90
    Confetti Chocolate Chip Cookies, 157
    Dandy Candy Oatmeal Cookies, 95
    Decadent Blonde Brownies, 22
    Double Chocolate Banana Cookies, 90
    Double Chocolate Cherry Cookies, 145
    Double Chocolate Chip Cookies, 100

Chocolate Chips (continued)
Double Chocolate Chunk Cookies, 142
Double Chocolate Cookies, 94
Double Chocolate Dream Cookies, 88
Double Chocolate Mint Chip Cookies, 105
Dreamy Chocolate Chip Cookies, 83
Forgotten Chips Cookies, 101
Fruit and Nut Chippers, 81
Gold Mine Nuggets, 85
Grandpa Would Have Loved These Cookies, 107
Heavenly Oatmeal Hearts, 89
Jeremy's Famous Turtles, 167
Jumbo Chunky Cookies, 92
Jumbo Corn Flake Cookies, 104
Kate's Chocolate Chip Cookies, 99
Kids' Favorite Jumbo Chippers, 85
Magic Cookie Bars, 55
Marble Squares, 51
Mini Chocolate Clouds, 211
Mini Morsel Meringue Wreaths, 204
Minted Chocolate Chip Brownies, 10
No-Bake Cherry Crisps, 171
No-Fuss Bar Cookies, 113
Oatmeal Candied Chippers, 96
Oatmeal Toffee Lizzies, 148
Orange-Walnut Chippers, 93
Original Toll House® Chocolate Chip Cookies, 196
Peanut Butter Chocolate Chip Cookies, 103
Peanut Butter Chocolate Chippers, 125
Pecan Florentines, 177
Pudding Drop Cookies, 103
"Radical" Peanut Butter Pizza Cookies, 150
Reese's® Cookies, 78
Rocky Road Brownies, 36
Special Treat No-Bake Squares, 118
Triple Layer Chocolate Bars, 53
Ultimate Chippers, 78
Ultimate Chocolate Chip Cookies, 96
Yummy Chocolate Chip Flower Cookies, 166
Chocolate Chunk Blonde Brownies, 14
Chocolate Crunch Cookies, 98
Chocolate-Dipped Almond Horns, 174
Chocolate-Dipped Brandy Snaps, 172
Chocolate-Dipped Cinnamon Thins, 160
Chocolate-Dipped Sandwich Macaroons, 82
Chocolate-Drizzled Peanut Bars, 46
Chocolate-Filled Bonbons, 155
Chocolate Filled Walnut-Oatmeal Bars, 53
Chocolate Filling, 53

Chocolate-Frosted Lebkuchen, 203
Chocolate Frosting, 195
Chocolate Fruit Bars, 60
Chocolate Glaze: 46, 49, 155
Chocolate Gingerbread Cookies, 184
Chocolate Macaroon Squares, 30
Chocolate Mint Cheesecake Bars, 49
Chocolate Mint Cookies, 132
Chocolate Mint Meltaways, 133
Chocolate Mint Sandwiches, 139
Chocolate Mint Snow-Top Cookies, 110
Chocolate Mint Sugar Cookie Drops, 105
Chocolate Oatmeal Chippers, 98
Chocolate Orange Granola Cookies, 94
Chocolate Peanut Butter Cup Cookies, 178
Chocolate Peanut Butter Squares, 205
Chocolate-Pecan Angels, 115
Chocolate Pecan Pie Squares, 58
Chocolate Pinwheel Cookies, 148
Chocolate Raspberry Coconut Squares, 42
Chocolate Sandwich Cookies, 147
Chocolate Scotcheroos, 99
Chocolate Streusel Bars, 72
Chocolate Sugar Spritz, 166
Chocolate Thumbprints, 141
Chocolatey Rocky Road Brownies, 28
Chunky Chocolate Cookies, 116
Cinnamon
Chocolate-Dipped Cinnamon Thins, 160
Cinnamon Stars, 151
Cinnamon-Chocolate Cutouts, 140
Cinnamon-Chocolate Cutouts, 140
Cinnamon Stars, 151
Circus Cookies, 125
Cocoa
Baked Truffle Treasures, 110
Best Brownies, 17
Black and White Cut-Outs, 169
Brownie Cheesecake Bars, 26
Brownie Cookies-on-a-Stick, 192
Chocolate Cheesecake Bars, 66
Chocolate Chip Chocolate Cookies, 95
Chocolate Fruit Bars, 60
Chocolate Gingerbread Cookies, 184
Chocolate Oatmeal Chippers, 98
Chocolate Sandwich Cookies, 147
Chocolate Streusel Bars, 72
Cocoa Almond Cut-out Cookies, 155
Cocoa Cream Cheese Cookies, 182
Cocoa-Pecan Kiss Cookies, 150
Creamy Brownie Frosting, 17
Double Chocolate Cherry Cookies, 145
Fudgy Almond Bars, 54

Cocoa (continued)
Fudgy Mocha Brownies with a Crust, 20
Fudgy Mocha Frosting, 20
Mini Chocolate Clouds, 211
Oatmeal Brownies, 20
Peanut Butter and Chocolate Cookie Sandwich Cookies, 128
Triple Layer Chocolate Bars, 53
Ultimate Designer Brownies, 33
Cocoa Almond Cut-out Cookies, 155
Cocoa Cream Cheese Cookies, 182
Cocoa-Pecan Kiss Cookies, 150
Coconut
Almond Toffee Squares, 45
Angel Pillows, 206
Baked Truffle Treasures, 110
Cherry Chewbilees, 192
Chocolate Chip Cordials, 173
Chocolate Chip Macaroons, 127
Chocolate Macaroon Squares, 30
Chocolate Raspberry Coconut Squares, 42
Coconut Chocolate Chip Cookies, 90
Coconut Crowned Cappuccino Brownies, 17
Coconut-Pecan Brownies, 26
Corn Flake Macaroons, 130
Date-Nut Macaroons, 125
Double "Topped" Brownies, 19
Jumbo Chunky Cookies, 92
Macadamia Bites, 136
Magic Cookie Bars, 55
No-Bake Cherry Crisps, 171
No-Fuss Bar Cookies, 113
Oatmeal Shaggies Cookies, 136
Orange Drop Cookies, 133
Peachy Oatmeal Bars, 75
Raspberry Coconut Layer Bars, 40
Special Treat No-Bake Squares, 118
Tropical Sun Bars, 77
Coconut Chocolate Chip Cookies, 90
Coconut Crowned Cappuccino Brownies, 17
Coconut-Pecan Brownies, 26
Confectioner's Sugar Glaze, 188
Confetti Chocolate Chip Cookies, 157
Cookie Filling, 144
Cookie Glaze, 208
Corn Flake Macaroons, 130
Cranberries: Cranberry Jewel Bars, 67
Cream Cheese
Almond Cream Cookies, 210
Angel Pillows, 206
Black & White Cheesecake Brownies, 37
Blueberry Cheesecake Bars, 76
Brownie Cheesecake Bars, 26

Cream Cheese *(continued)*
Brownie Sandwich Cookies, 137
Cherry Chewbilees, 192
Cheese Crunchers, 61
Chewy Oatmeal-Apricot-Date Bars, 48
Chippy Cheeseys, 42
Choco Cheesecake Squares, 68
Chocolate Cheesecake Bars, 66
Chocolate Mint Cheesecake Bars, 49
Chocolate Peanut Butter Squares, 205
Chocolate Streusel Bars, 72
Cocoa Cream Cheese Cookies, 182
Cream Cheese Cookies, 113
Extra Moist & Chunky Brownies, 22
Four-Layer Oatmeal Bars, 65
Fudgy Cheesecake Swirl Brownies, 38
German Sweet Chocolate Cream
Cheese Brownies, 15
Irish Brownies, 24
Irish Cream Frosting, 24
Kahlúa® Pumpkin Squares with
Praline Topping, 40
Lemon Nut Bars, 56
Lemon Raspberry Cheesecake Bars, 54
Marble Squares, 51
Orange Chess Bars, 45
"Philly" Apricot Cookies, 137
Rich 'n' Creamy Brownie Bars, 12
Special Treat No-Bake Squares, 118
Walnut Shortbread Bars, 49
Cream Cheese Cookies, 113
Creamy Brownie Frosting, 17
Creamy Mint Filling, 140
Creamy Vanilla Frosting: 70, 195
Crust: Bar Cookie Crust, 46

D

Dandy Candy Oatmeal Cookies, 95
Date Menenas, 152
Date-Nut Macaroons, 125
Dates
Chewy Oatmeal-Apricot-Date Bars,
48
Date Menenas, 152
Date-Nut Macaroons, 125
Holiday Citrus Logs, 201
Pecan Date Bars, 63
Decadent Blonde Brownies, 22
Decorator Icing, 140
Double Chocolate Banana Cookies, 90
Double Chocolate Cherry Cookies, 145
Double Chocolate Chip Cookies, 100
Double Chocolate Chunk Cookies, 142
Double Chocolate Cookies, 94
Double Chocolate Dream Cookies, 88

Double Chocolate Mint Chip Cookies,
105
Double-Dipped Chocolate-Peanut
Butter Cookies, 158
Double-Dipped Hazelnut Crisps, 176
Double "Topped" Brownies, 19
Dreamy Chocolate Chip Cookies, 83
Drop Cookies
Almond Delightful Cookies, 82
Almond Milk Chocolate Chippers, 87
Baker's® Chocolate Chip Cookies, 88
Banana Chocolate Chip Softies, 103
Brian's Buffalo Cookies, 80
Butterscotch Fruit Drops, 211
Butterscotch Granola Cookies, 105
Butterscotch Lemon Cookies, 86
Butterscotch Walnut Crisps, 85
"Buttery" Drop Cookies, 195
Caramel Pecan Cookies, 157
Child's Choice, 101
Choco-Scutterbotch, 104
Chocolate Almond Cookie Bites, 120
Chocolate Butter-Pecan Crescents, 113
Chocolate Cherry Drops, 201
Chocolate Chip Chocolate Cookies, 95
Chocolate Chip Cookies, 106
Chocolate Chip Crispers, 83
Chocolate Chip Macaroons, 127
Chocolate Chip Oatmeal Raisin
Cookies, 106
Chocolate Chip Pretzel Cookies, 92
Chocolate Crunch Cookies, 98
Chocolate-Frosted Lebkuchen, 203
Chocolate Mint Meltaways, 133
Chocolate Oatmeal Chippers, 98
Chocolate Orange Granola Cookies,
94
Chocolate-Pecan Angels, 115
Chocolate Scotcheroos, 99
Chunky Chocolate Cookies, 116
Circus Cookies, 125
Coconut Chocolate Chip Cookies, 90
Confetti Chocolate Chip Cookies, 157
Corn Flake Macaroons, 130
Cream Cheese Cookies, 113
Dandy Candy Oatmeal Cookies, 95
Double Chocolate Banana Cookies, 90
Double Chocolate Chip Cookies, 100
Double Chocolate Chunk Cookies, 142
Double Chocolate Cookies, 94
Double Chocolate Dream Cookies, 88
Double Chocolate Mint Chip Cookies,
105
Dreamy Chocolate Chip Cookies, 83
Forgotten Chips Cookies, 101
Fruit and Nut Chippers, 81
Fudgy Raisin Pixies, 123
Gold Mine Nuggets, 85

Drop Cookies *(continued)*
Grandpa Would Have Loved These
Cookies, 107
Jumbo Chunky Cookies, 92
Jumbo Corn Flake Cookies, 104
Kate's Chocolate Chip Cookies, 99
Kids' Favorite Jumbo Chippers, 85
Mini Chocolate Clouds, 211
Mocha Cookies, 116
Oatmeal Candied Chippers, 96
Oatmeal Honey Cookies, 114
Oatmeal Scotchies™, 86
Oatmeal Shaggies Cookies, 136
Oatmeal Supremes, 118
Old-Fashioned Oatmeal Cookies, 123
Orange Drop Cookies, 133
Orange Pecan Gems, 126
Orange-Walnut Chippers, 93
Original Toll House® Chocolate Chip
Cookies, 196
Peanut Butter Chewies, 120
Peanut Butter Chocolate Chip
Cookies, 103
Pecan Drops, 108
Pineapple Carrot Cookies, 126
Pudding Drop Cookies, 103
Quick Chocolate Softies, 108
Reese's® Cookies, 78
Ultimate Chippers, 78
Ultimate Chocolate Chip Cookies, 96

E

Easter Egg Cookies, 177
Elegant Lace Cookie Cups, 164
English Toffee Bars, 66
Extra Moist & Chunky Brownies, 22

F

Fancy Walnut Brownies, 27
Fillings
Chocolate Filling, 53
Cookie Filling, 144
Creamy Mint Filling, 140
Fluffy White Frosting, 185
Forgotten Chips Cookies, 101
Four-Layer Oatmeal Bars, 65
Frosted Butter Cookies, 152
Frosted Maraschino Brownies, 21
Frosted Peanut Butter Peanut Brittle
Cookies, 154
Frostings (*see also* **Glazes**)
Almond Frosting, 134

Frostings (*continued*)
    Chocolate Frosting, 195
    Creamy Brownie Frosting, 17
    Creamy Vanilla Frosting: 70, 195
    Decorator Icing, 140
    Fluffy White Frosting, 185
    Fudgy Mocha Frosting, 20
    Irish Cream Frosting, 24
Fruit and Nut Chippers, 81
Fudge-wiches, 61
Fudgy Almond Bars, 54
Fudgy Bittersweet Brownie Pie, 13
Fudgy Cheesecake Swirl Brownies, 38
Fudgy Mocha Brownies with a Crust, 20
Fudgy Mocha Frosting, 20
Fudgy Raisin Pixies, 123
Fudgy Walnut Cookie Wedges, 43

G

German Sweet Chocolate Cream Cheese
    Brownies, 15
Gingerbread
    Banana Gingerbread Bars, 76
    Chocolate Gingerbread Cookies, 184
    Spicy Gingerbread Cookies, 180
Glazed Pecan Halves, 44
Glazed Sugar Cookies, 197
Glazes
    Bittersweet Glaze, 203
    Chocolate Chip Glaze, 198
    Chocolate Glaze: 46, 49, 155
    Cookie Glaze, 208
    Confectioner's Sugar Glaze, 188
    Kahlúa® Glaze, 14
    Mocha Glaze, 209
    Toffee Topping, 66
    Vanilla Glaze, 33
Gold Mine Nuggets, 85
Gorp Bars, 70
Grandpa Would Have Loved These
    Cookies, 107
Granola
    Butterscotch Granola Cookies, 106
    Chocolate Orange Granola Cookies,
    94

H

Hanukkah Cookies, 206
Happy Pumpkin Faces, 183
Heavenly Oatmeal Hearts, 89
Hidden Treasures, 162
Holiday Almond Wreaths, 192

Holiday Citrus Logs, 201
Honey
    Honey Carrot Cookies, 122
    Honey-Ginger Bourbon Balls,
    203
    Oatmeal Honey Cookies, 114
Honey Carrot Cookies, 122
Honey-Ginger Bourbon Balls, 203

I

Irish Brownies, 24
Irish Cream Frosting, 24

J

Jammy Fantasia, 191
Jeremy's Famous Turtles, 167
Jumbo Chunky Cookies, 92
Jumbo Corn Flake Cookies, 104

K

Kahlúa® Glaze, 14
Kahlúa® Mudslide Brownies, 14
Kahlúa® Pumpkin Squares with Praline
    Topping, 40
Kate's Chocolate Chip Cookies, 99
Kids' Favorite Jumbo Chippers, 85
Kittens and Mittens, 208
Kringle's Cutouts, 207

L

Lemon
    Butterscotch Lemon Cookies, 86
    Chocolate-Frosted Lebkuchen, 203
    Lemon Blossom Cookies, 205
    Lemon Nut Bars, 56
    Lemon Pecan Crescents, 144
    Lemon Raspberry Cheesecake Bars,
    54
    Lemon Wafers, 111
Lemon Blossom Cookies, 205
Lemon Nut Bars, 56
Lemon Pecan Crescents, 144
Lemon Raspberry Cheesecake Bars,
    54
Lemon Wafers, 111
Linzer Hearts, 184

M

Macadamia Bites, 136
Macadamia Nuts
    Chocolate Chunk Cookies, 63
    Decadent Blonde Brownies, 22
    Dreamy Chocolate Chip Cookies, 83
    Macadamia Bites, 136
Magic Cookie Bars, 55
Marble Squares, 51
Marshmallow Krispie Bars, 56
Marshmallows
    Caramel Marshmallow Bars, 73
    Chocolatey Rocky Road Brownies, 28
    Fluffy White Frosting, 185
    Gorp Bars, 70
    Marshmallow Krispie Bars, 56
    Marshmallow Sandwich Cookies,
    121
    Mississippi Mud Brownies, 22
    Rocky Road Brownies, 36
    Sweets-for-the-Sweet Brownies, 18
Marshmallow Sandwich Cookies, 121
Mini Chocolate Clouds, 211
Mini Morsel Meringue Wreaths, 204
Mini Pecan Tarts, 164
Mint
    Chocolate Mint Cheesecake Bars, 49
    Chocolate Mint Cookies, 132
    Chocolate Mint Meltaways, 133
    Chocolate Mint Sandwiches, 139
    Chocolate Mint Snow-Top Cookies,
    110
    Chocolate Mint Sugar Cookie Drops,
    105
    Creamy Mint Filling, 140
    Double Chocolate Mint Chip Cookies,
    105
    Mint Chocolate Pinwheels, 174
    Minted Chocolate Chip Brownies, 10
    Minty Fudge Brownies, 37
    Peppermint Refrigerator Slices, 190
    Scrumptious Minted Brownies, 25
Mint Chocolate Pinwheels, 174
Minted Chocolate Chip Brownies, 10
Minty Fudge Brownies, 37
Mississippi Mud Brownies, 22
Mocha
    Black Russian Brownies, 27
    Cappuccino Brownies, 30
    Fudgy Mocha Brownies with a Crust,
    20
    Kahlúa® Mudslide Brownies, 14
    Mocha Cookies, 116
    Mocha Glaze, 209
    Triple Chocolate Pretzels, 209
Mocha Cookies, 116
Mocha Glaze, 209

N

Nerds® Sprinkle Cookies, 111
No-Bake Cherry Crisps, 171
No-Bake Peanutty Cookies, 127
No-Fuss Bar Cookies, 113
Norwegian Almond Bars, 58
Norwegian Molasses Cookies, 188
Nuts (*see also* **individual types**)
    Double-Dipped Hazelnut Crisps, 176
    Fruit and Nut Chippers, 81
    Praline Brownies, 21
    Streusel Caramel Bars, 52

O

Oatmeal Brownies, 20
Oatmeal Candied Chippers, 96
Oatmeal Honey Cookies, 114
Oatmeal Scotchies™, 86
Oatmeal Shaggies Cookies, 136
Oatmeal Supremes, 118
Oatmeal Toffee Lizzies, 148
Oats
    Apple Crumb Squares, 75
    Brian's Buffalo Cookies, 80
    Butter-Flavored Brickle Drizzles, 147
    Butterscotch Granola Cookies, 105
    Butterscotch Walnut Crisps, 85
    Chewy Oatmeal-Apricot-Date Bars, 48
    Child's Choice, 101
    Choco Peanut Butter Dreams, 213
    Chocolate 'n' Oat Bars, 56
    Chocolate Apple Crisp, 67
    Chocolate Chip Oatmeal Raisin Cookies, 106
    Chocolate Oatmeal Chippers, 98
    Chocolate Filled Walnut-Oatmeal Bars, 53
    Cranberry Jewel Bars, 67
    Dandy Candy Oatmeal Cookies, 95
    Double Chocolate Banana Cookies, 90
    Four-Layer Oatmeal Bars, 65
    Fudge-wiches, 61
    Gold Mine Nuggets, 85
    Grandpa Would Have Loved These Cookies, 107
    Happy Pumpkin Faces, 183
    Heavenly Oatmeal Hearts, 89
    Jammy Fantasia, 191
    Jeremy's Famous Turtles, 167
    Lemon Nut Bars, 56
    Mint Chocolate Pinwheels, 174
    Oatmeal Brownies, 20
    Oatmeal Candied Chippers, 96
    Oatmeal Honey Cookies, 114

Oats (*continued*)
    Oatmeal Scotchies™, 86
    Oatmeal Shaggies Cookies, 136
    Oatmeal Supremes, 118
    Oatmeal Toffee Lizzies, 148
    Oats 'n' Pumpkin Pinwheels, 145
    Old-Fashioned Oatmeal Cookies, 123
    Peachy Oatmeal Bars, 75
    Peanut Butter & Jelly Cookies, 171
    Peanutty Picnic Brownies, 10
    Radical Peanut Butter Pizza Cookies, 150
    Roasted Honey Nut Sandwich Cookies, 144
    Santa's Thumbprints, 197
    Snow Covered Almond Crescents, 131
Oats 'n' Pumpkin Pinwheels, 145
Old-Fashioned Ice Cream Sandwiches, 117
Old-Fashioned Oatmeal Cookies, 123
Orange
    Chocolate-Frosted Lebkuchen, 203
    Chocolate Orange Granola Cookies, 94
    Circus Cookies, 125
    Orange & Chocolate Ribbon Cookies, 139
    Orange Chess Bars, 45
    Orange Drop Cookies, 133
    Orange Pecan Gems, 126
    Orange Shortbread Squares, 63
    Orange-Walnut Chippers, 93
    Vanilla Chip Orange Brownies, 38
Orange & Chocolate Ribbon Cookies, 139
Orange Chess Bars, 45
Orange Drop Cookies, 133
Orange Pecan Gems, 126
Orange Shortbread Squares, 63
Orange-Walnut Chippers, 93
Original Toll House® Chocolate Chip Cookies, 196
Outrageous Brownies, 18

P

Peaches
    Four-Layer Oatmeal Bars, 65
    Peachy Oatmeal Bars, 75
Peanut Butter/Peanut Butter Chips
    Brownie Candy Cups, 15
    Buckeye Cookie Bars, 19
    Caramel Pecan Cookies, 157
    Cheery Chocolate Teddy Bear Cookies, 114
    Chewy Choco-Peanut Pudgies, 134

Peanut Butter/Peanut Butter Chips
    (*continued*)
    Choco Peanut Butter Dreams, 213
    Chocolate Fruit Bars, 60
    Chocolate Peanut Butter Cup Cookies, 178
    Chocolate Peanut Butter Squares, 205
    Chocolate Thumbprints, 141
    Cookie Filling, 144
    Dandy Candy Oatmeal Cookies, 95
    Double-Dipped Chocolate-Peanut Butter Cookies, 158
    Frosted Peanut Butter Peanut Brittle Cookies, 154
    Kids' Favorite Jumbo Chippers, 85
    Marshmallow Krispie Bars, 56
    No-Bake Peanutty Cookies, 127
    Peanut Butter and Chocolate Cookie Sandwich Cookies, 128
    Peanut Butter & Jelly Cookies, 171
    Peanut Butter Bars, 59
    Peanut Butter Brickle Cookies, 115
    Peanut Butter Brownie Cups, 39
    Peanut Butter Chewies, 120
    Peanut Butter Chips and Jelly Bars, 64
    Peanut Butter Chocolate Chip Cookies, 103
    Peanut Butter Chocolate Chippers, 125
    Peanut Butter Paisley Brownies, 12
    Peanut Butter Reindeer, 188
    Peanut Butter Stars, 131
    Peanut Butter Sugar Cookies, 200
    Peanutty Picnic Brownies, 10
    "Radical" Peanut Butter Pizza Cookies, 150
    Reese's® Cookies, 78
    Roasted Honey Nut Sandwich Cookies, 144
    Streusel Peanut Butter Bars, 71
Peanut Butter and Chocolate Cookie Sandwich Cookies, 128
Peanut Butter & Jelly Cookies, 171
Peanut Butter Bars, 59
Peanut Butter Brickle Cookies, 115
Peanut Butter Brownie Cups, 39
Peanut Butter Chewies, 120
Peanut Butter Chips and Jelly Bars, 64
Peanut Butter Chocolate Chip Cookies, 103
Peanut Butter Chocolate Chippers, 125
Peanut Butter Paisley Brownies, 12
Peanut Butter Reindeer, 188
Peanut Butter Stars, 131
Peanut Butter Sugar Cookies, 200
Peanuts
    Caramel Marshmallow Bars, 73
    Chewy Choco-Peanut Pudgies, 134

Peanuts (*continued*)
Chocolate-Drizzled Peanut Bars, 46
Chocolate Peanut Butter Cup Cookies, 178
Chocolatey Rocky Road Brownies, 28
Frosted Peanut Butter Peanut Brittle Cookies, 154
Streusel Peanut Butter Bars, 71
Peanutty Picnic Brownies, 10
Pecan Date Bars, 63
Pecan Drops, 108
Pecan Florentines, 177
Pecan Pie Bars, 44
Pecans
Butter Pecan Squares, 63
Candy Bar Cookies, 68
Caramel Pecan Cookies, 157
Chocolate Butter-Pecan Crescents, 113
Chocolate Caramel-Pecan Bars, 51
Chocolate-Pecan Angels, 115
Chocolate Pecan Pie Squares, 58
Cocoa-Pecan Kiss Cookies, 150
Coconut-Pecan Brownies, 26
Date-Nut Macaroons, 125
English Toffee Bars, 66
Glazed Pecan Halves, 44
Jeremy's Famous Turtles, 167
Lemon Pecan Crescents, 144
Mini Pecan Tarts, 164
Orange Pecan Gems, 126
Pecan Date Bars, 63
Pecan Drops, 108
Pecan Florentines, 177
Pecan Pie Bars, 44
Ultimate Chocolate Chip Cookies, 96
Peppermint Refrigerator Slices, 190
"Philly" Apricot Cookies, 137
Pineapple
Banana Split Bars, 70
Four-Layer Oatmeal Bars, 65
Gold Mine Nuggets, 85
Pineapple Almond Shortbread Bars, 72
Pineapple Carrot Cookies, 126
Pineapple Almond Shortbread Bars, 72
Pineapple Carrot Cookies, 126
Pinwheels and Checkerboards, 130
Praline Brownies, 21
Pudding Drop Cookies, 103
Pumpkin
Kahlúa® Pumpkin Squares with Praline Topping, 40
Oats 'n' Pumpkin Pinwheels, 145
Pumpkin Cheesecake Bars, 44
Pumpkin Jingle Bars, 55
Pumpkin Cheesecake Bars, 44
Pumpkin Jingle Bars, 55

Q

Quick Chocolate Softies, 108

R

"Radical" Peanut Butter Pizza Cookies, 150
Raisins
Butterscotch Granola Cookies, 106
Chocolate Chip Oatmeal Raisin Cookies, 106
Fudgy Raisin Pixies, 123
Grandpa Would Have Loved These Cookies, 107
Oatmeal Honey Cookies, 114
Old-Fashioned Oatmeal Cookies, 123
Pineapple Carrot Cookies, 126
Raspberries
Austrian Tea Cookies, 170
Chocolate Raspberry Coconut Squares, 42
Lemon Raspberry Cheesecake Bars, 54
Linzer Hearts, 184
Raspberry Almond Sandwich Cookies, 163
Raspberry Coconut Layer Bars, 40
Raspberry Freckles, 149
Raspberry Almond Sandwich Cookies, 163
Raspberry Coconut Layer Bars, 40
Raspberry Freckles, 149
Reese's® Cookies, 78
Rich 'n' Creamy Brownie Bars, 12
Rich Chocolate Caramel Brownies, 35
Roasted Honey Nut Sandwich Cookies, 144
Rocky Road Brownies, 36

S

Sandwich Cookies
Brownie Sandwich Cookies, 137
Chocolate Chip Sandwich Cookies, 156
Chocolate-Dipped Sandwich Macaroons, 82
Chocolate Mint Sandwiches, 139
Chocolate Sandwich Cookies, 147
Marshmallow Sandwich Cookies, 121
Old-Fashioned Ice Cream Sandwiches, 117
Peanut Butter and Chocolate Cookie Sandwich Cookies, 128

Sandwich Cookies (*continued*)
Raspberry Almond Sandwich Cookies, 163
Roasted Honey Nut Sandwich Cookies, 144
Santa's Thumbprints, 197
Scrumptious Minted Brownies, 25
Shaped Cookies
Almond Cream Cookies, 210
Almond Hearts, 178
Almond Shortbread Cookies, 134
Angel Pillows, 206
Anise Cookie Cordials, 81
Austrian Tea Cookies, 170
Autumn Mobile, 212
Baked Truffle Treasures, 110
Biscochitos, 142
Black and White Cut-Outs, 169
Brownie Cookies-on-a-Stick, 193
Butter Cookies, 212
Caramel Lace Chocolate Chip Cookies, 161
Cherry Surprises, 160
Cherry Thumbprint Cookies, 210
Chewy Choco-Peanut Pudgies, 134
Choco Peanut Butter Dreams, 213
Chocolate Chip Cordials, 173
Chocolate-Dipped Almond Horns, 174
Chocolate-Dipped Brandy Snaps, 172
Chocolate-Dipped Cinnamon Thins, 160
Chocolate-Filled Bonbons, 155
Chocolate Gingerbread Cookies, 184
Chocolate Mint Cookies, 132
Chocolate Mint Snow-Top Cookies, 110
Chocolate Mint Sugar Cookie Drops, 105
Chocolate Peanut Butter Cup Cookies, 178
Chocolate Pinwheel Cookies, 148
Chocolate Sugar Spritz, 166
Chocolate Thumbprints, 141
Cinnamon-Chocolate Cutouts, 140
Cinnamon Stars, 151
Cocoa Almond Cut-out Cookies, 155
Cocoa Cream Cheese Cookies, 182
Cocoa-Pecan Kiss Cookies, 150
Date Menenas, 152
Date-Nut Macaroons, 125
Double Chocolate Cherry Cookies, 145
Double-Dipped Chocolate-Peanut Butter Cookies, 158
Double-Dipped Hazelnut Crisps, 176
Easter Egg Cookies, 177
Elegant Lace Cookie Cups, 164

Shaped Cookies (*continued*)
Frosted Butter Cookies, 152
Frosted Peanut Butter Peanut Brittle
    Cookies, 154
Glazed Sugar Cookies, 197
Hanukkah Cookies, 206
Happy Pumpkin Faces, 183
Heavenly Oatmeal Hearts, 89
Hidden Treasures, 162
Holiday Almond Wreaths, 192
Holiday Citrus Logs, 201
Honey Carrot Cookies, 122
Honey-Ginger Bourbon Balls, 203
Jeremy's Famous Turtles, 167
Kittens and Mittens, 208
Kringle's Cutouts, 207
Lemon Blossom Cookies, 205
Lemon Pecan Crescents, 144
Lemon Wafers, 111
Linzer Hearts, 184
Macadamia Bites, 136
Mini Morsel Meringue Wreaths, 204
Mini Pecan Tarts, 164
Mint Chocolate Pinwheels, 174
Nerds® Sprinkle Cookies, 111
No-Bake Cherry Crisps, 171
No-Bake Peanutty Cookies, 127
Norwegian Molasses Cookies, 188
Oatmeal Toffee Lizzies, 148
Oats 'n' Pumpkin Pinwheels, 145
Orange & Chocolate Ribbon Cookies,
    139
Peanut Butter & Jelly Cookies, 171
Peanut Butter Brickle Cookies, 115
Peanut Butter Chocolate Chippers,
    125
Peanut Butter Reindeer, 188
Peanut Butter Stars, 131
Peanut Butter Sugar Cookies, 200
Pecan Florentines, 177
Peppermint Refrigerator Slices, 190
"Philly" Apricot Cookies, 137
Pinwheels and Checkerboards, 130
"Radical" Peanut Butter Pizza
    Cookies, 150
Raspberry Freckles, 149
Santa's Thumbprints, 197
Snowballs, 200
Snow Covered Almond Crescents,
    131

Shaped Cookies (*continued*)
Soft Spicy Molasses Cookies, 122
Spicy Gingerbread Cookies, 180
Spooky Ghost Cookies, 185
Spritz Christmas Trees, 204
Sugar Cookie Wreaths, 182
Surprise Cookies, 179
Toasted Anise Biscuits, 156
Triple Chocolate Pretzels, 209
Two-Toned Spritz Cookies, 162
Versatile Cut-Out Cookies, 186
Watermelon Slices, 172
Yule Tree Namesakes, 190
Yummy Chocolate Chip Flower
    Cookies, 166
Snowballs, 200
Snow Covered Almond Crescents,
    131
Soft Spicy Molasses Cookies, 122
Sour Cream Walnut Brownies, 31
Special Treat No-Bake Squares, 118
Spicy Gingerbread Cookies, 180
Spooky Ghost Cookies, 185
Spritz Christmas Trees, 204
Strawberry Streusel Bars, 75
Streusel Caramel Bars, 52
Streusel Peanut Butter Bars, 71
Sugar Cookie Wreaths, 182
Surprise Cookies, 179
Sweets-for-the-Sweet Brownies, 18

T

Tex-Mex Brownies, 39
Toasted Anise Biscuits, 156
Toffee Topping, 66
Triple Chocolate Pretzels, 209
Triple Layer Chocolate Bars, 53
Tropical Sun Bars, 77
Two-Toned Spritz Cookies, 162

U

Ultimate Chippers, 78
Ultimate Chocolate Chip Cookies, 96
Ultimate Designer Brownies, 33

V

Vanilla
Creamy Vanilla Frosting: 70, 195
Vanilla Glaze, 33
Vanilla Chip Orange Brownies, 38
Vanilla Glaze, 33
Versatile Cut-Out Cookies, 186

W

Walnut Shortbread Bars, 49
Walnut Toffee Bars, 73
Walnuts
Butterscotch Walnut Crisps, 85
Cherry Chewbilees, 192
Cheese Crunchers, 61
Chocolate Filled Walnut-Oatmeal
    Bars, 53
Chunky Chocolate Cookies, 116
Fancy Walnut Brownies, 27
Fudgy Walnut Cookie Wedges, 43
Oatmeal Supremes, 118
Orange-Walnut Chippers, 93
Sour Cream Walnut Brownies, 31
Walnut Shortbread Bars, 49
Walnut Toffee Bars, 73
Watermelon Slices, 172
White Chocolate
Confetti Chocolate Chip Cookies,
    157
Heavenly Oatmeal Hearts, 89
Peanut Butter Sugar Cookies, 200
Quick Chocolate Softies, 108
Raspberry Freckles, 149
Vanilla Chip Orange Brownies, 38
White Chocolate Brownies, 32
White Chocolate Chunk Brownies, 25
White Chocolate Brownies, 32
White Chocolate Chunk Brownies, 25

Y

Yule Tree Namesakes, 190
Yummy Chocolate Chip Flower
    Cookies, 166

METRIC CONVERSION CHART

VOLUME MEASUREMENTS (dry)

⅛ teaspoon = 0.5 mL
¼ teaspoon = 1 mL
½ teaspoon = 2 mL
¾ teaspoon = 4 mL
1 teaspoon = 5 mL
1 tablespoon = 15 mL
2 tablespoons = 30 mL
¼ cup = 60 mL
⅓ cup = 75 mL
½ cup = 125 mL
⅔ cup = 150 mL
¾ cup = 175 mL
1 cup = 250 mL
2 cups = 1 pint = 500 mL
3 cups = 750 mL
4 cups = 1 quart = 1 L

VOLUME MEASUREMENTS (fluid)

1 fluid ounce (2 tablespoons) = 30 mL
4 fluid ounces (½ cup) = 125 mL
8 fluid ounces (1 cup) = 250 mL
12 fluid ounces (1½ cups) = 375 mL
16 fluid ounces (2 cups) = 500 mL

WEIGHTS (mass)

½ ounce = 15 g
1 ounce = 30 g
3 ounces = 90 g
4 ounces = 120 g
8 ounces = 225 g
10 ounces = 285 g
12 ounces = 360 g
16 ounces = 1 pound = 450 g

DIMENSIONS

1/16 inch = 2 mm
⅛ inch = 3 mm
¼ inch = 6 mm
½ inch = 1.5 cm
¾ inch = 2 cm
1 inch = 2.5 cm

OVEN TEMPERATURES

250°F = 120°C
275°F = 140°C
300°F = 150°C
325°F = 160°C
350°F = 180°C
375°F = 190°C
400°F = 200°C
425°F = 220°C
450°F = 230°C

BAKING PAN SIZES

Utensil	Size in Inches/Quarts	Metric Volume	Size in Centimeters
Baking or Cake Pan (square or rectangular)	8×8×2	2 L	20×20×5
	9×9×2	2.5 L	22×22×5
	12×8×2	3 L	30×20×5
	13×9×2	3.5 L	33×23×5
Loaf Pan	8×4×3	1.5 L	20×10×7
	9×5×3	2 L	23×13×7
Round Layer Cake Pan	8×1½	1.2 L	20×4
	9×1½	1.5 L	23×4
Pie Plate	8×1¼	750 mL	20×3
	9×1¼	1 L	23×3
Baking Dish or Casserole	1 quart	1 L	—
	1½ quart	1.5 L	—
	2 quart	2 L	—